HERA KLES

BOOK 3

WRITTEN AND ILLUSTRATED BY

EDOUARD COUR

English translation by JEREMY MELLOUL
Localization, layout, and editing by MIKE KENNEDY

LION
FORGE™

MAGNETIC™

ISBN: 978-1-942367-51-2

Library of Congress Control Number: 2018931353

Printed in China.

10 9 8 7 6 5 4 3 2 1

A big thank you to all my family, close friends (you know who you are, you're already in the previous volumes!), and all the other people who believed in me. Without your support, this crazy project would never have made it this far.

This album is dedicated to my father, my grandmother Renee, my grandfather Michel, and to all the humans who have lived the adventure of life from one end to the other.

Happy reading,

— Edouard Cour

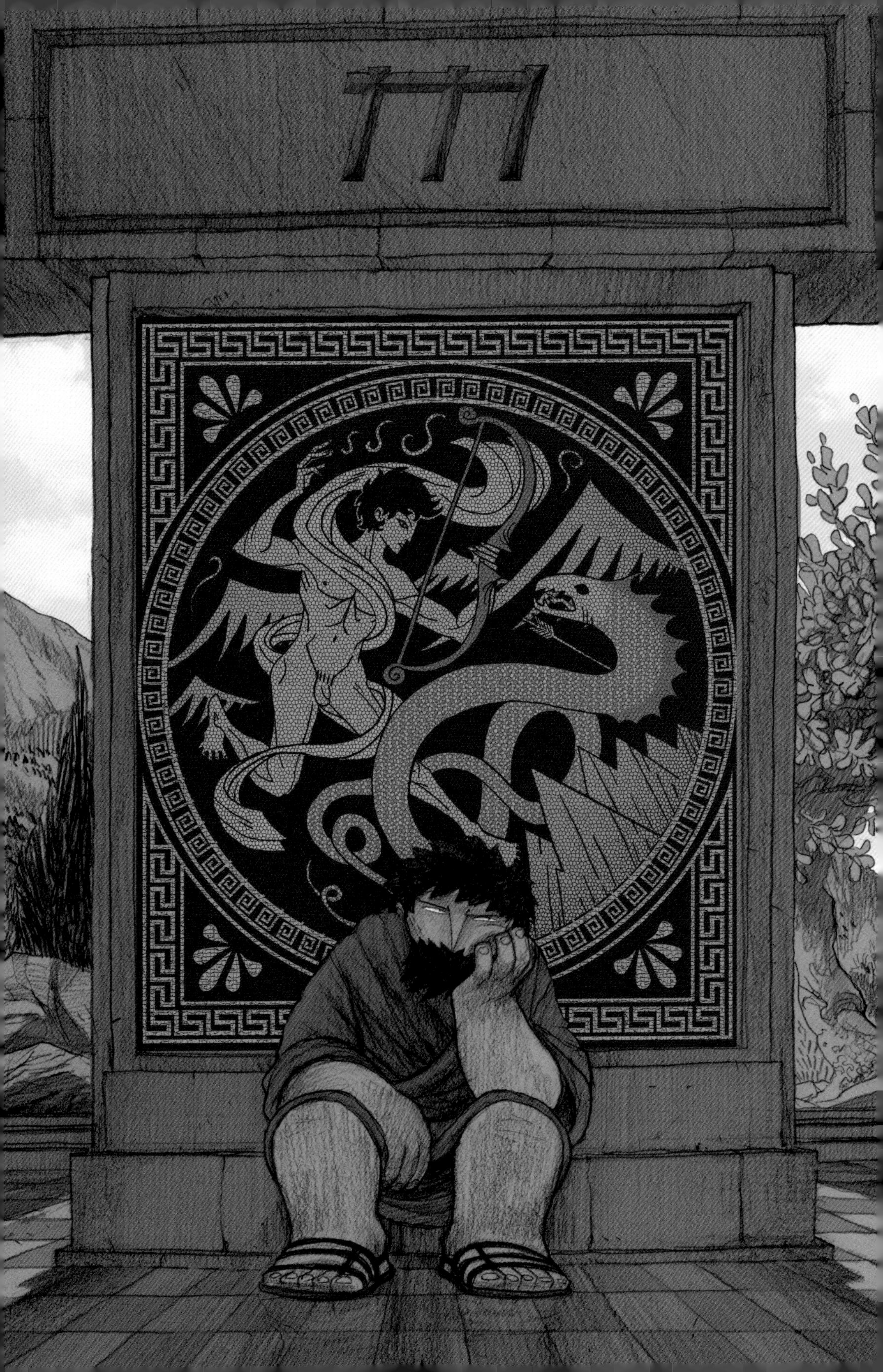

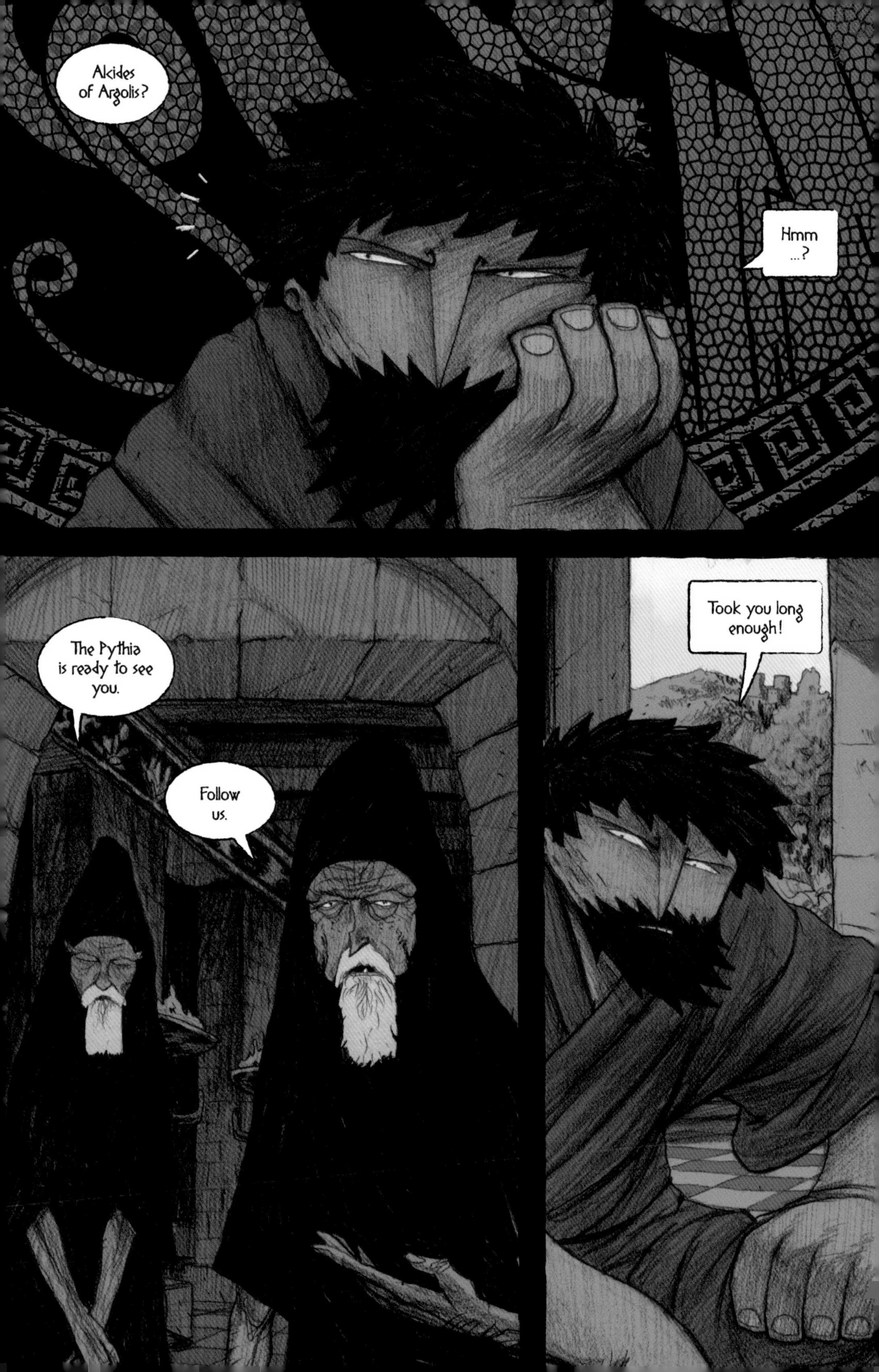
Alcides of Argolis?
Hmm ...?
The Pythia is ready to see you.
Follow us.
Took you long enough!

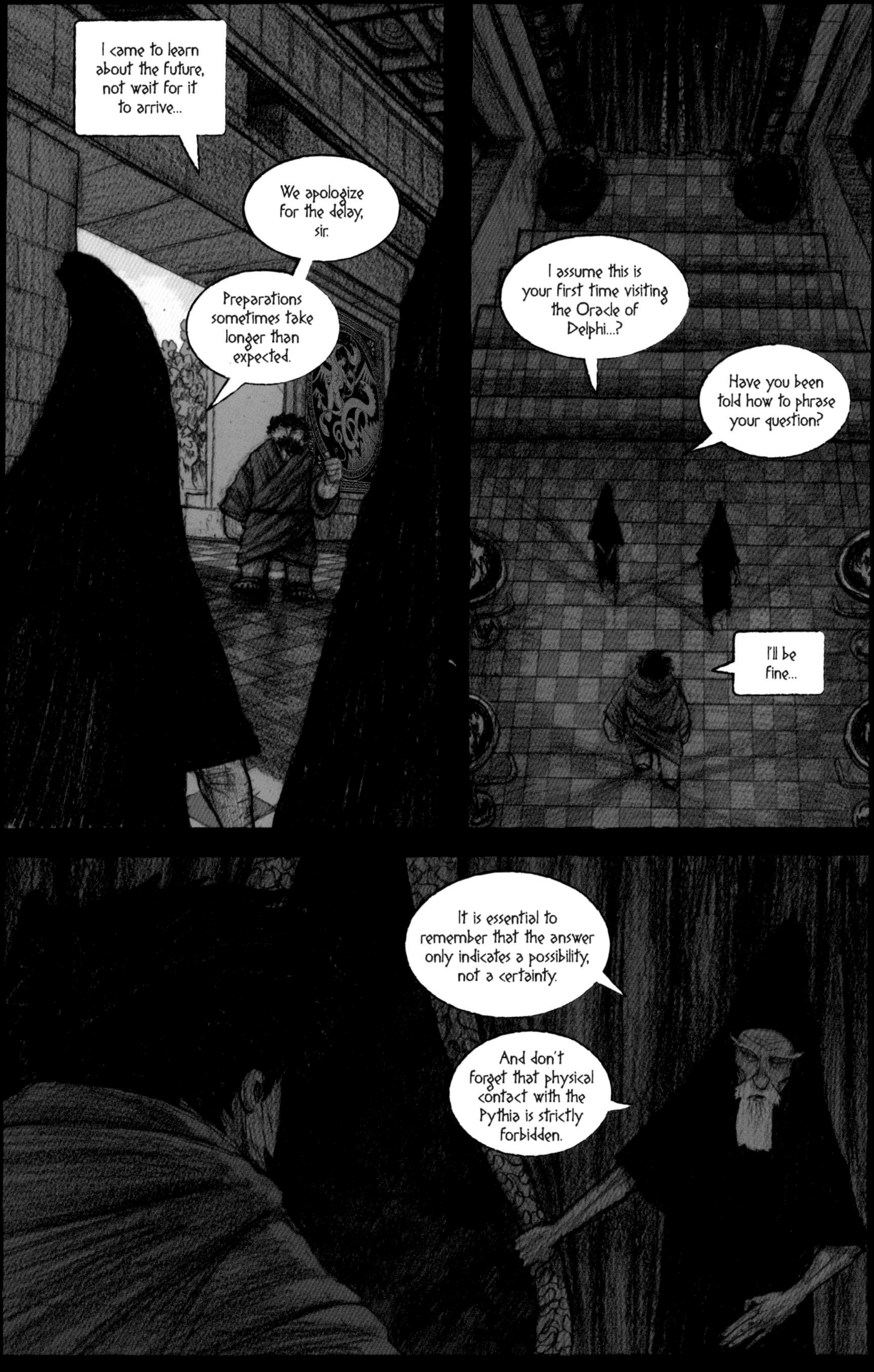
I came to learn about the future, not wait for it to arrive...
We apologize for the delay, sir.
Preparations sometimes take longer than expected.
I assume this is your first time visiting the Oracle of Delphi...?
Have you been told how to phrase your question?
I'll be fine...
It is essential to remember that the answer only indicates a possibility, not a certainty.
And don't forget that physical contact with the Pythia is strictly forbidden.

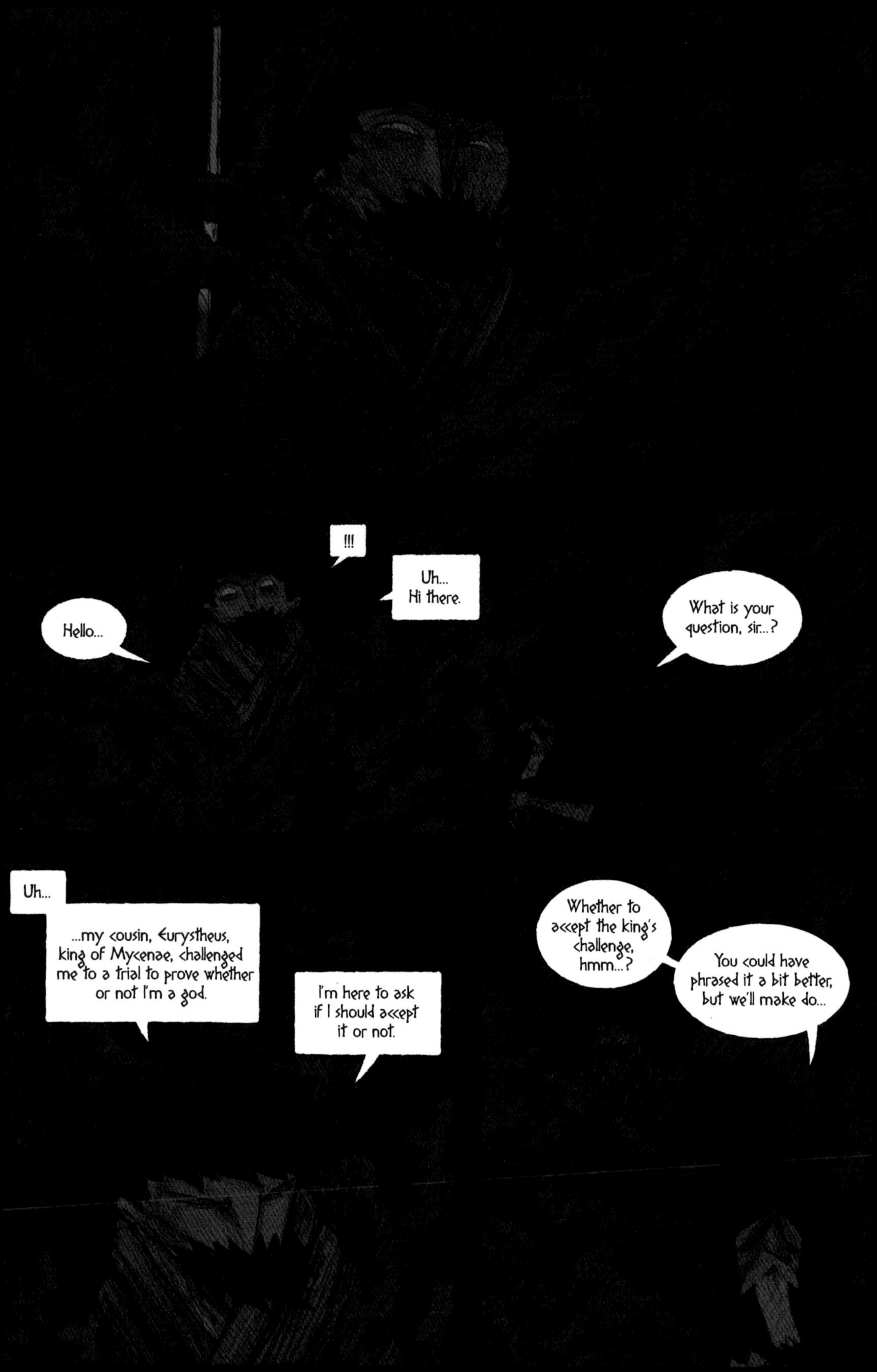
!!!
Uh... Hi there.
Hello...
What is your question, sir...?
Uh...
...my cousin, Eurystheus, king of Mycenae, challenged me to a trial to prove whether or not I'm a god.
I'm here to ask if I should accept it or not.
Whether to accept the king's challenge, hmm...?
You could have phrased it a bit better, but we'll make do...

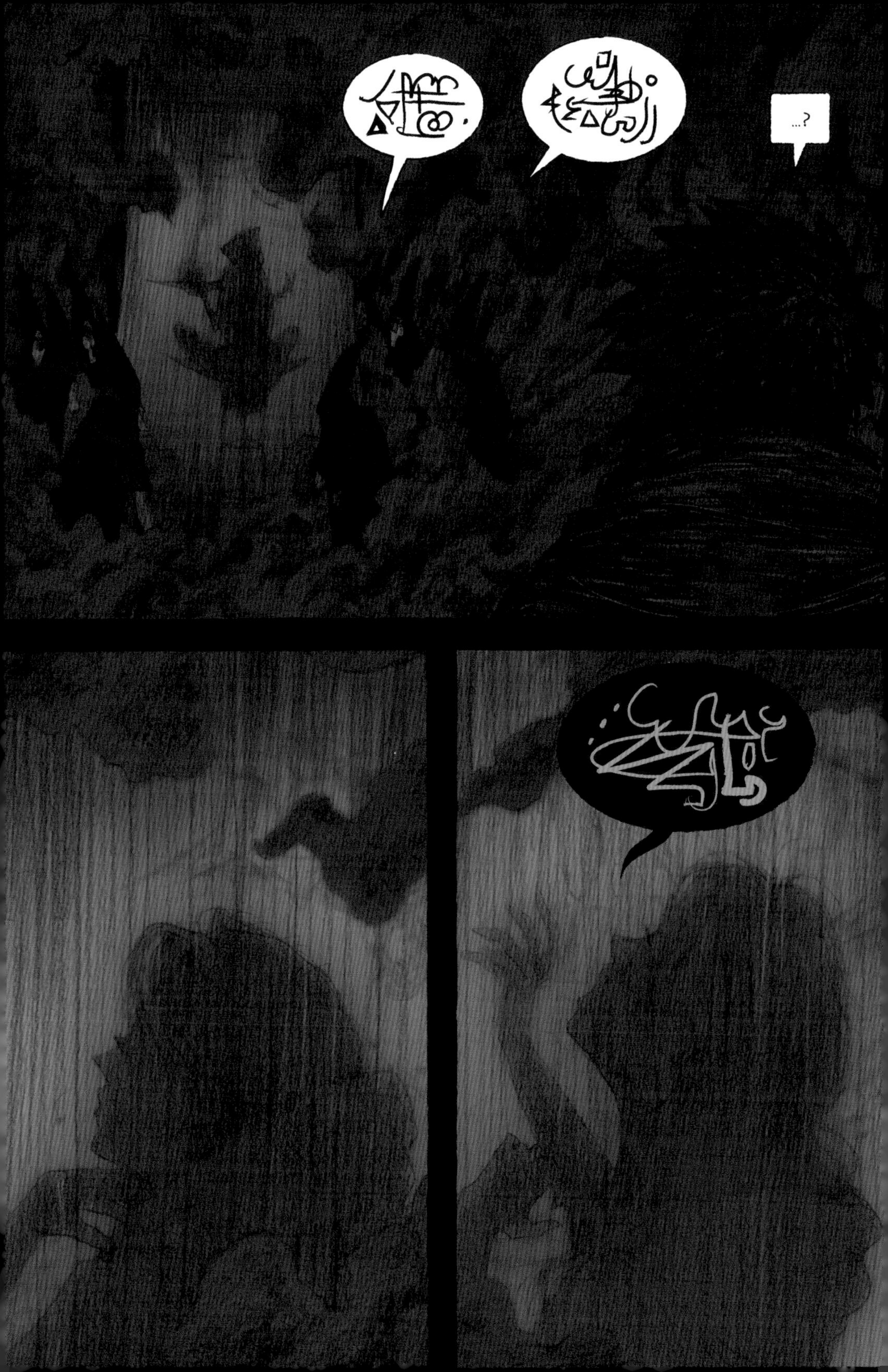
...?

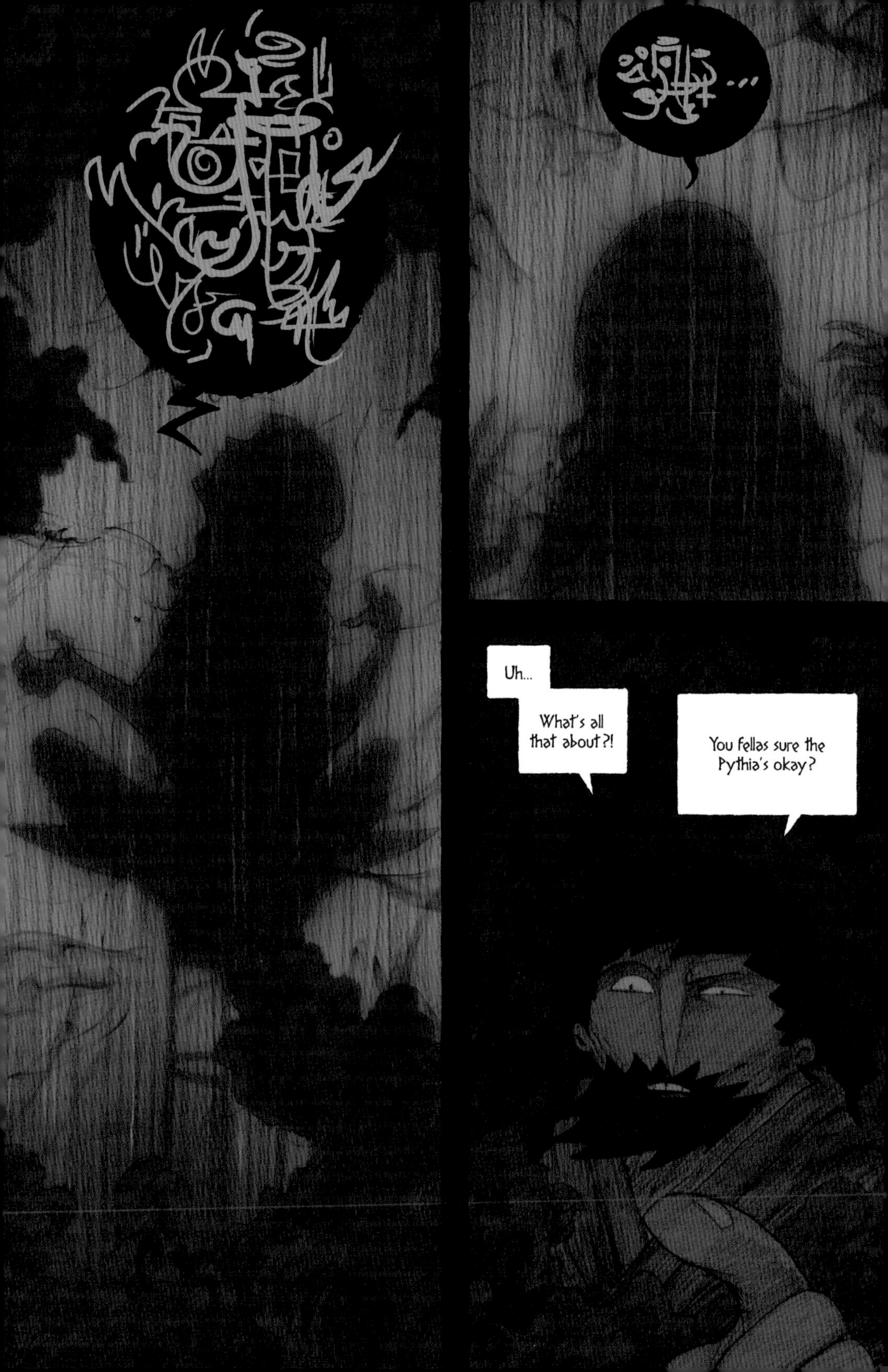
Uh...
What's all that about?!
You fellas sure the Pythia's okay?

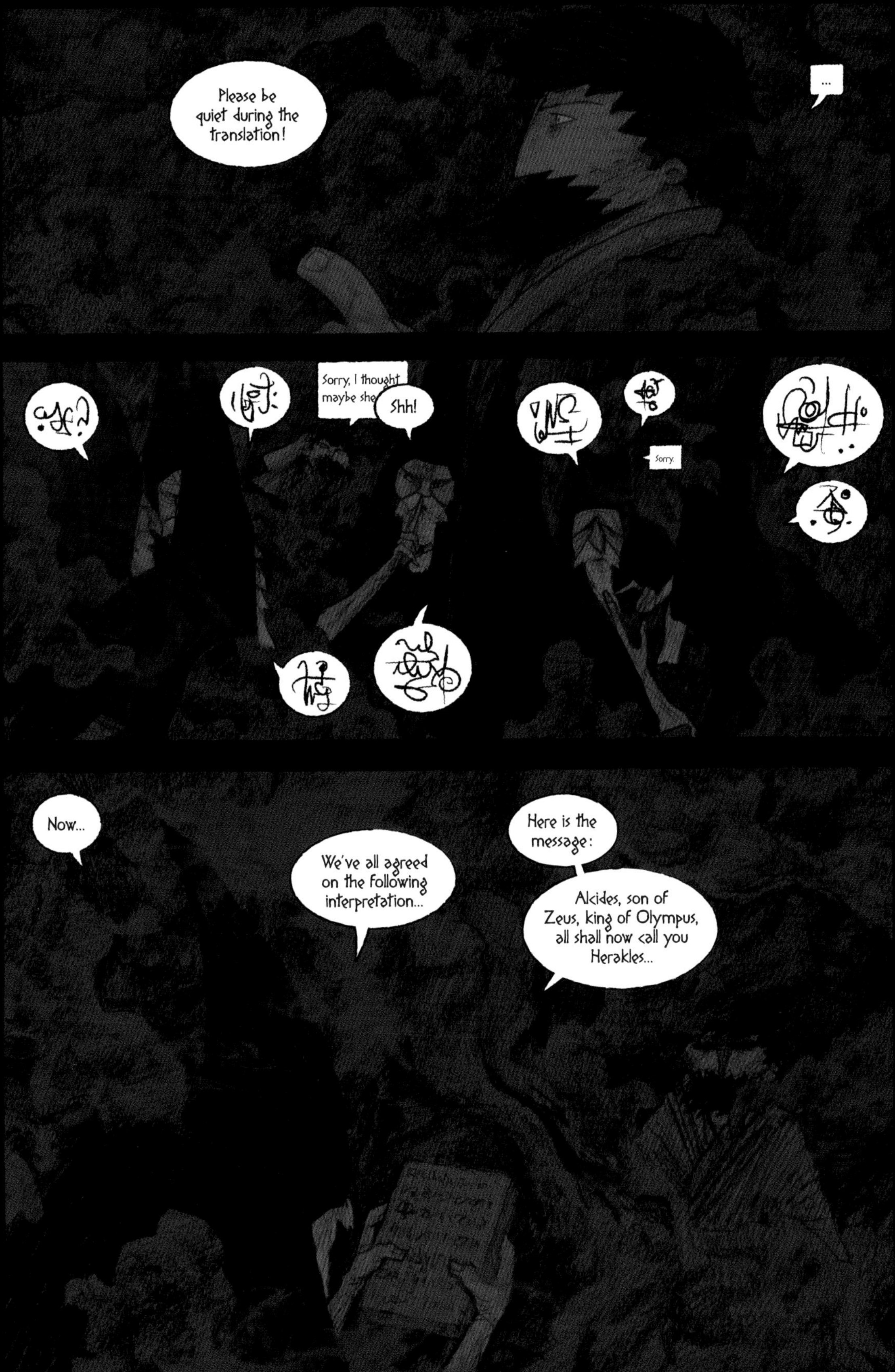
Please be quiet during the translation!
...
Sorry, I thought maybe she
Shh!
Sorry.
Now...
We've all agreed on the following interpretation...
Here is the message:
Alkides, son of Zeus, king of Olympus, all shall now call you Herakles...

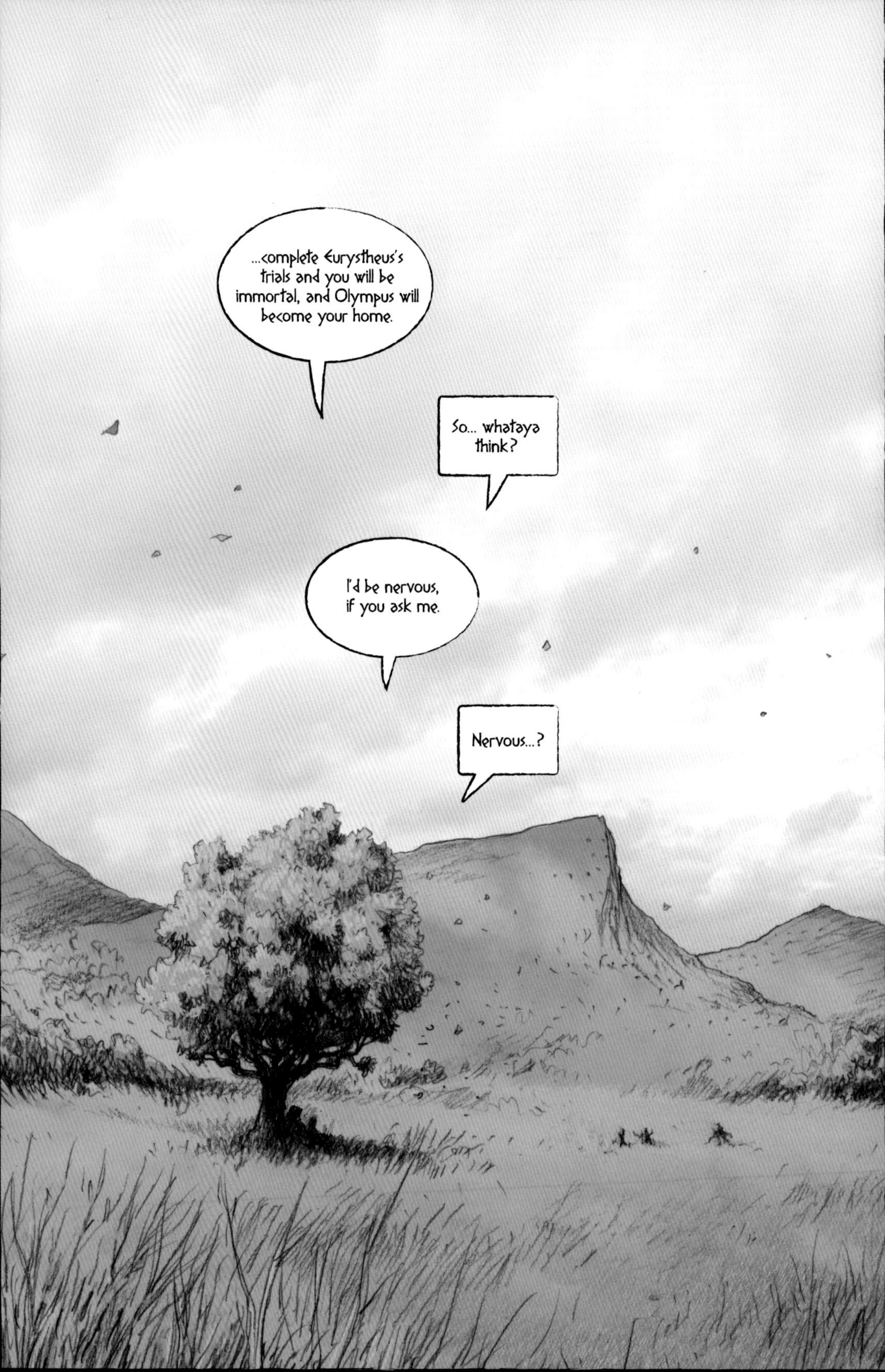
...complete Eurystheus's trials and you will be immortal, and Olympus will become your home.
So... whataya think?
I'd be nervous, if you ask me.
Nervous...?

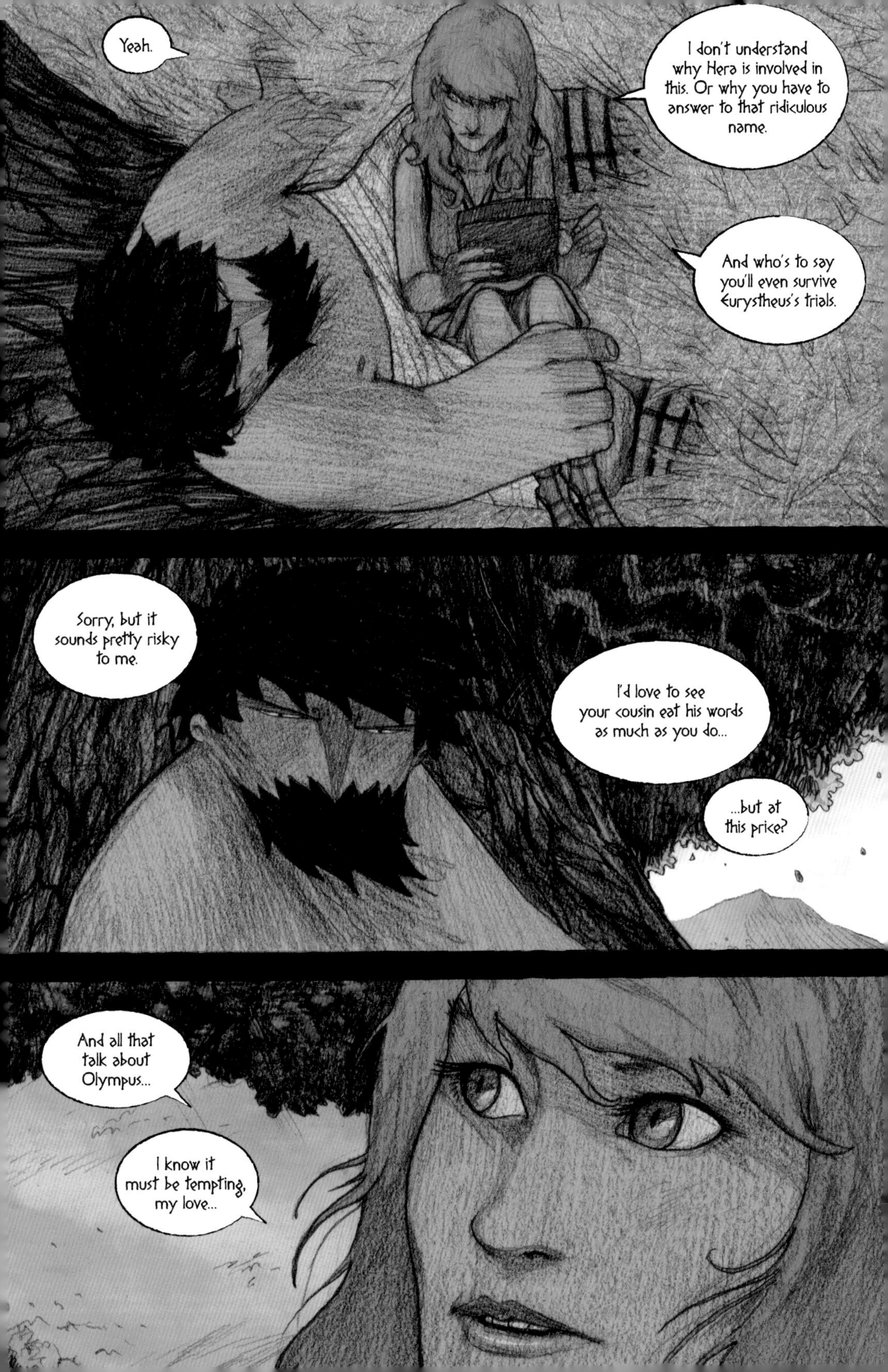
Yeah.
I don't understand why Hera is involved in this. Or why you have to answer to that ridiculous name.
And who's to say you'll even survive Eurystheus's trials.
Sorry, but it sounds pretty risky to me.
I'd love to see your cousin eat his words as much as you do...
...but at this price?
And all that talk about Olympus...
I know it must be tempting, my love...

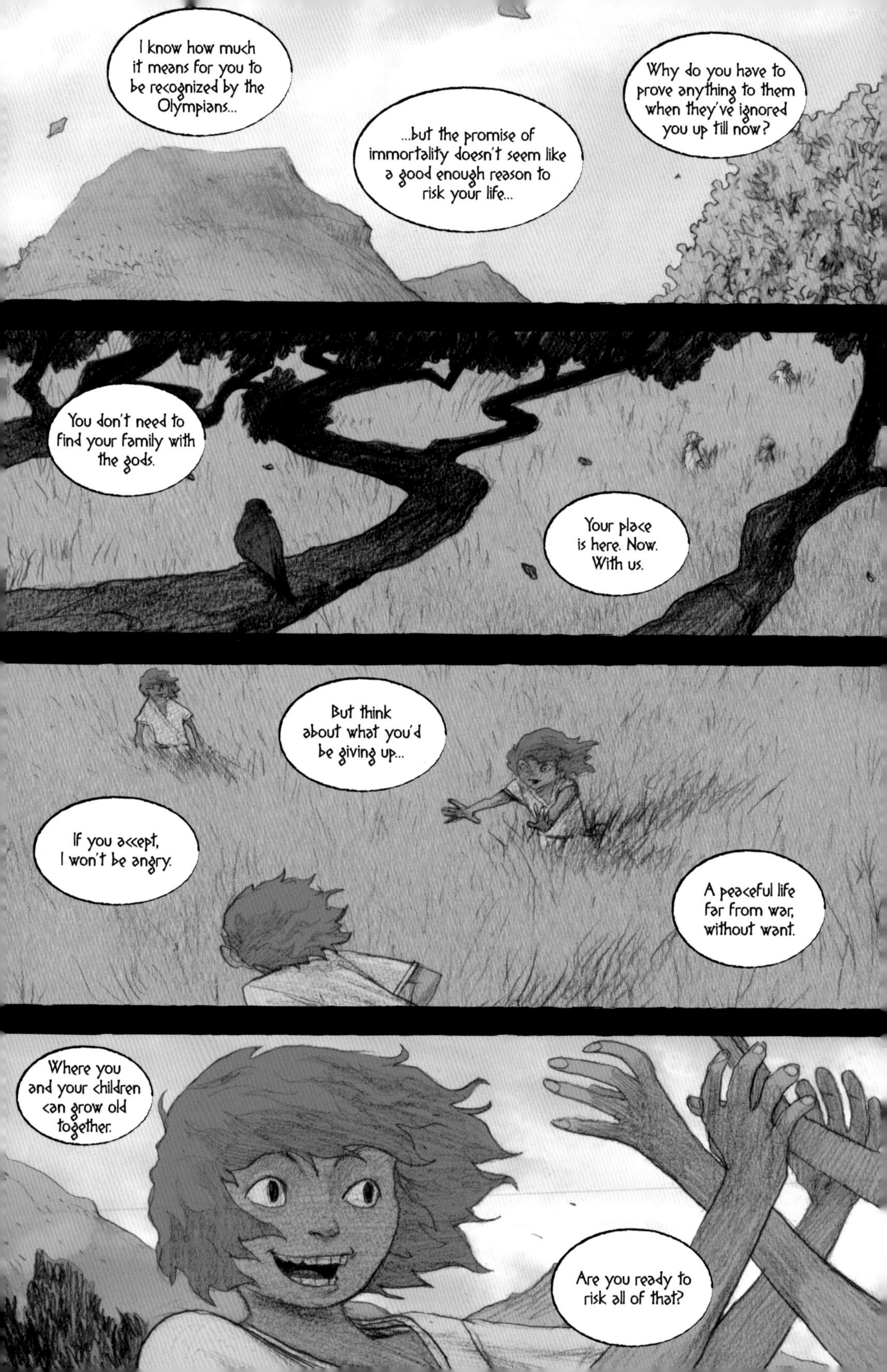
I know how much it means for you to be recognized by the Olympians...
...but the promise of immortality doesn't seem like a good enough reason to risk your life...
Why do you have to prove anything to them when they've ignored you up till now?
You don't need to find your family with the gods.
Your place is here. Now. With us.
But think about what you'd be giving up...
If you accept, I won't be angry.
A peaceful life far from war, without want.
Where you and your children can grow old together.
Are you ready to risk all of that?

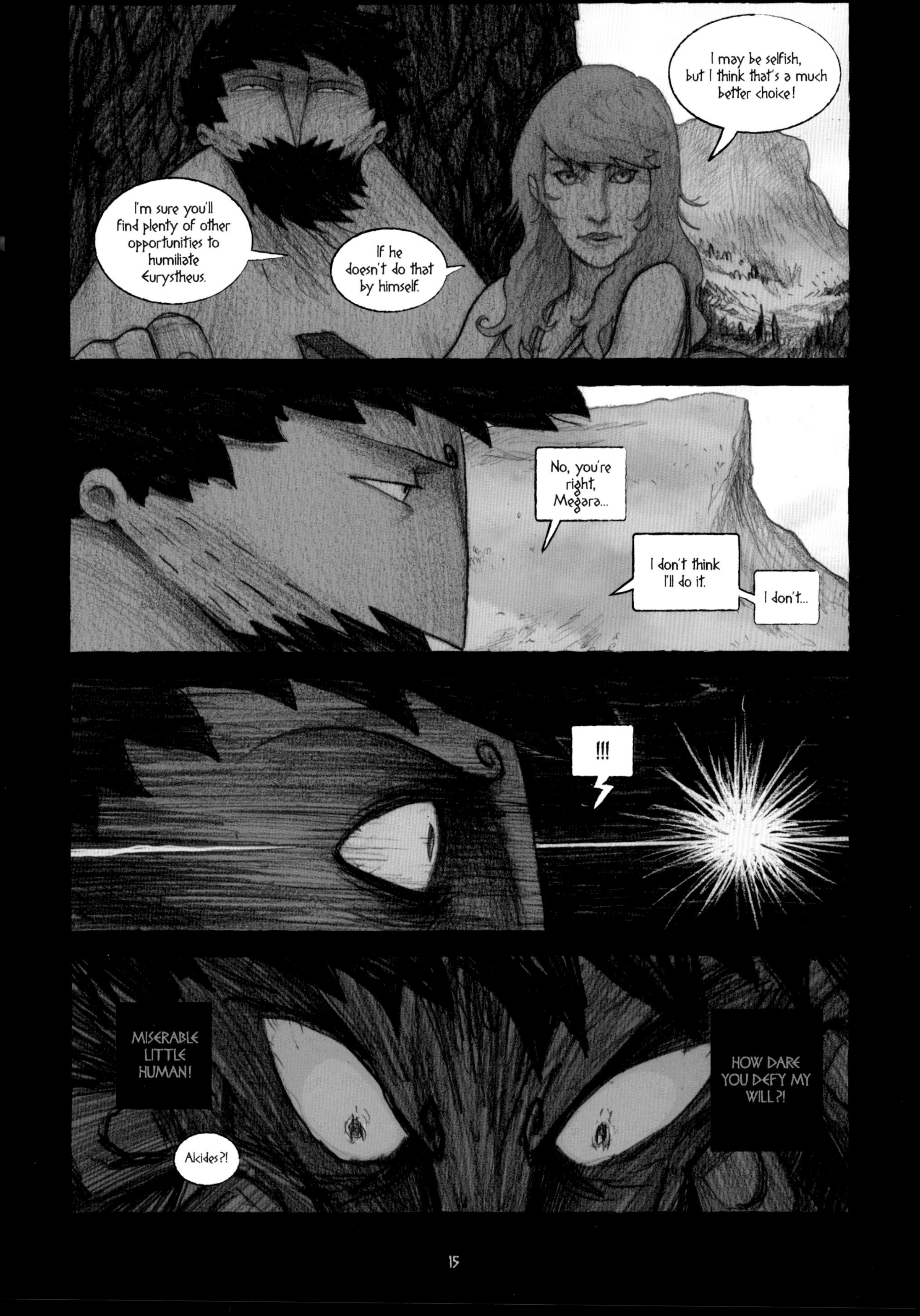
I may be selfish, but I think that's a much better choice!
I'm sure you'll find plenty of other opportunities to humiliate Eurystheus.
If he doesn't do that by himself.
No, you're right, Megara...
I don't think I'll do it.
I don't...
!!!
MISERABLE LITTLE HUMAN!
HOW DARE YOU DEFY MY WILL?!
Alcides?!

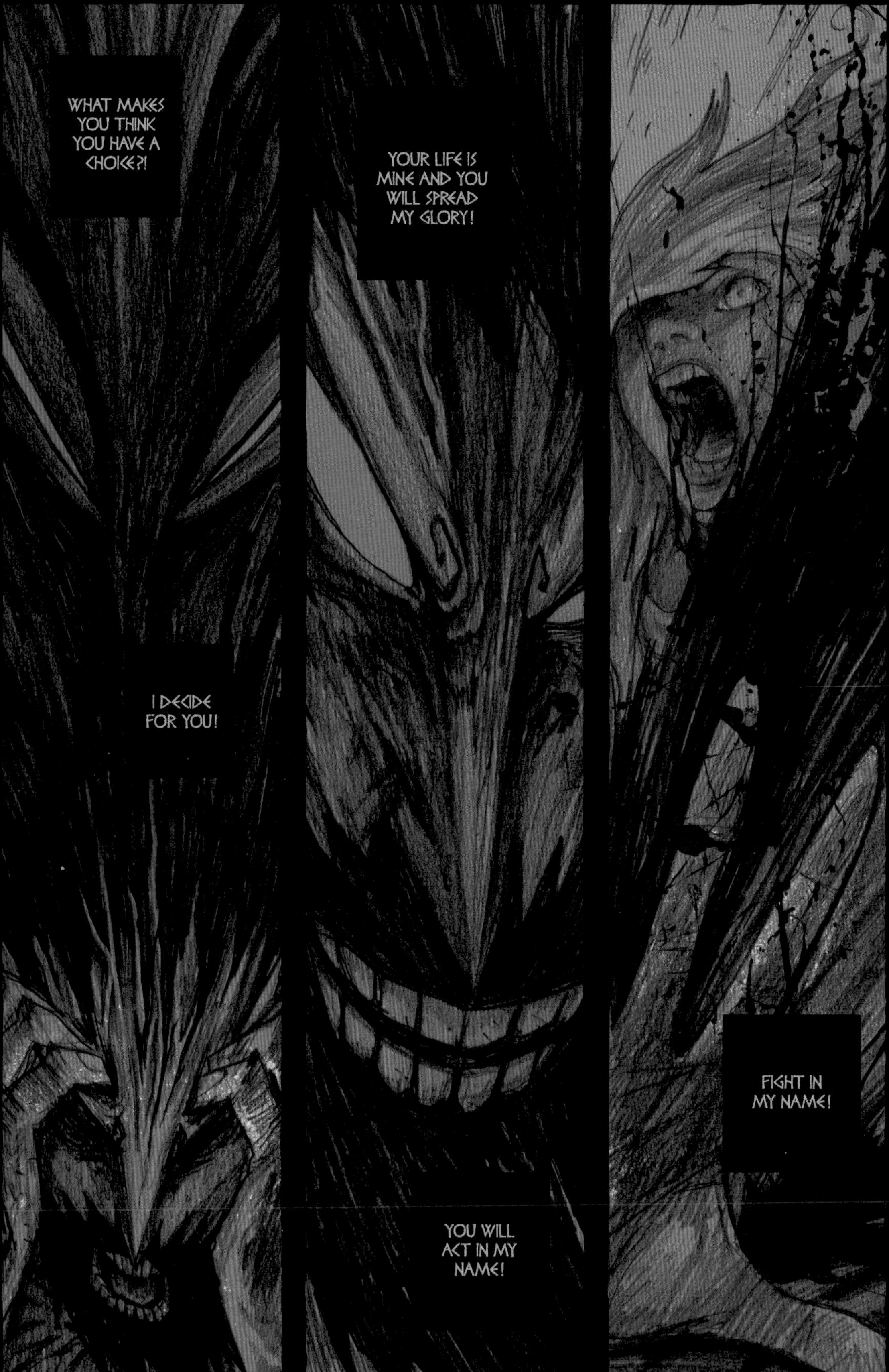
WHAT MAKES YOU THINK YOU HAVE A CHOICE?!
I DECIDE FOR YOU!
YOUR LIFE IS MINE AND YOU WILL SPREAD MY GLORY!
YOU WILL ACT IN MY NAME!
FIGHT IN MY NAME!

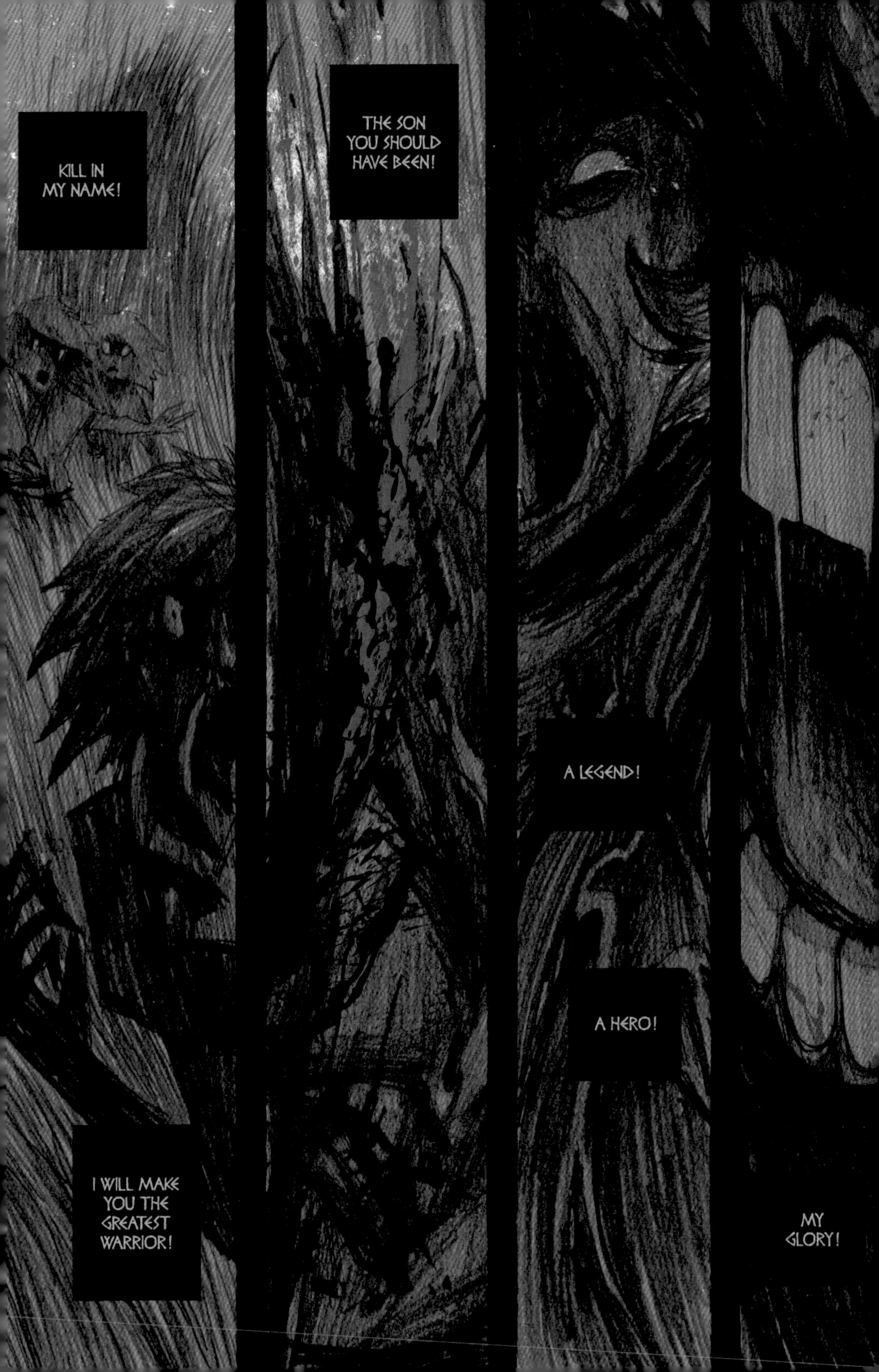
KILL IN MY NAME!
I WILL MAKE YOU THE GREATEST WARRIOR!
THE SON YOU SHOULD HAVE BEEN!
A LEGEND!
A HERO!
MY GLORY!

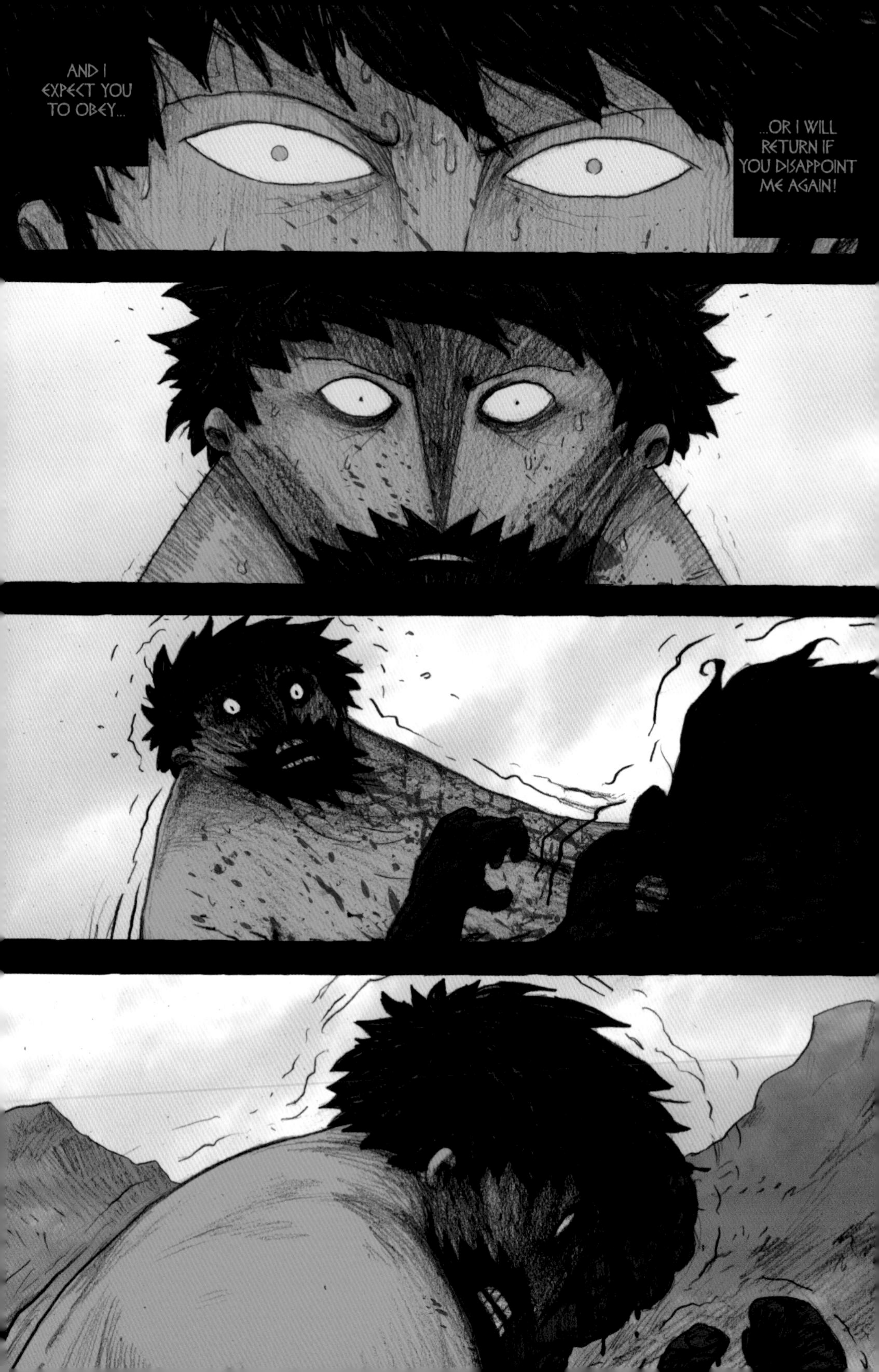
AND I EXPECT YOU TO OBEY...
...OR I WILL RETURN IF YOU DISAPPOINT ME AGAIN!

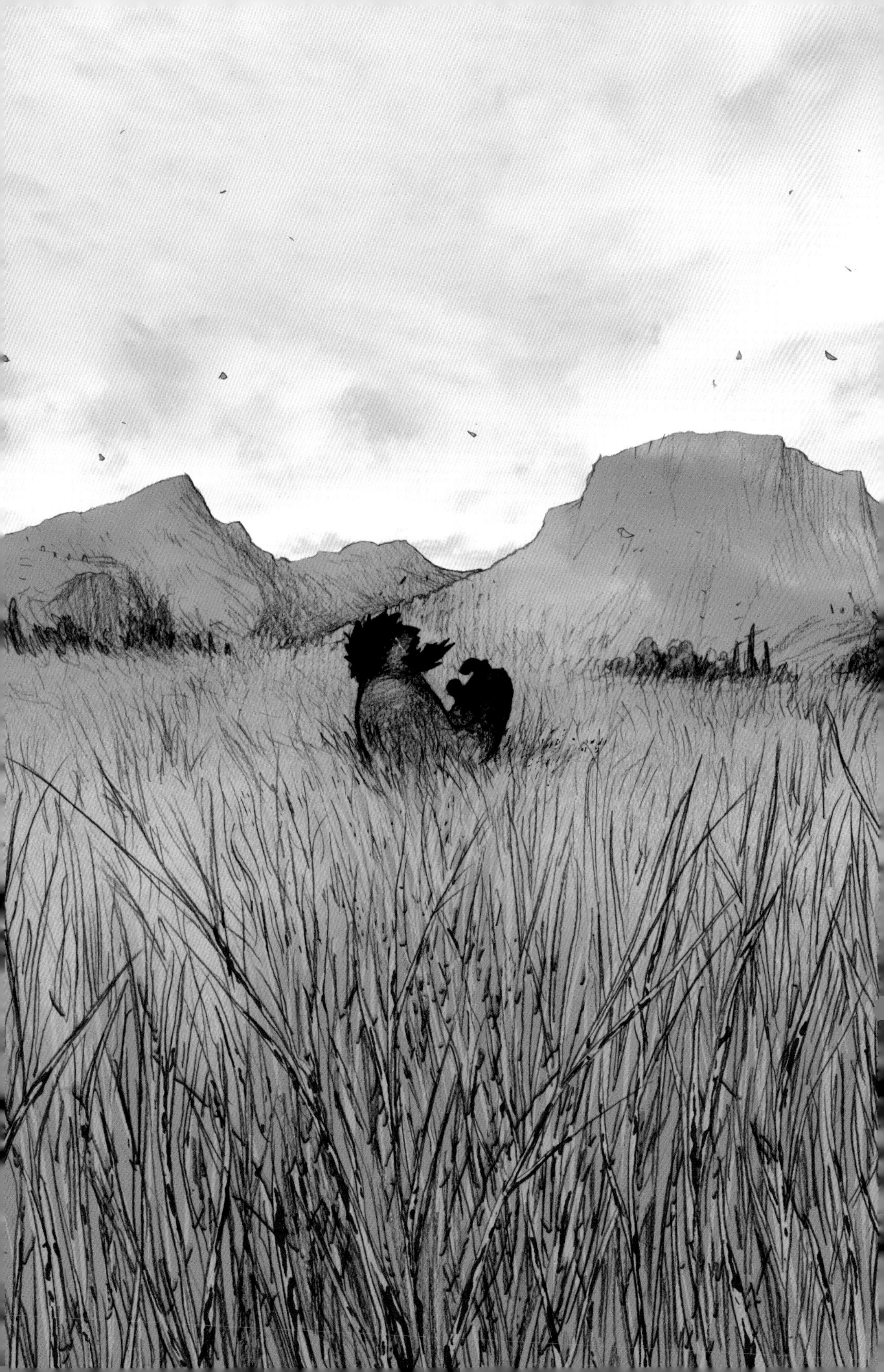

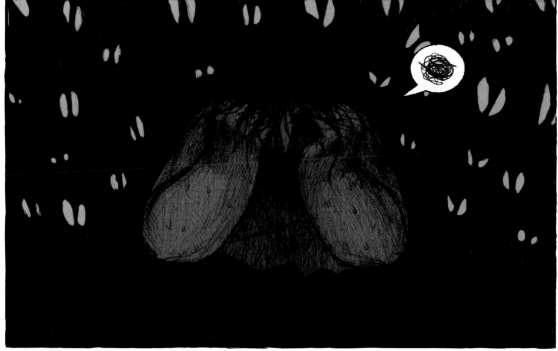

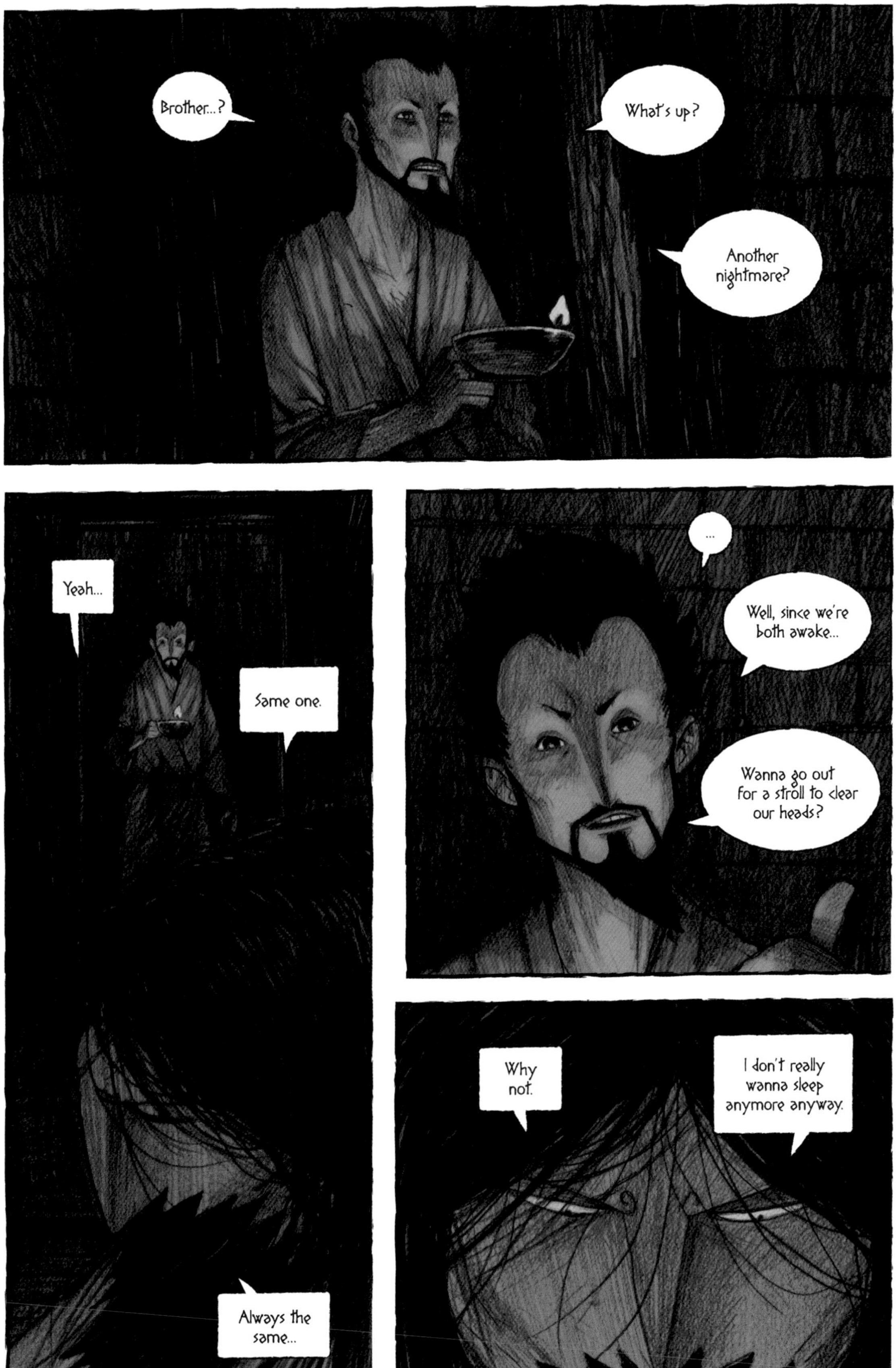

Brother...?
What's up?
Another nightmare?
Yeah...
Same one.
Always the same...
...
Well, since we're both awake...
Wanna go out for a stroll to clear our heads?
Why not.
I don't really wanna sleep anymore anyway.

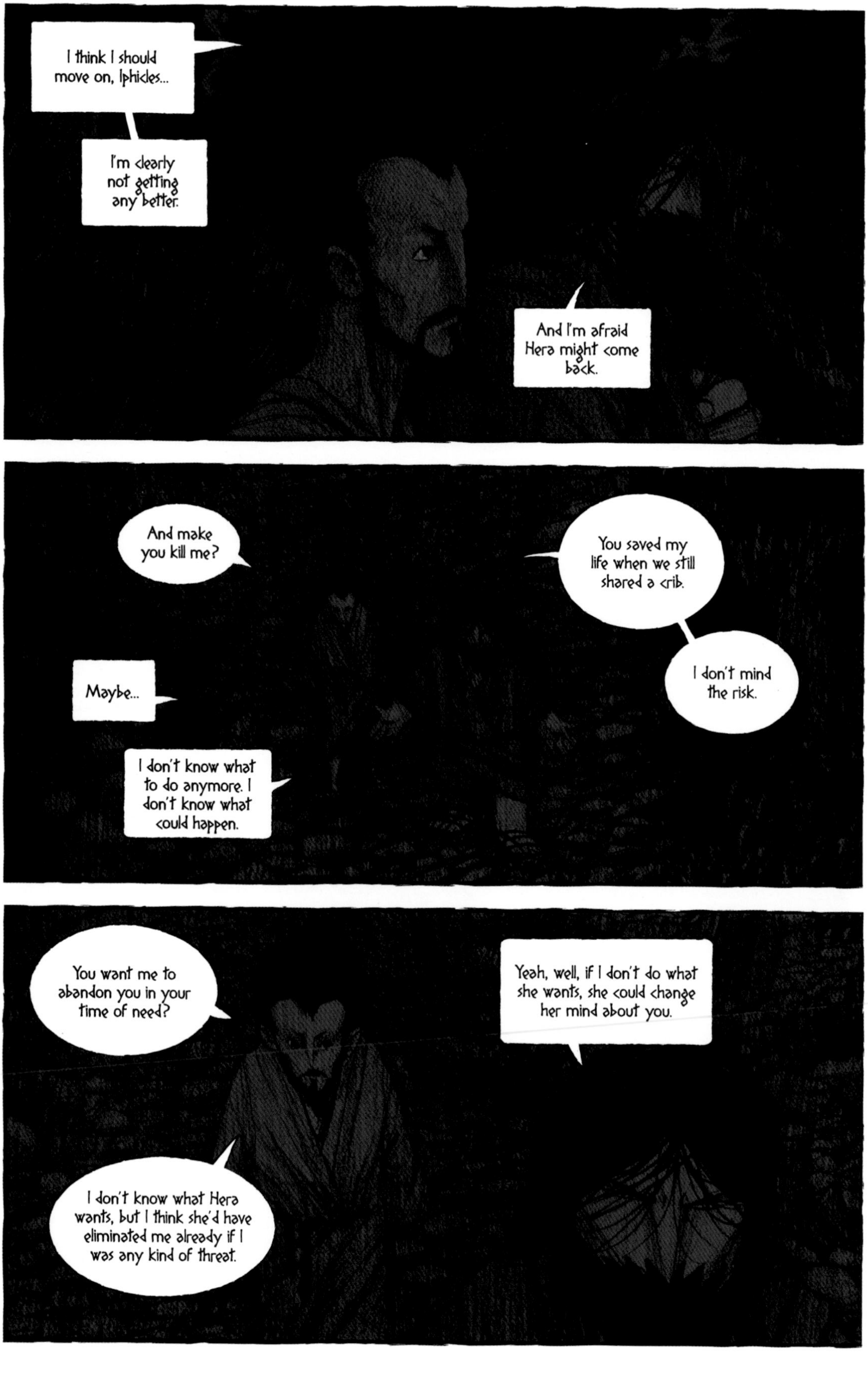
I think I should move on, Iphicles...
I'm clearly not getting any better.
And I'm afraid Hera might come back.
And make you kill me?
You saved my life when we still shared a crib.
I don't mind the risk.
Maybe...
I don't know what to do anymore. I don't know what could happen.
You want me to abandon you in your time of need?
Yeah, well, if I don't do what she wants, she could change her mind about you.
I don't know what Hera wants, but I think she'd have eliminated me already if I was any kind of threat.

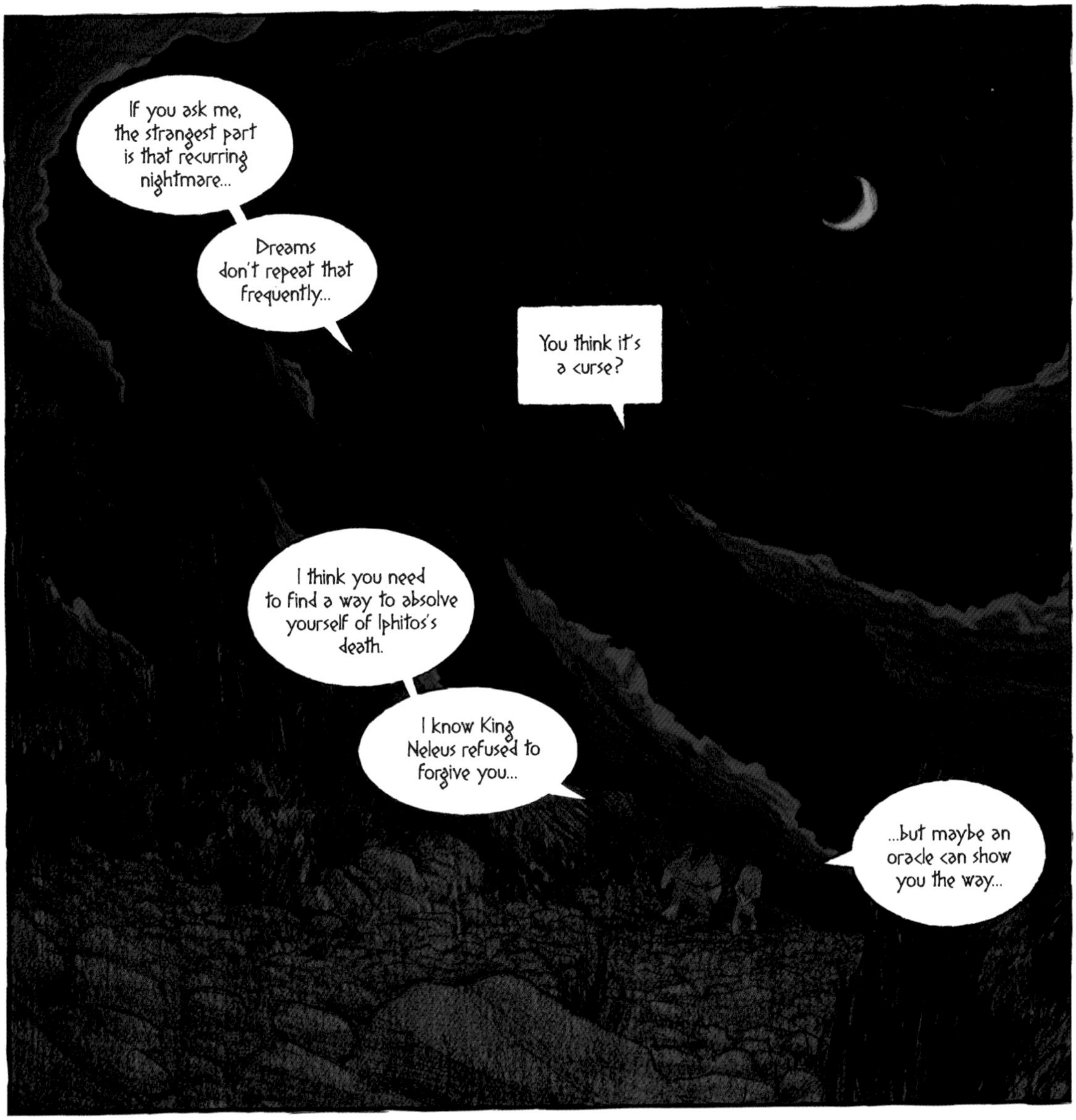
If you ask me, the strangest part is that recurring nightmare...
Dreams don't repeat that frequently...
You think it's a curse?
I think you need to find a way to absolve yourself of Iphitos's death.
I know King Neleus refused to forgive you...
...but maybe an oracle can show you the way...

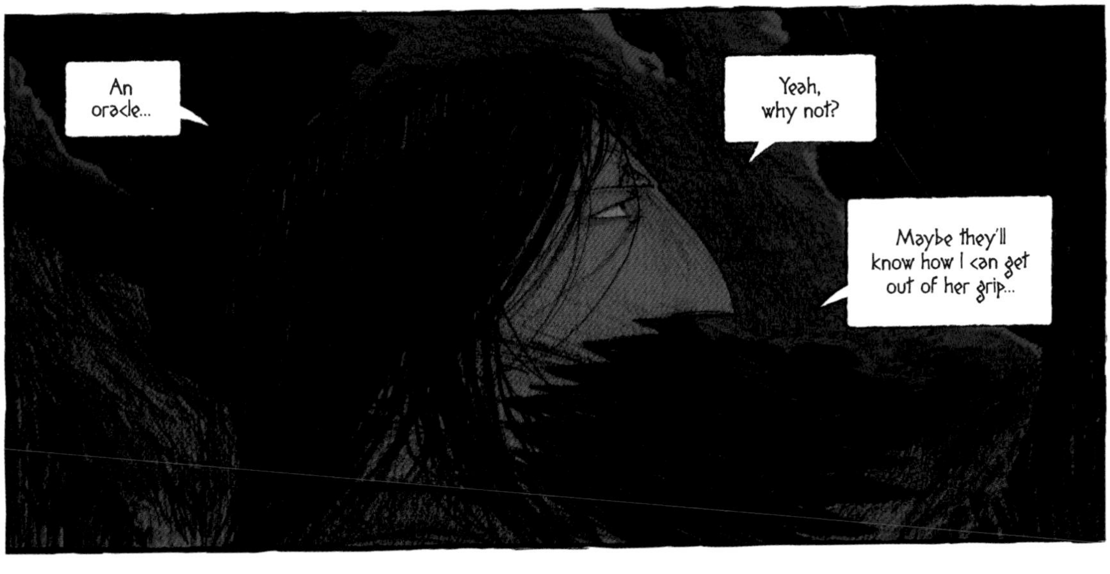
An oracle...
Yeah, why not?
Maybe they'll know how I can get out of her grip...

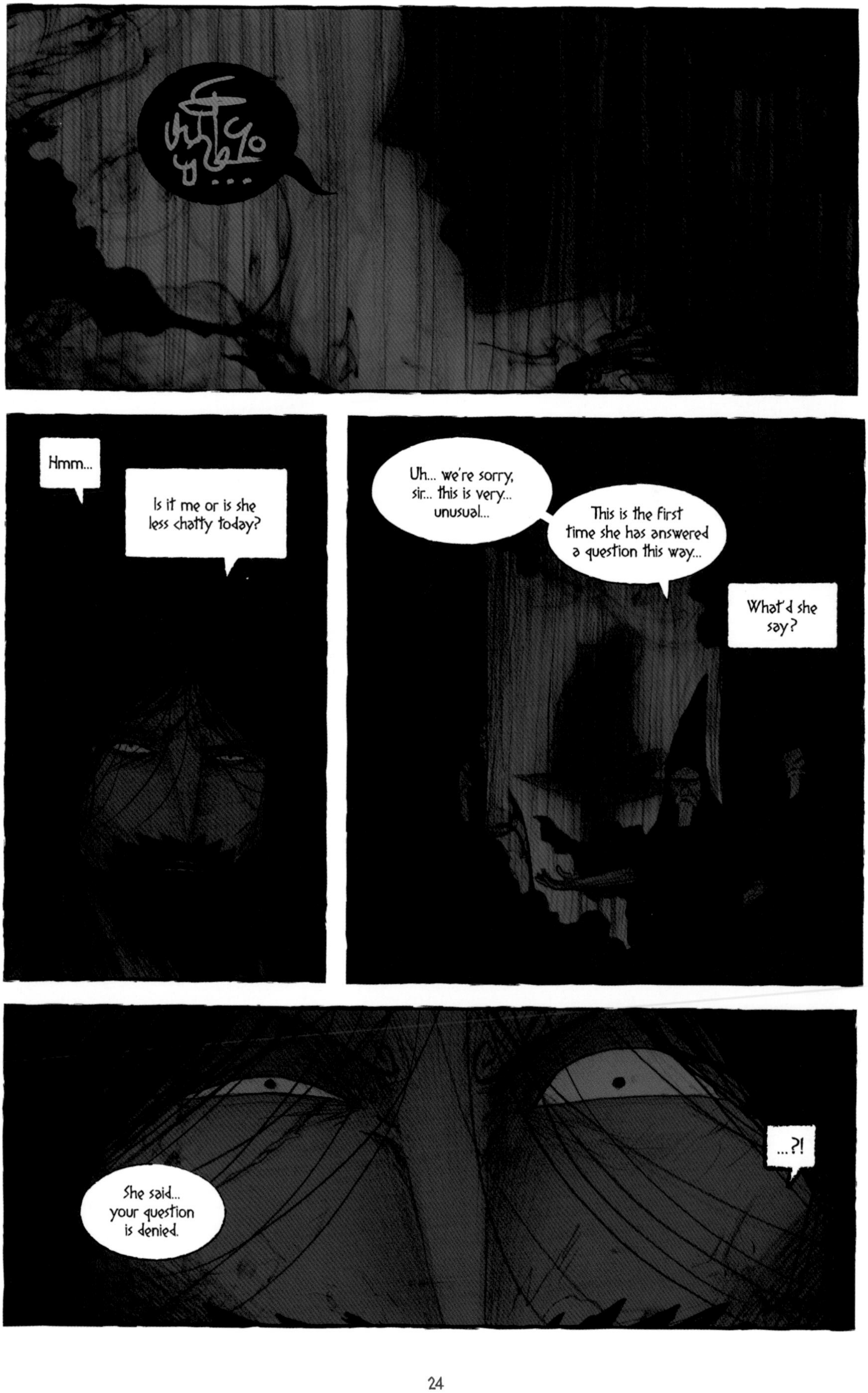
Hmm...
Is it me or is she less chatty today?
Uh... we're sorry, sir... this is very... unusual...
This is the first time she has answered a question this way...
What'd she say?
She said... your question is denied.
...?!

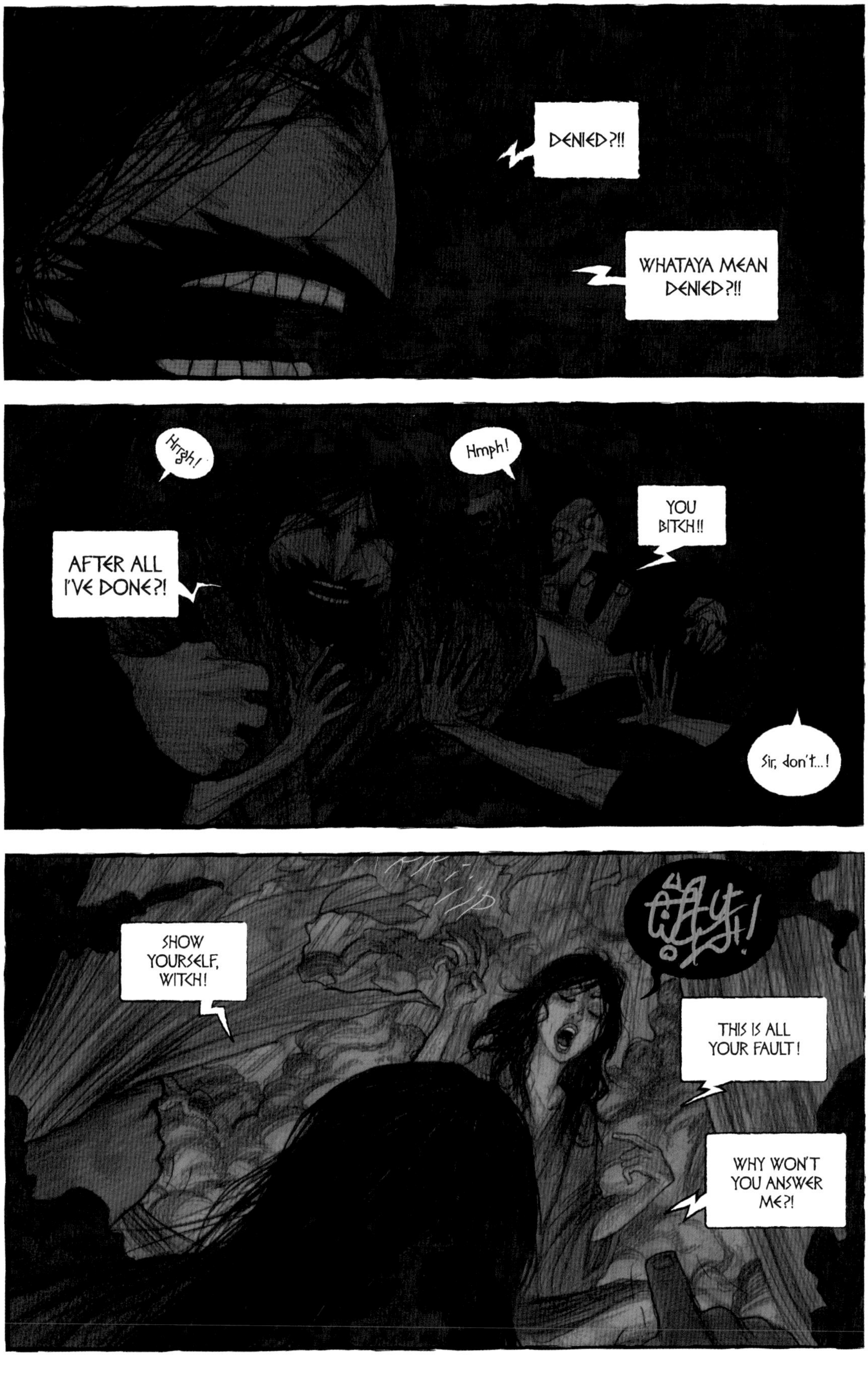
DENIED?!!
WHATAYA MEAN DENIED?!!
Hrrgh!
Hmph!
AFTER ALL I'VE DONE?!
YOU BITCH!!
Sir, don't...!
SHOW YOURSELF, WITCH!
THIS IS ALL YOUR FAULT!
WHY WON'T YOU ANSWER ME?!

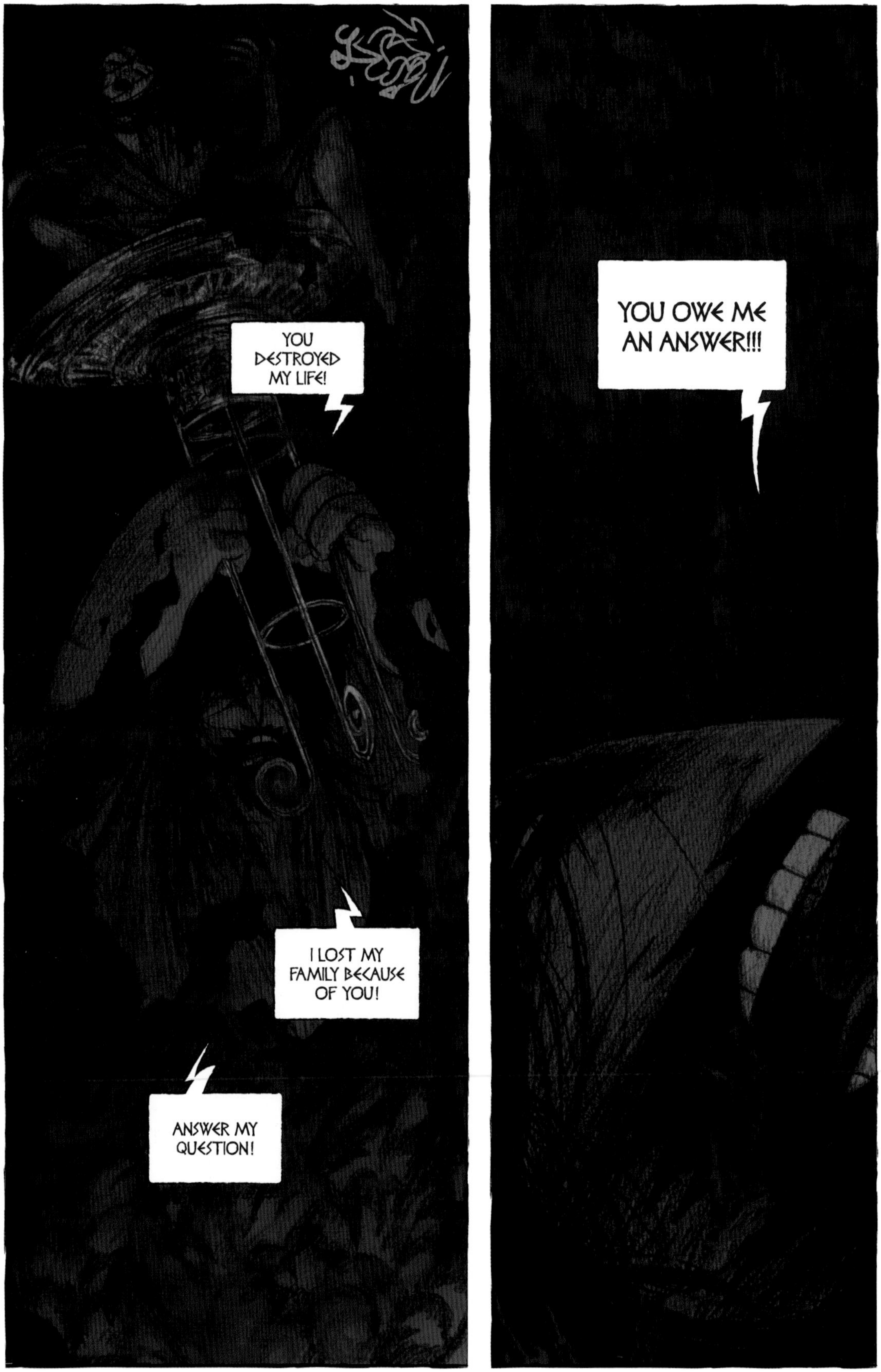
YOU DESTROYED MY LIFE!
I LOST MY FAMILY BECAUSE OF YOU!
ANSWER MY QUESTION!
YOU OWE ME AN ANSWER!!!

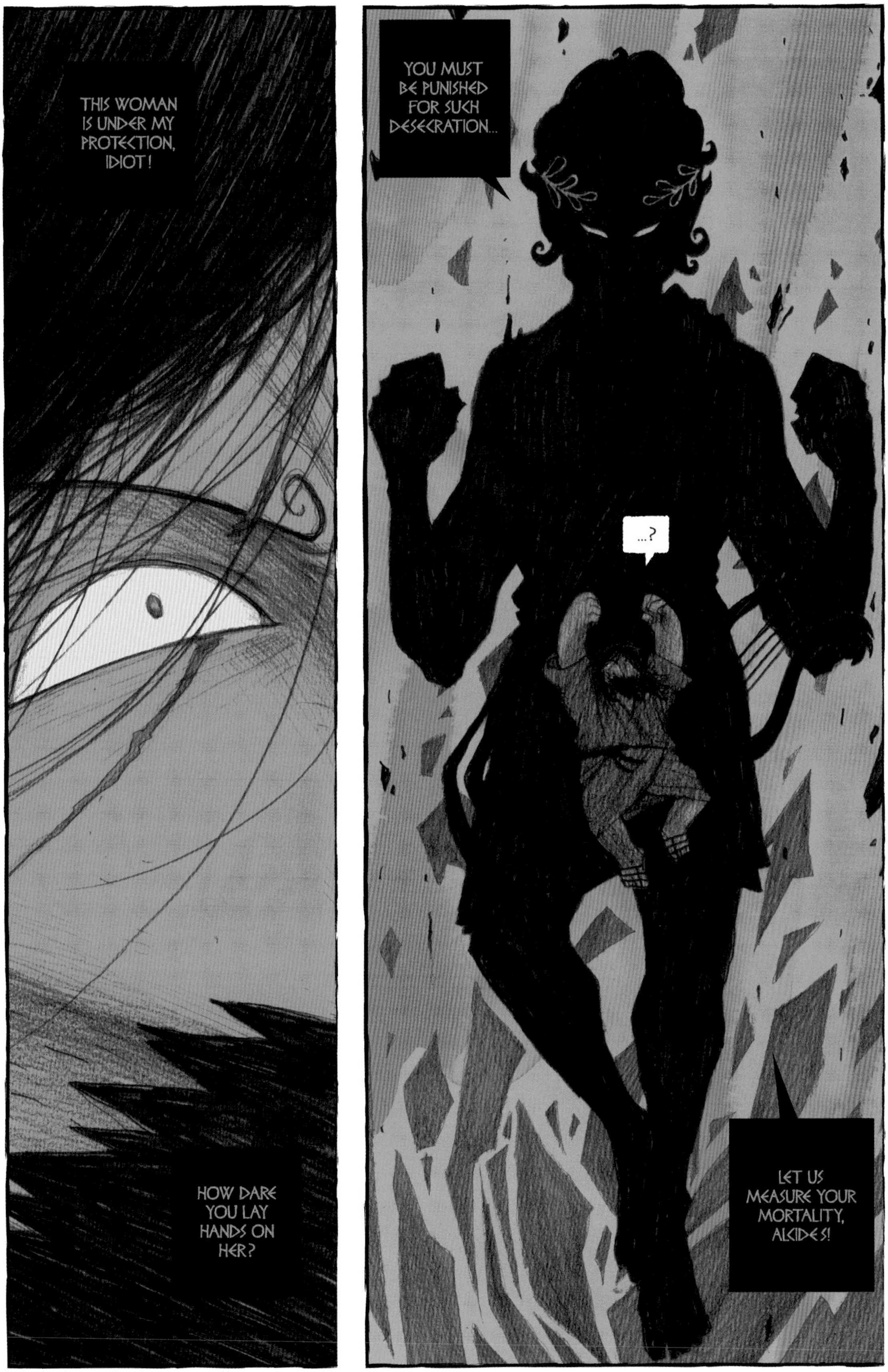
THIS WOMAN IS UNDER MY PROTECTION, IDIOT!
HOW DARE YOU LAY HANDS ON HER?
YOU MUST BE PUNISHED FOR SUCH DESECRATION...
...?
LET US MEASURE YOUR MORTALITY, ALCIDES!

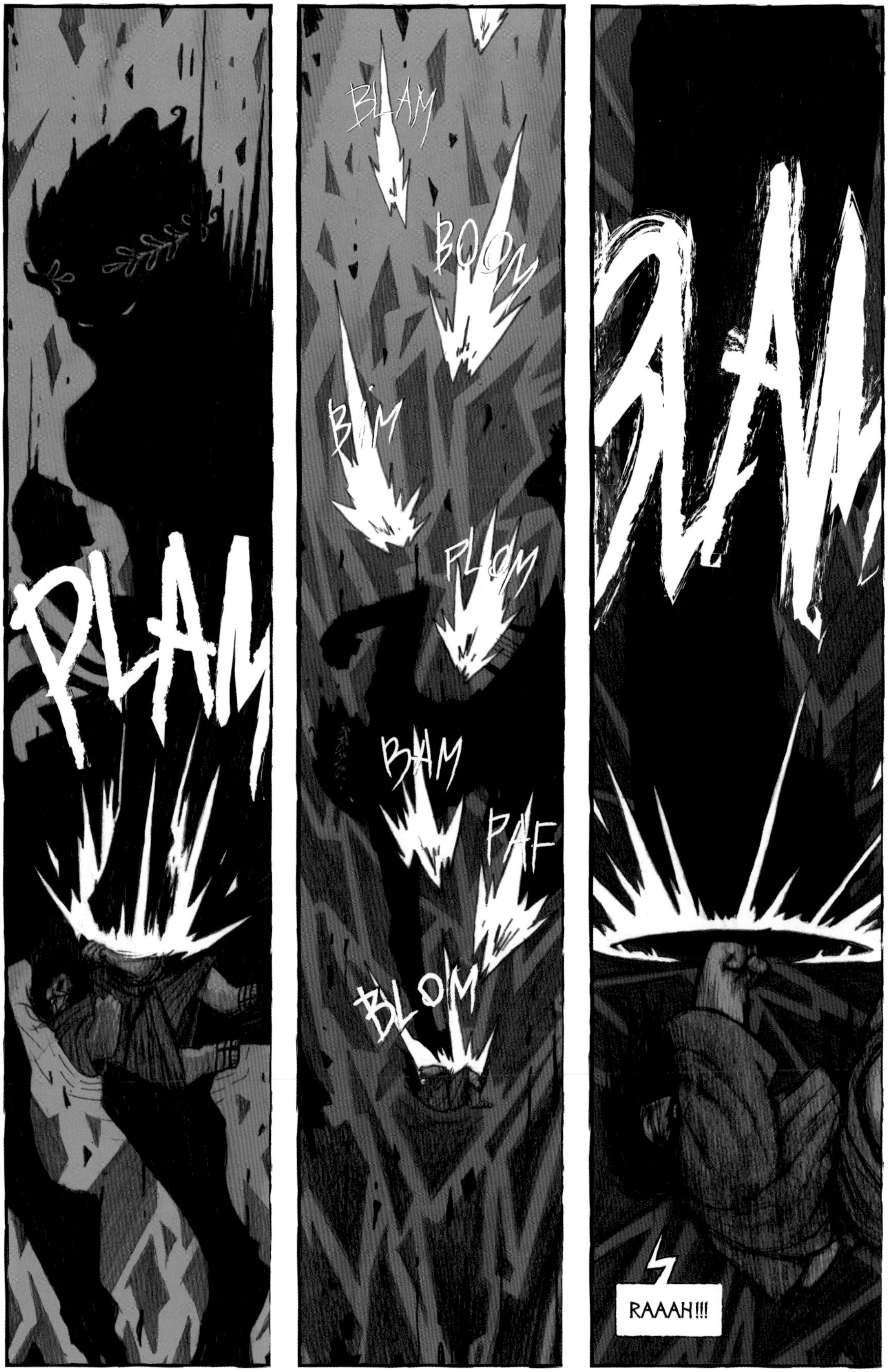
BLAM
BOOM
BIM
PLOM
BAM
PAF
BLOM
RAAAH!!!

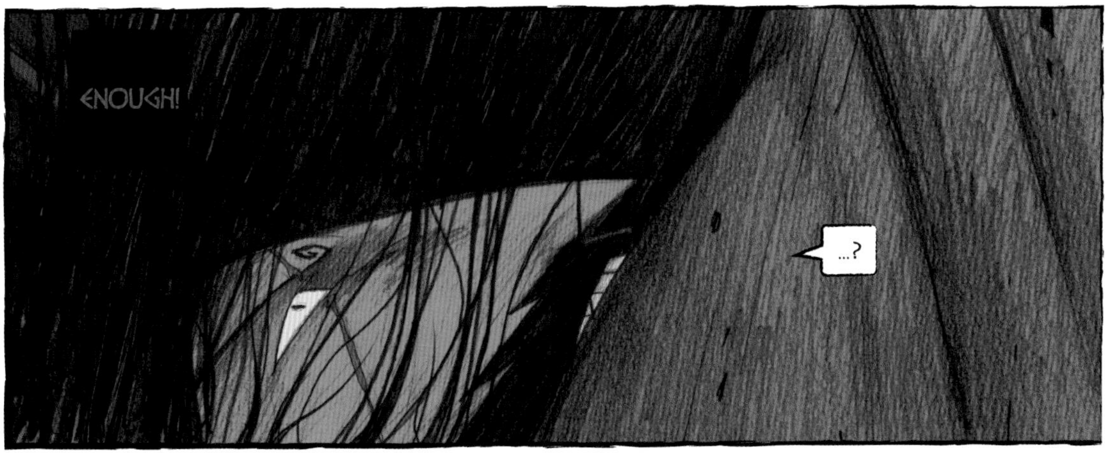
ENOUGH!
...?

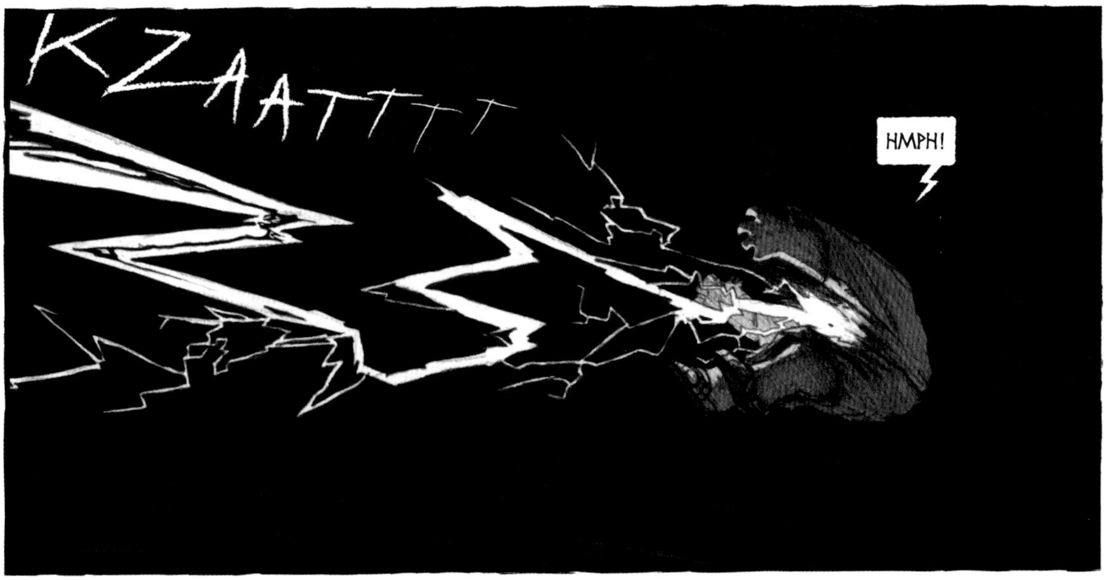
KZAATTTTT
HMPH!

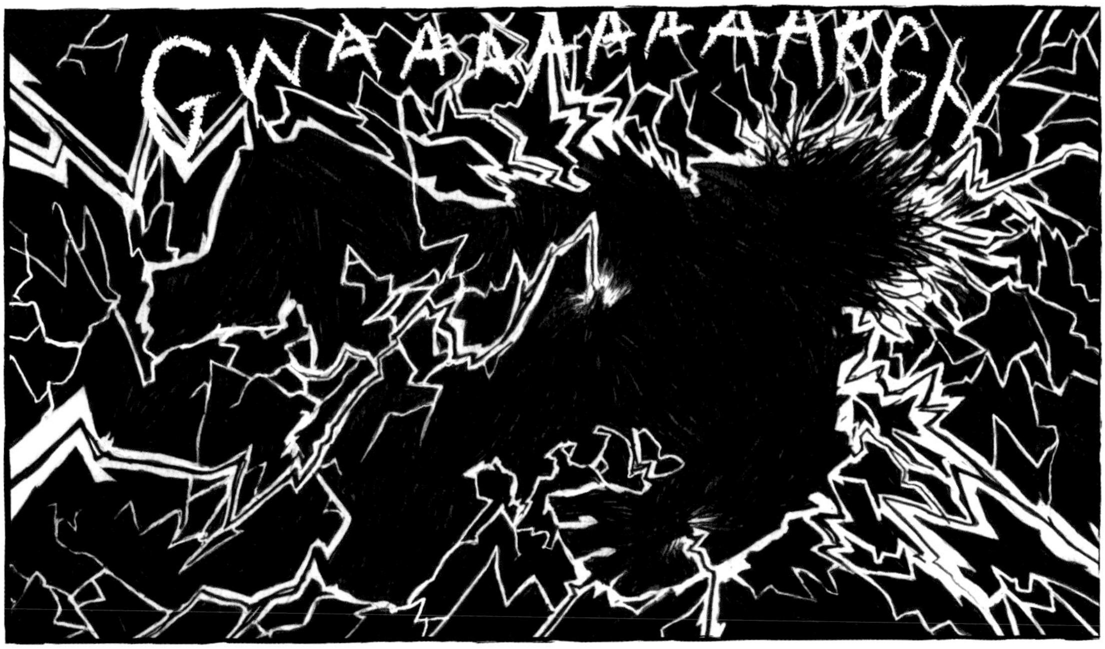
GWAAAAAAAARGH

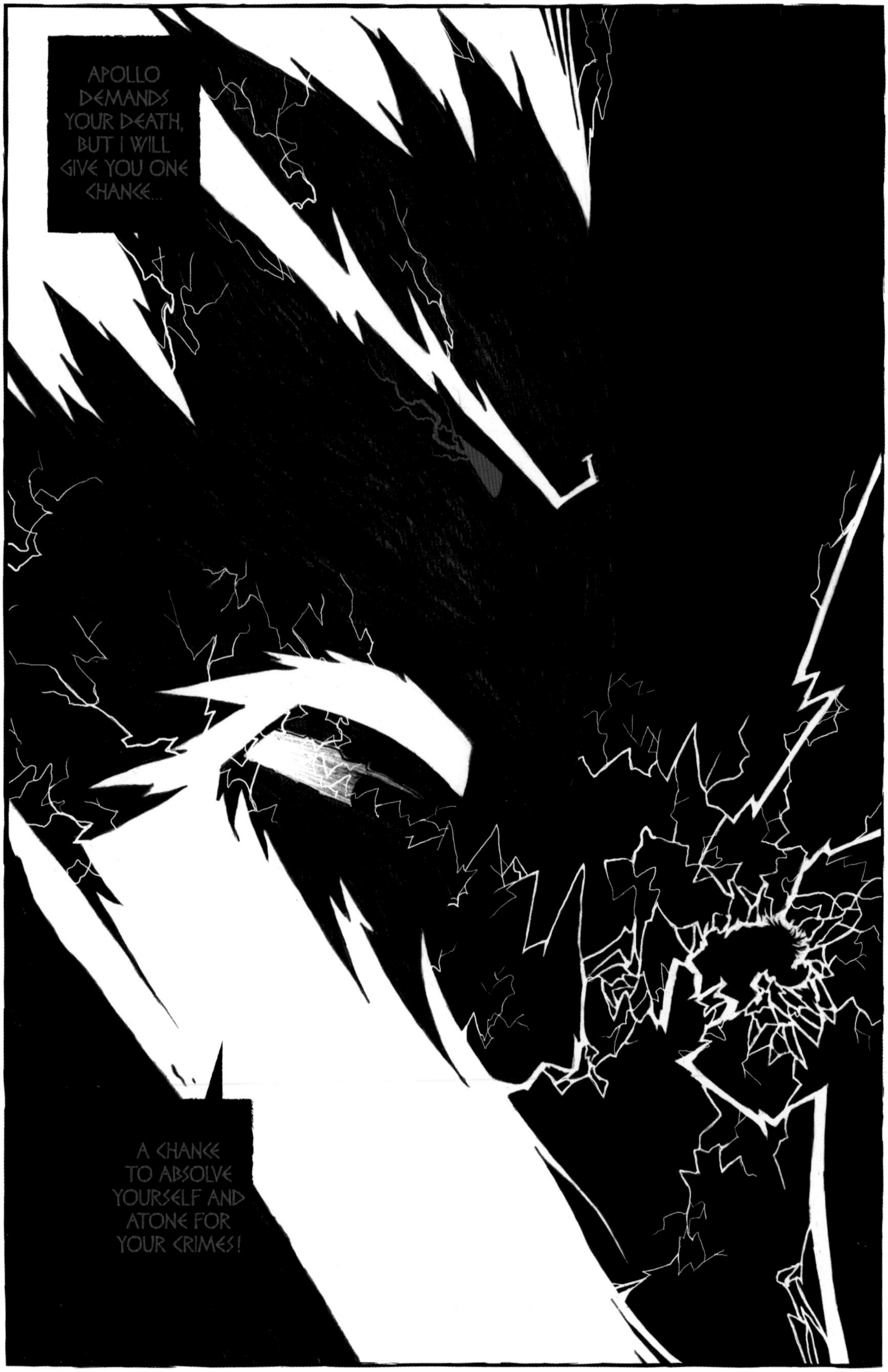
APOLLO DEMANDS YOUR DEATH, BUT I WILL GIVE YOU ONE CHANCE...
A CHANCE TO ABSOLVE YOURSELF AND ATONE FOR YOUR CRIMES!

YOU WILL BE CONDEMNED TO THREE YEARS OF SERVITUDE.

SOLD AS A SLAVE TO OMPHALE, QUEEN OF LYDIA.

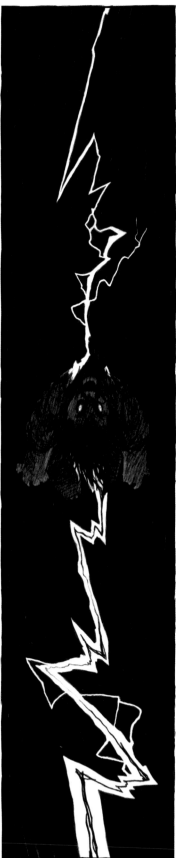

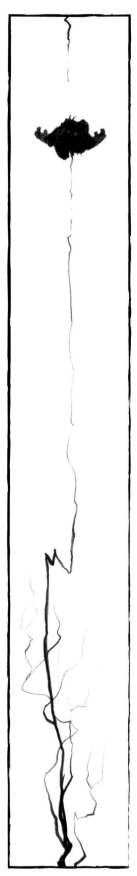

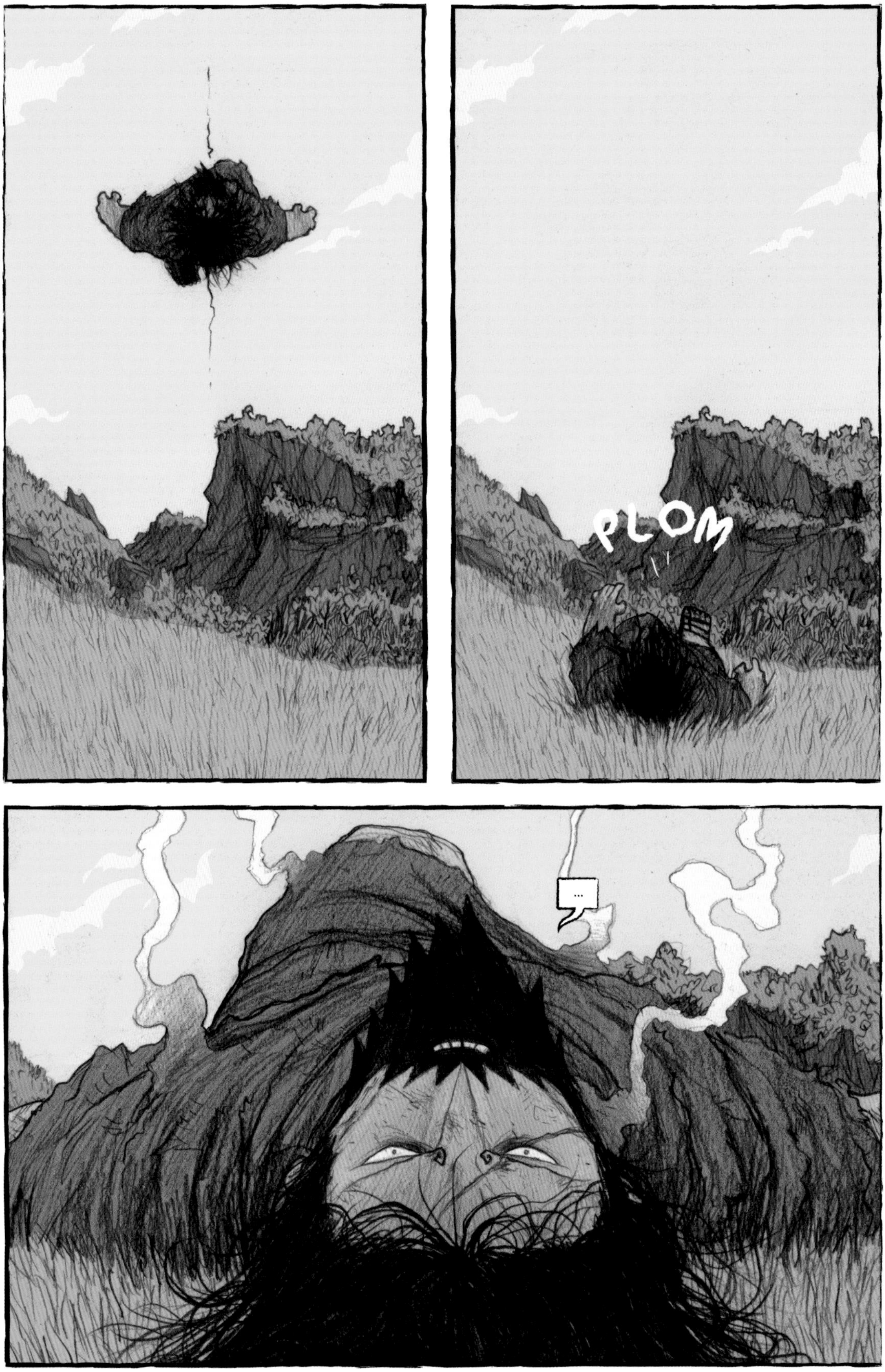
PLOM
...

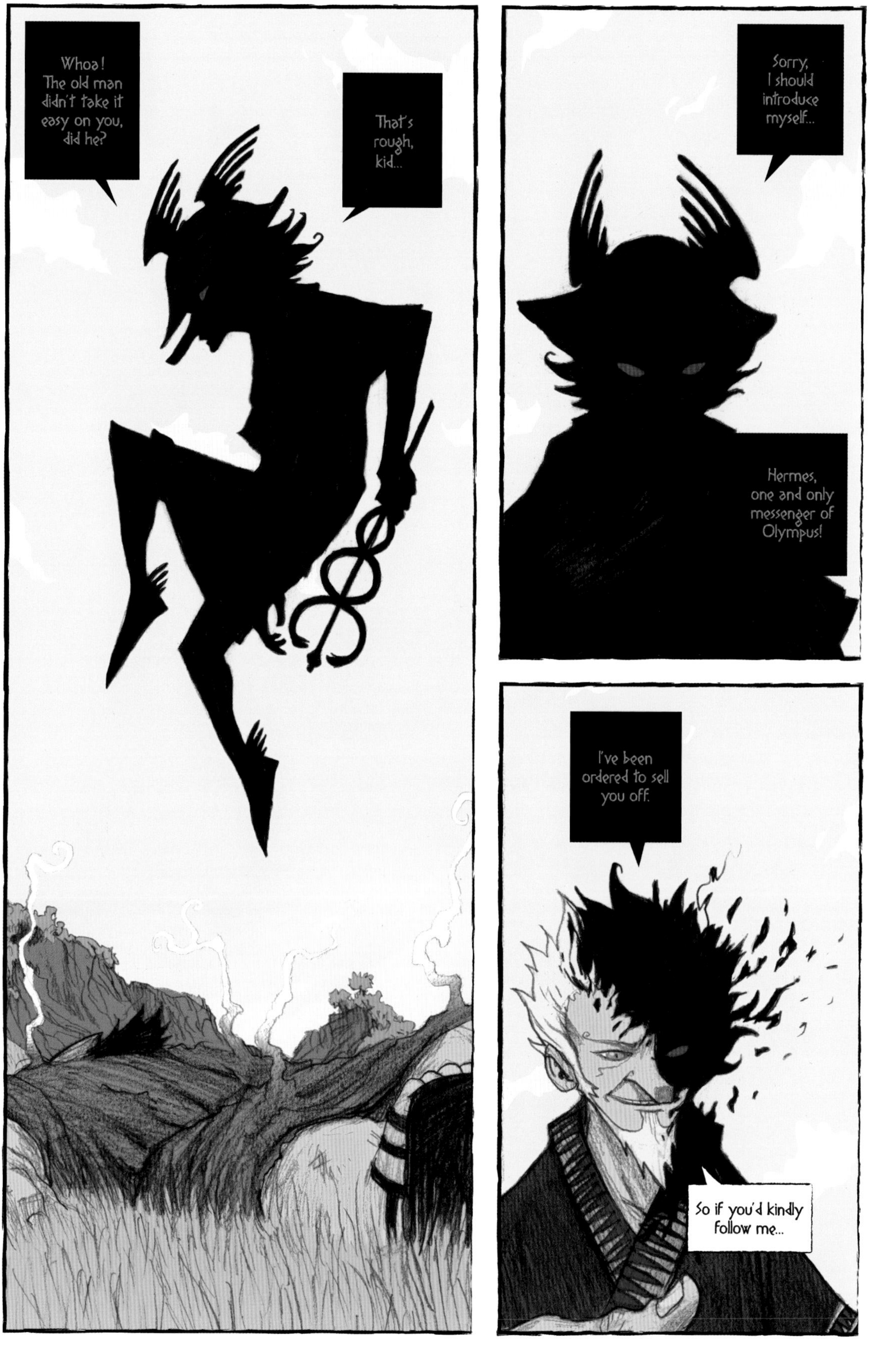

Whoa!
The old man didn't take it easy on you, did he?
That's rough, kid...
Sorry, I should introduce myself...
Hermes, one and only messenger of Olympus!
I've been ordered to sell you off.
So if you'd kindly follow me...

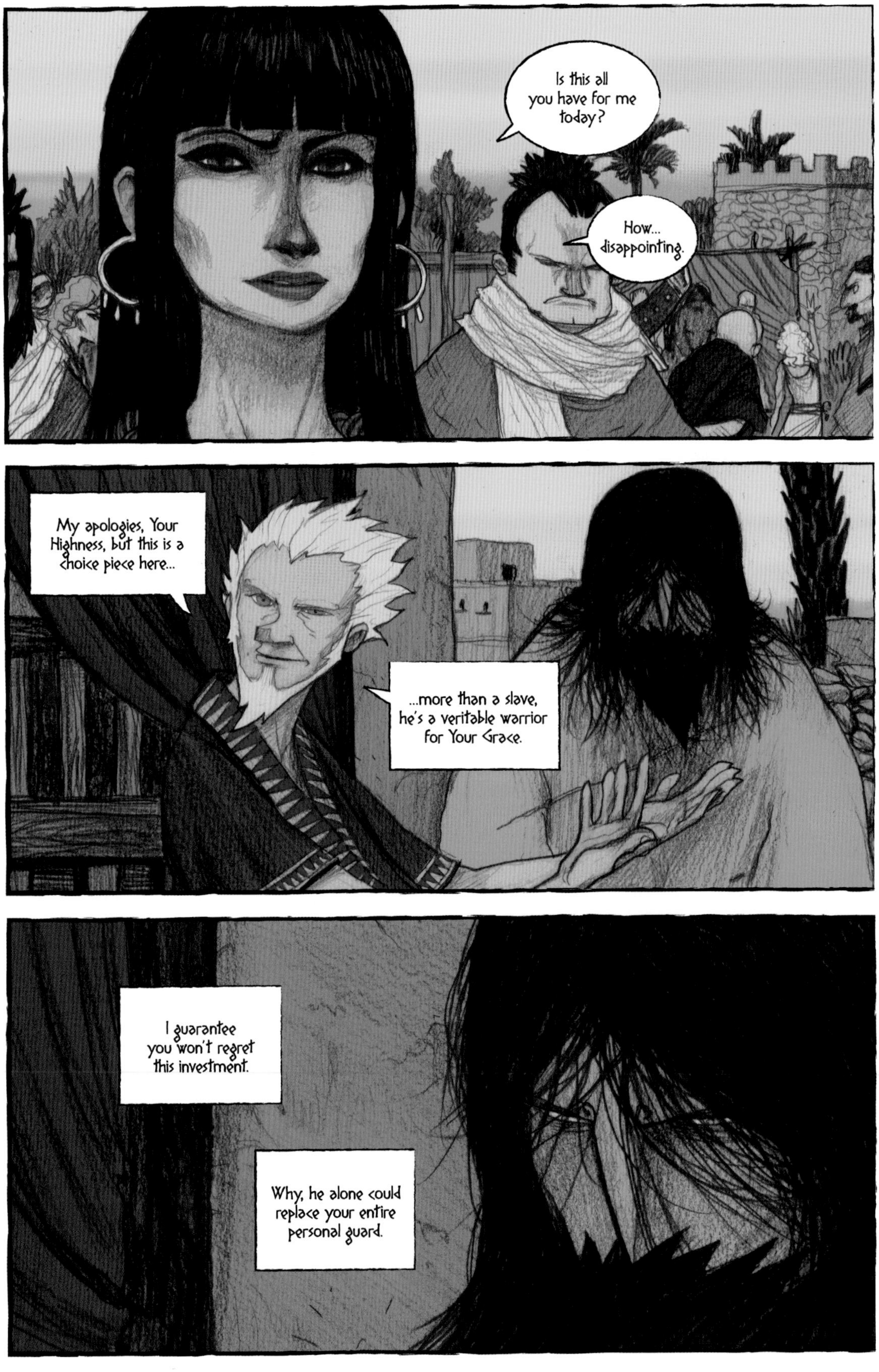
Is this all you have for me today?
How... disappointing.
My apologies, Your Highness, but this is a choice piece here...
...more than a slave, he's a veritable warrior for Your Grace.
I guarantee you won't regret this investment.
Why, he alone could replace your entire personal guard.

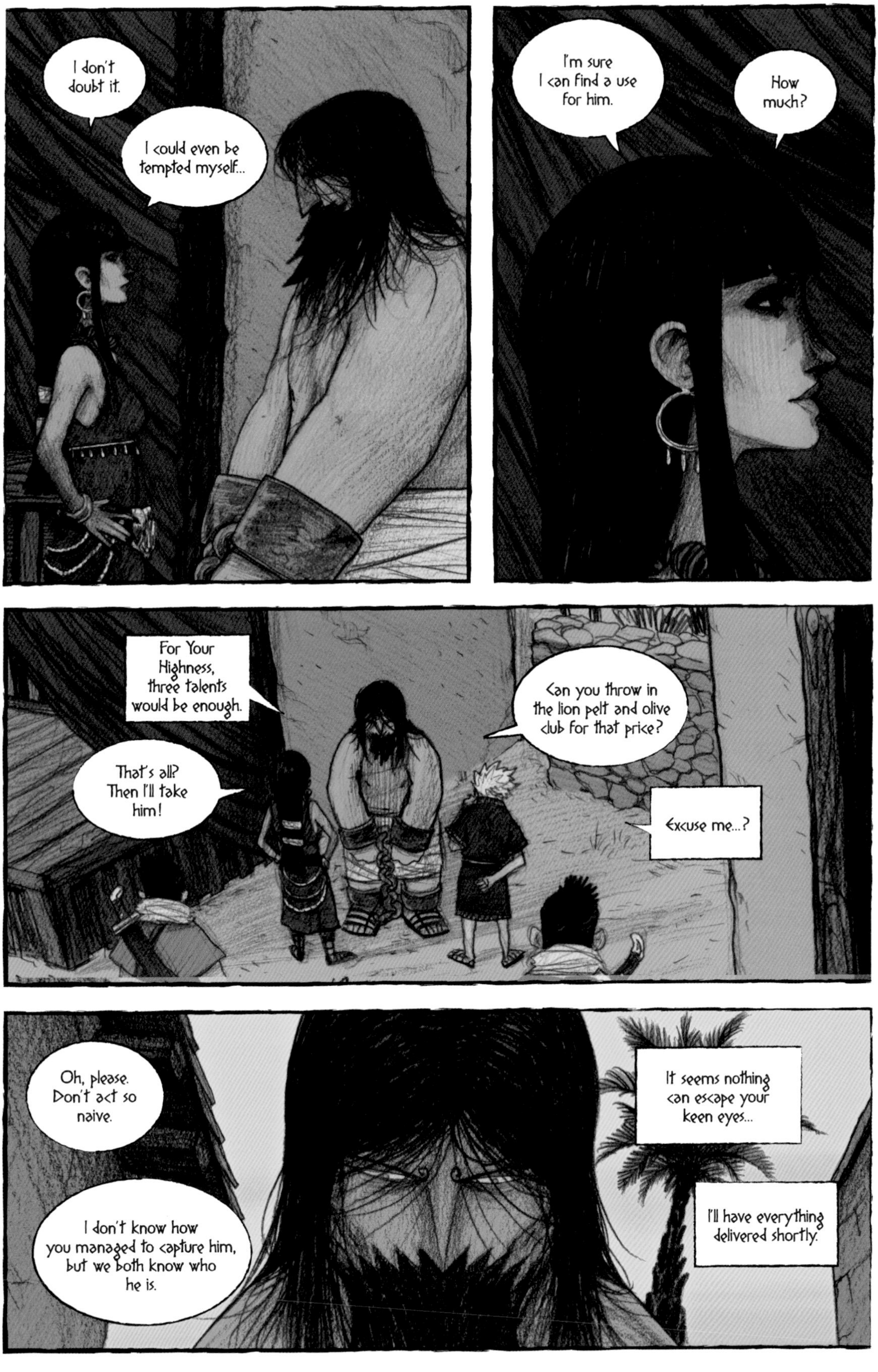
I don't doubt it.
I could even be tempted myself...
I'm sure I can find a use for him.
How much?
For Your Highness, three talents would be enough.
Can you throw in the lion pelt and olive club for that price?
That's all? Then I'll take him!
Excuse me...?
Oh, please. Don't act so naive.
I don't know how you managed to capture him, but we both know who he is.
It seems nothing can escape your keen eyes...
I'll have everything delivered shortly.

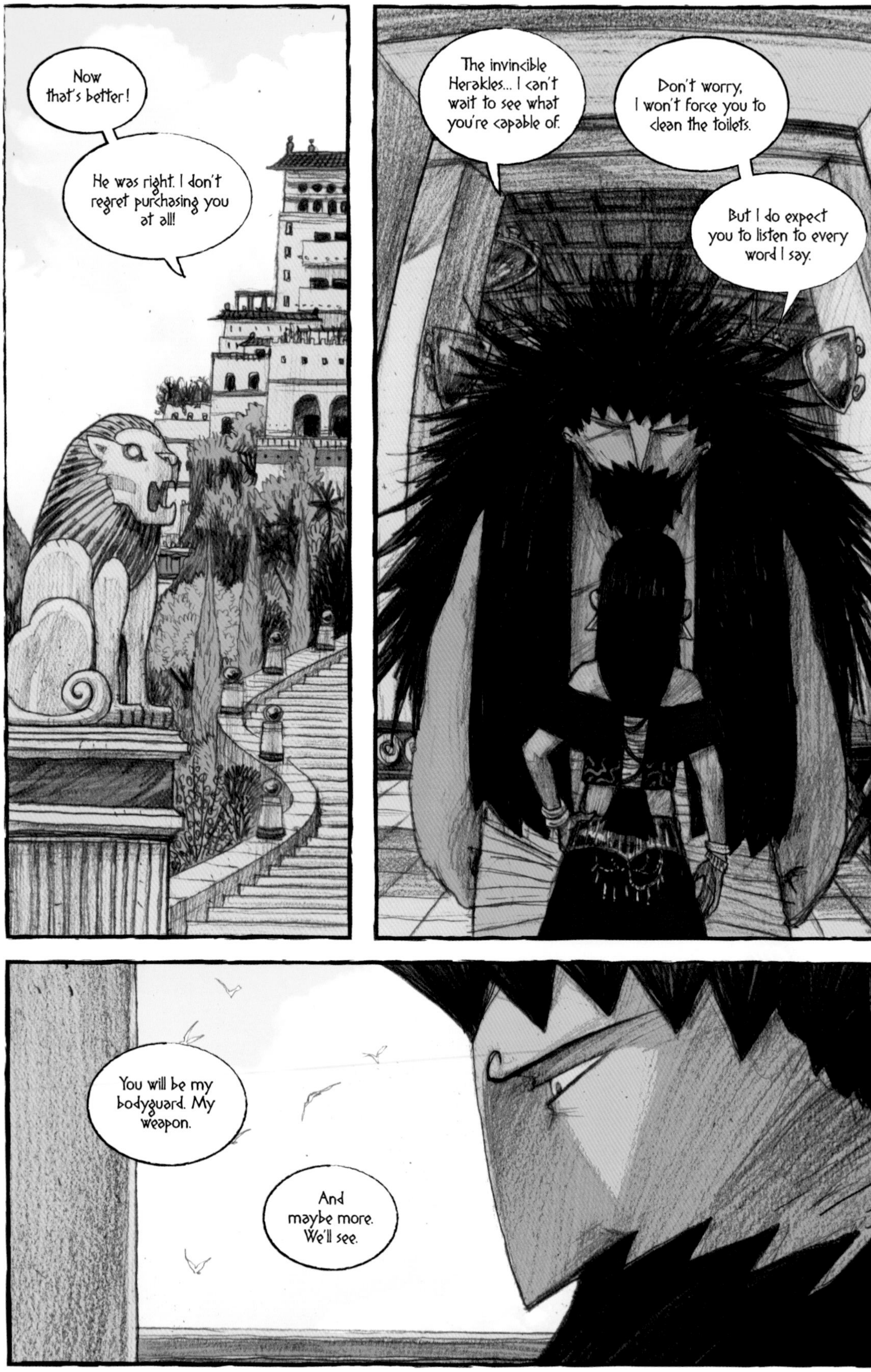
Now that's better!
He was right. I don't regret purchasing you at all!
The invincible Herakles... I can't wait to see what you're capable of.
Don't worry, I won't force you to clean the toilets.
But I do expect you to listen to every word I say.
You will be my bodyguard. My weapon.
And maybe more. We'll see.

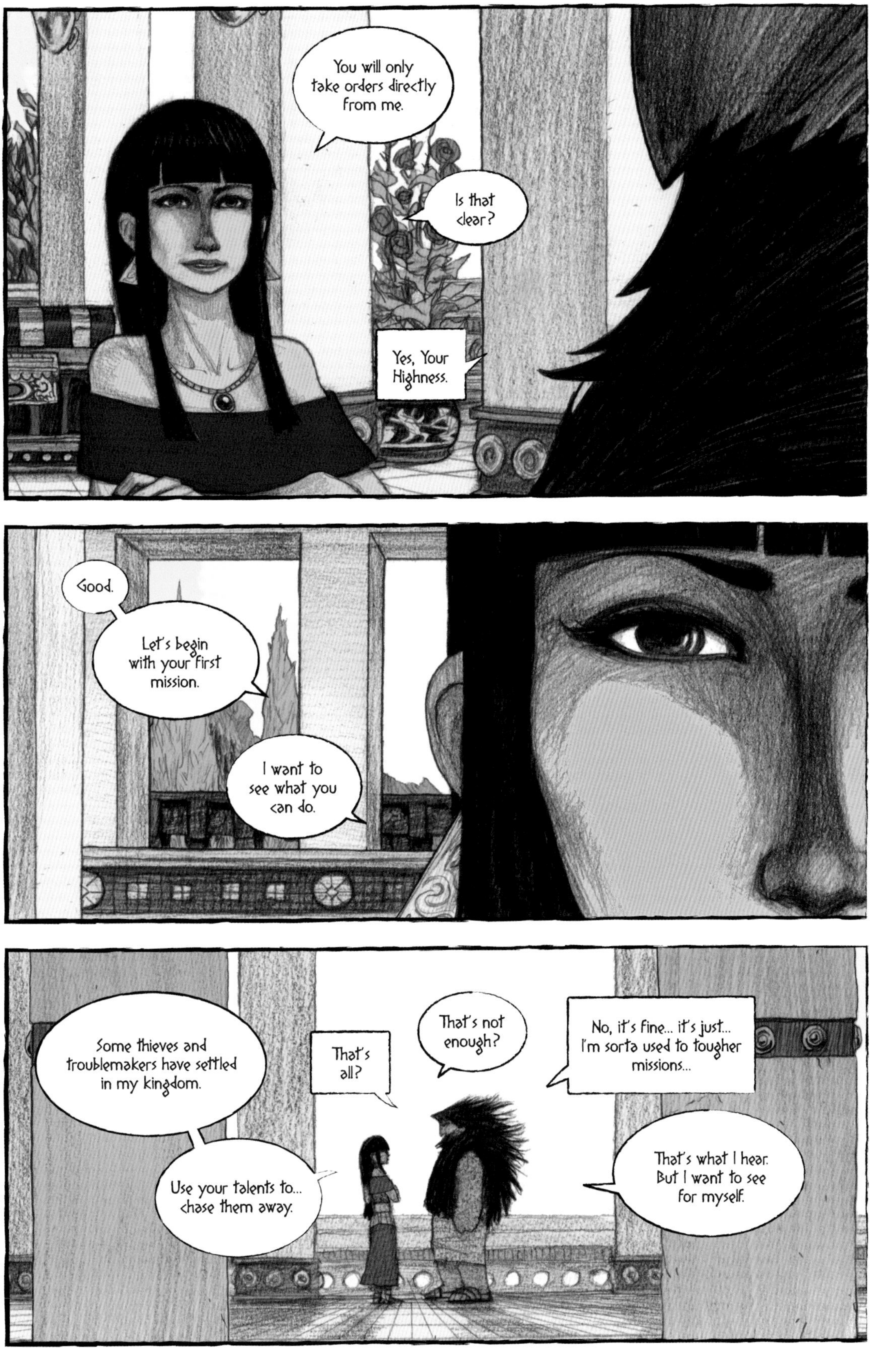
You will only take orders directly from me.
Is that clear?
Yes, Your Highness.
Good.
Let's begin with your first mission.
I want to see what you can do.
Some thieves and troublemakers have settled in my kingdom.
Use your talents to... chase them away.
That's all?
That's not enough?
No, it's fine... it's just... I'm sorta used to tougher missions...
That's what I hear. But I want to see for myself.

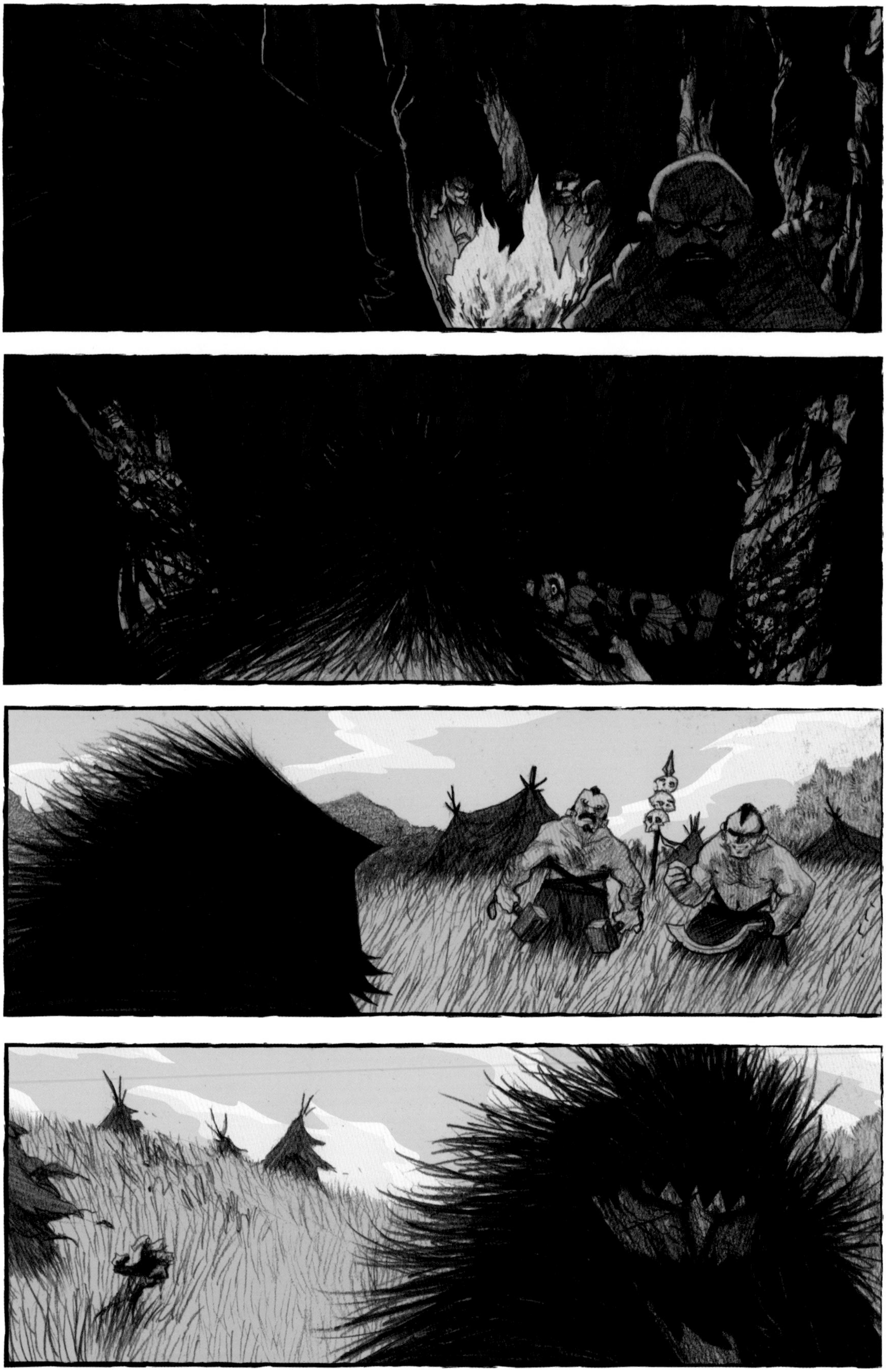

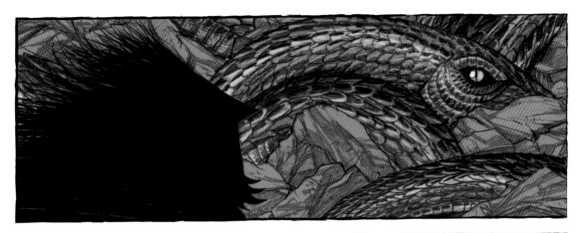

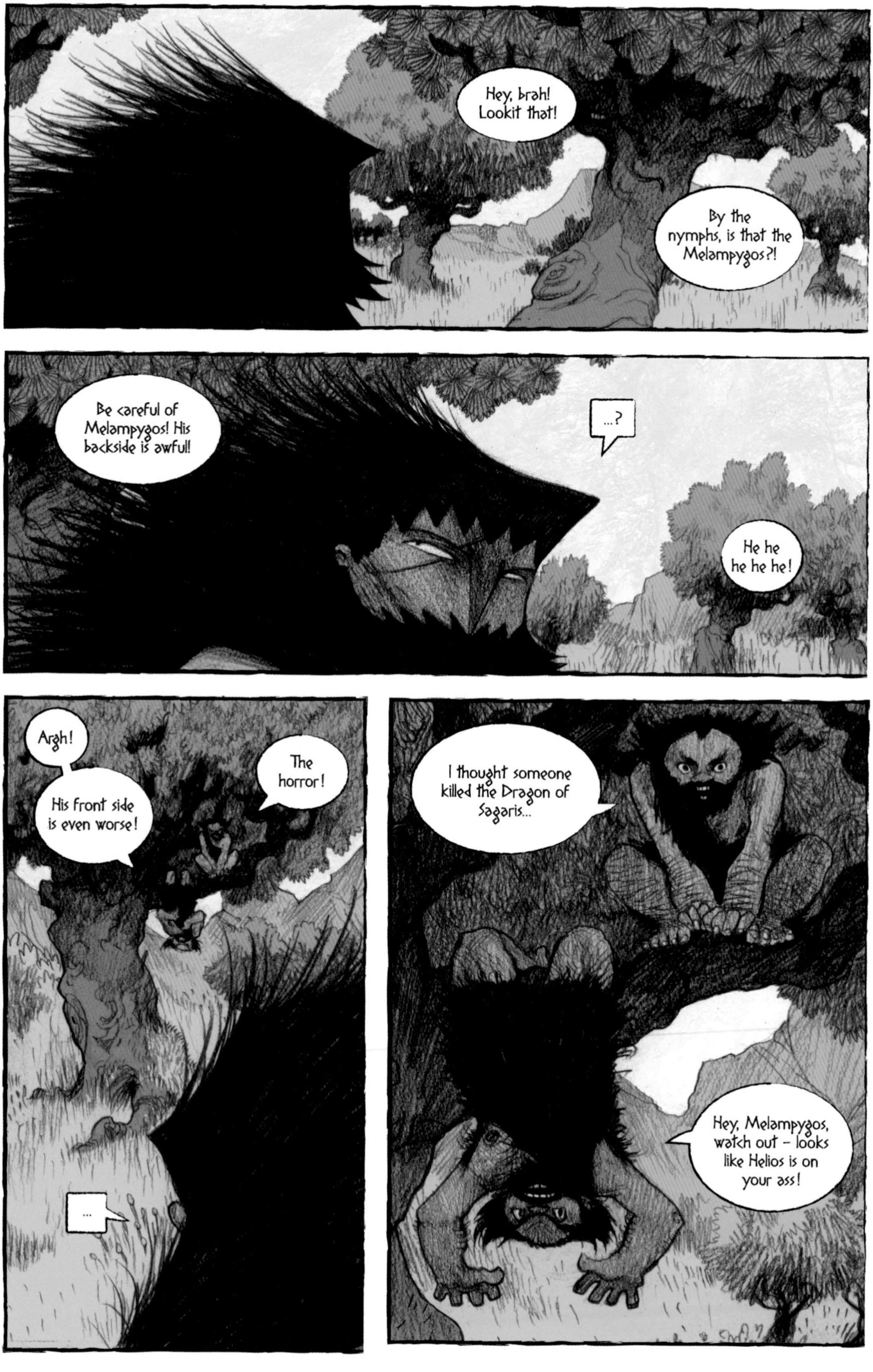
Hey, brah! Lookit that!
By the nymphs, is that the Melampygos?!
Be careful of Melampygos! His backside is awful!
...?
He he he he he!
Argh!
His front side is even worse!
The horror!
...
I thought someone killed the Dragon of Sagaris...
Hey, Melampygos, watch out – looks like Helios is on your ass!

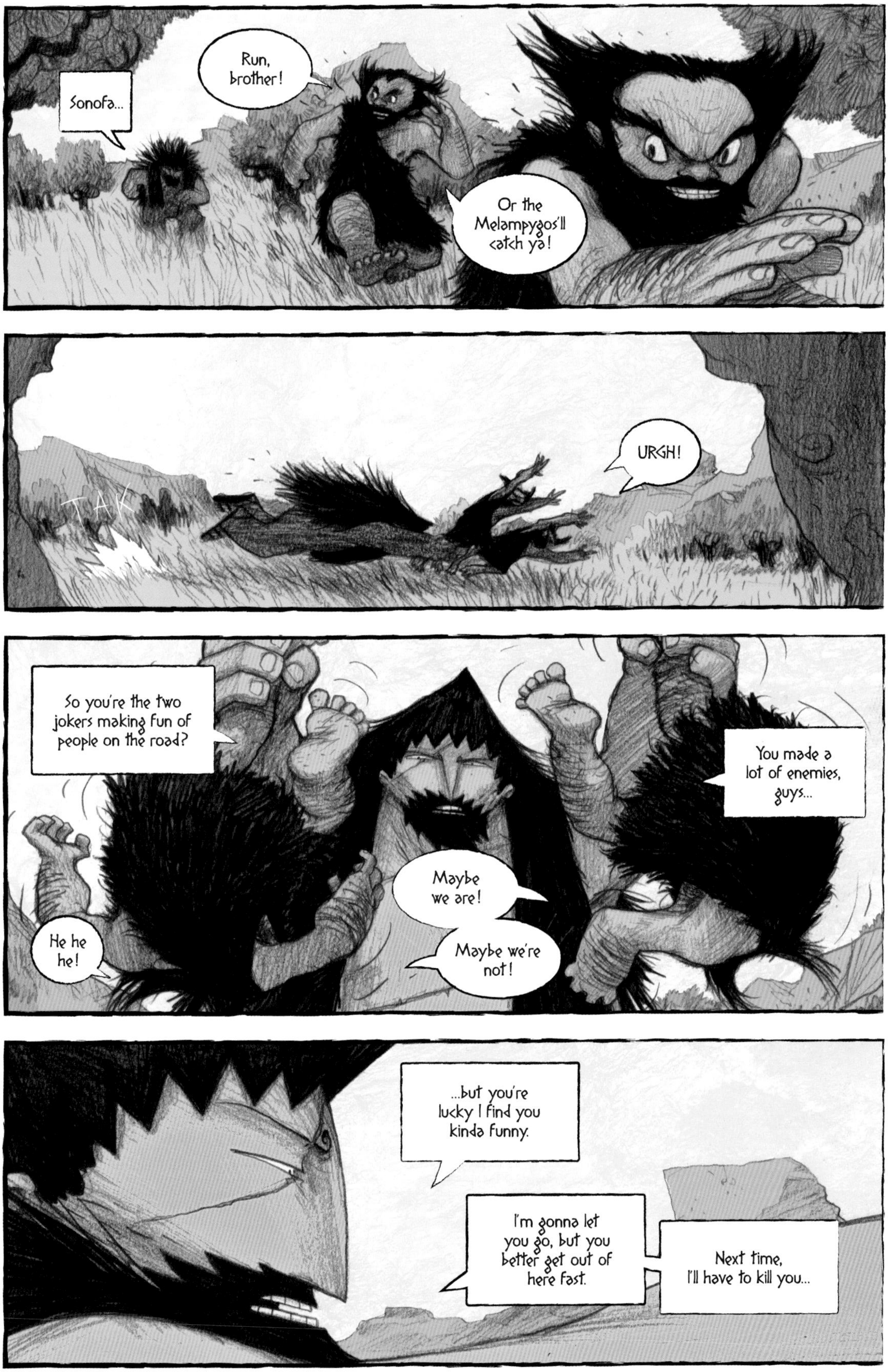
Sonofa...
Run, brother!
Or the Melampygos'll catch ya!
TAK
URGH!
So you're the two jokers making fun of people on the road?
You made a lot of enemies, guys...
Maybe we are!
Maybe we're not!
He he he!
...but you're lucky I find you kinda funny.
I'm gonna let you go, but you better get out of here fast.
Next time, I'll have to kill you...

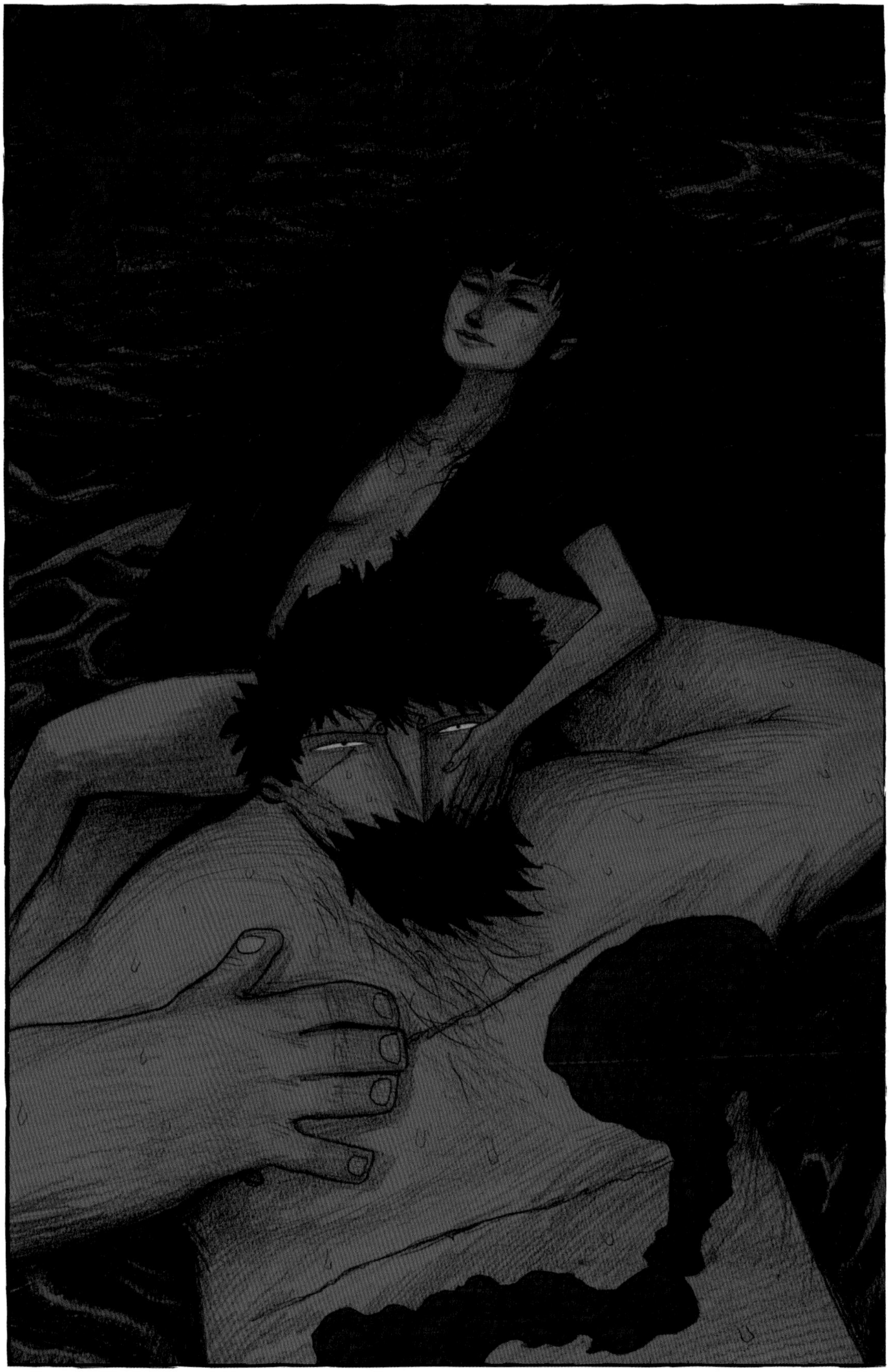

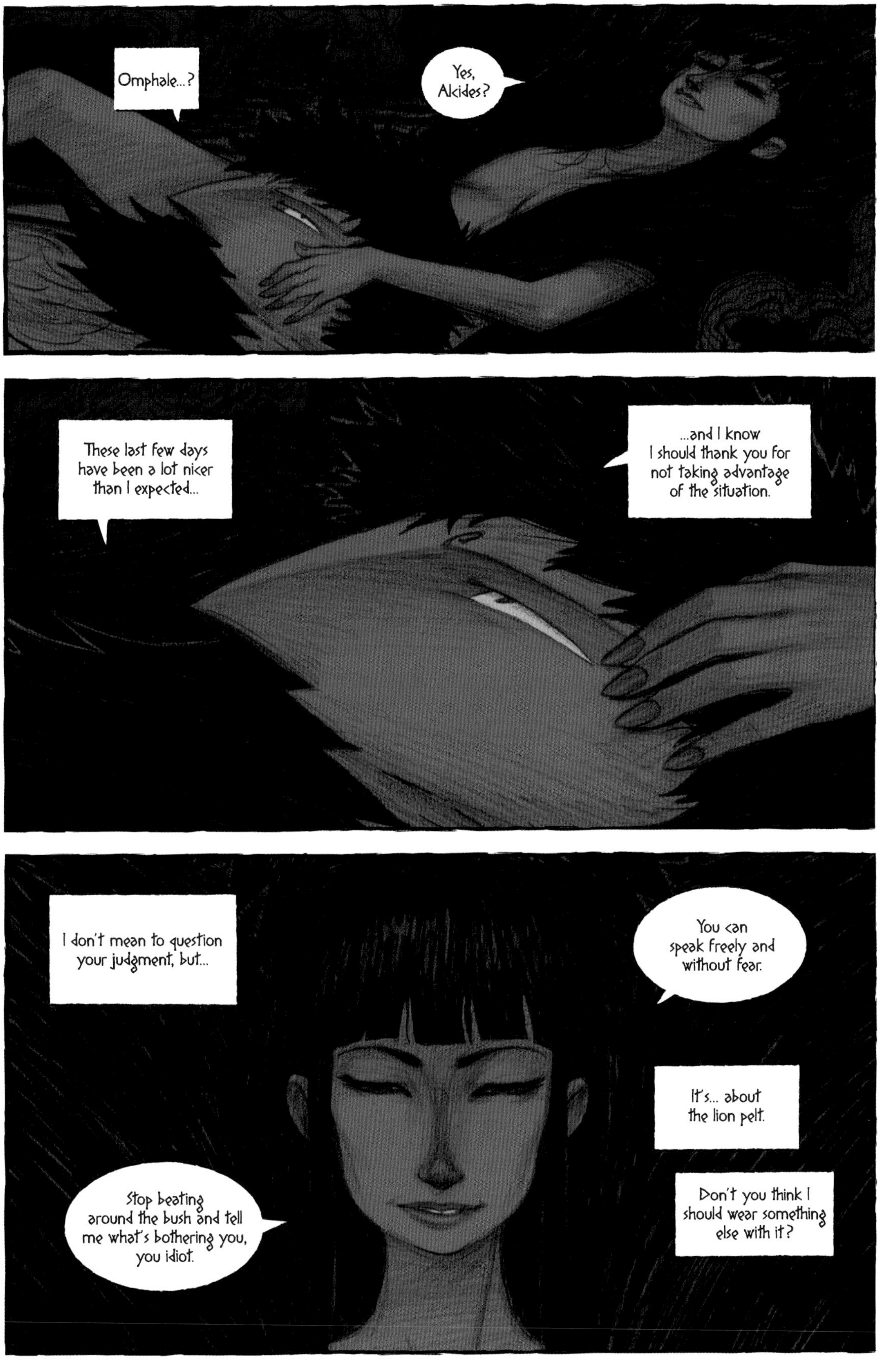
Omphale...?
Yes, Alkides?
These last few days have been a lot nicer than I expected...
...and I know I should thank you for not taking advantage of the situation.
I don't mean to question your judgment, but...
You can speak freely and without fear.
It's... about the lion pelt.
Don't you think I should wear something else with it?
Stop beating around the bush and tell me what's bothering you, you idiot.

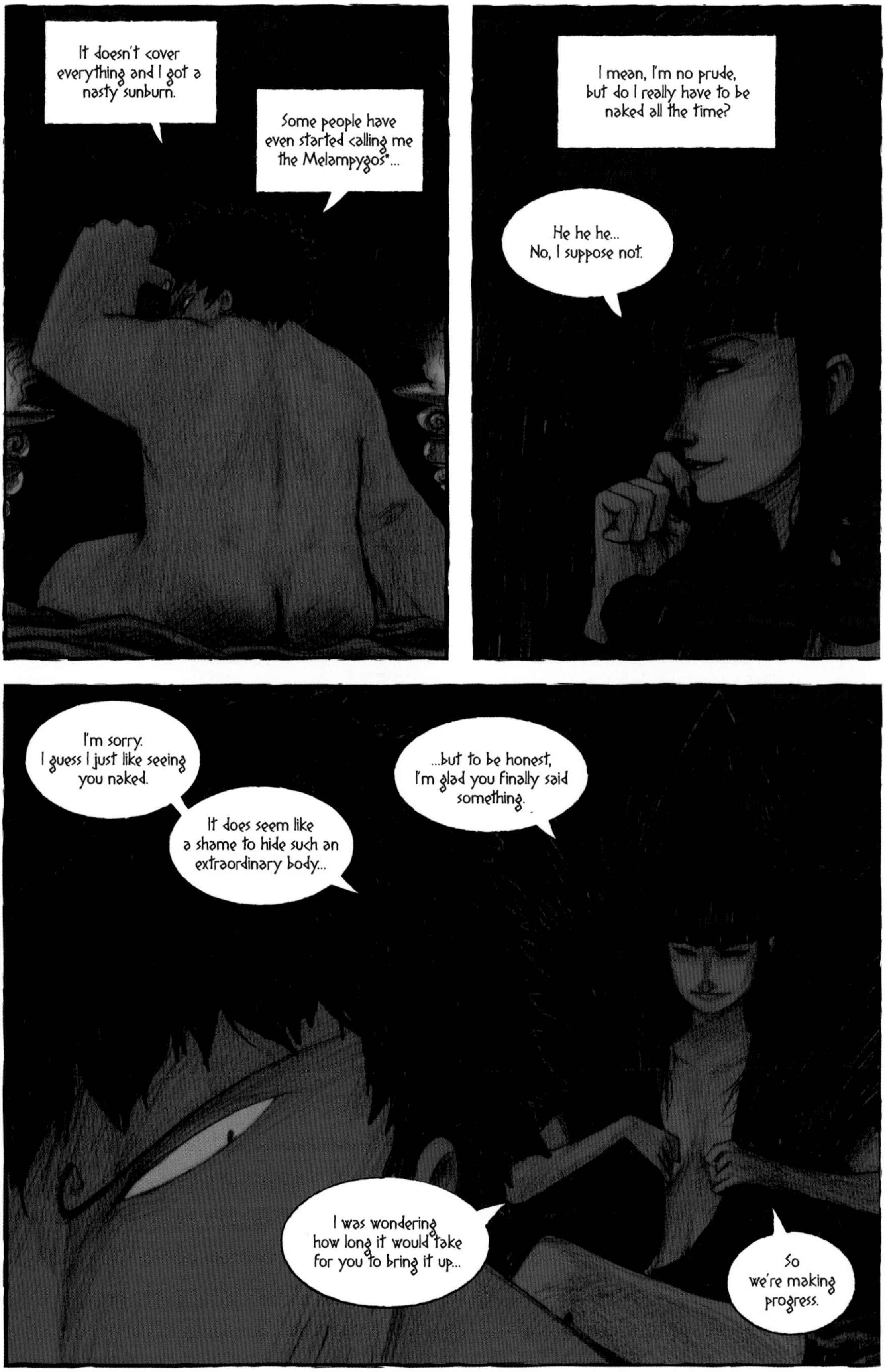
It doesn't cover everything and I got a nasty sunburn.
Some people have even started calling me the Melampygos*...
I mean, I'm no prude, but do I really have to be naked all the time?
He he he... No, I suppose not.
I'm sorry. I guess I just like seeing you naked.
It does seem like a shame to hide such an extraordinary body...
...but to be honest, I'm glad you finally said something.
I was wondering how long it would take for you to bring it up...
So we're making progress.

*black-ass

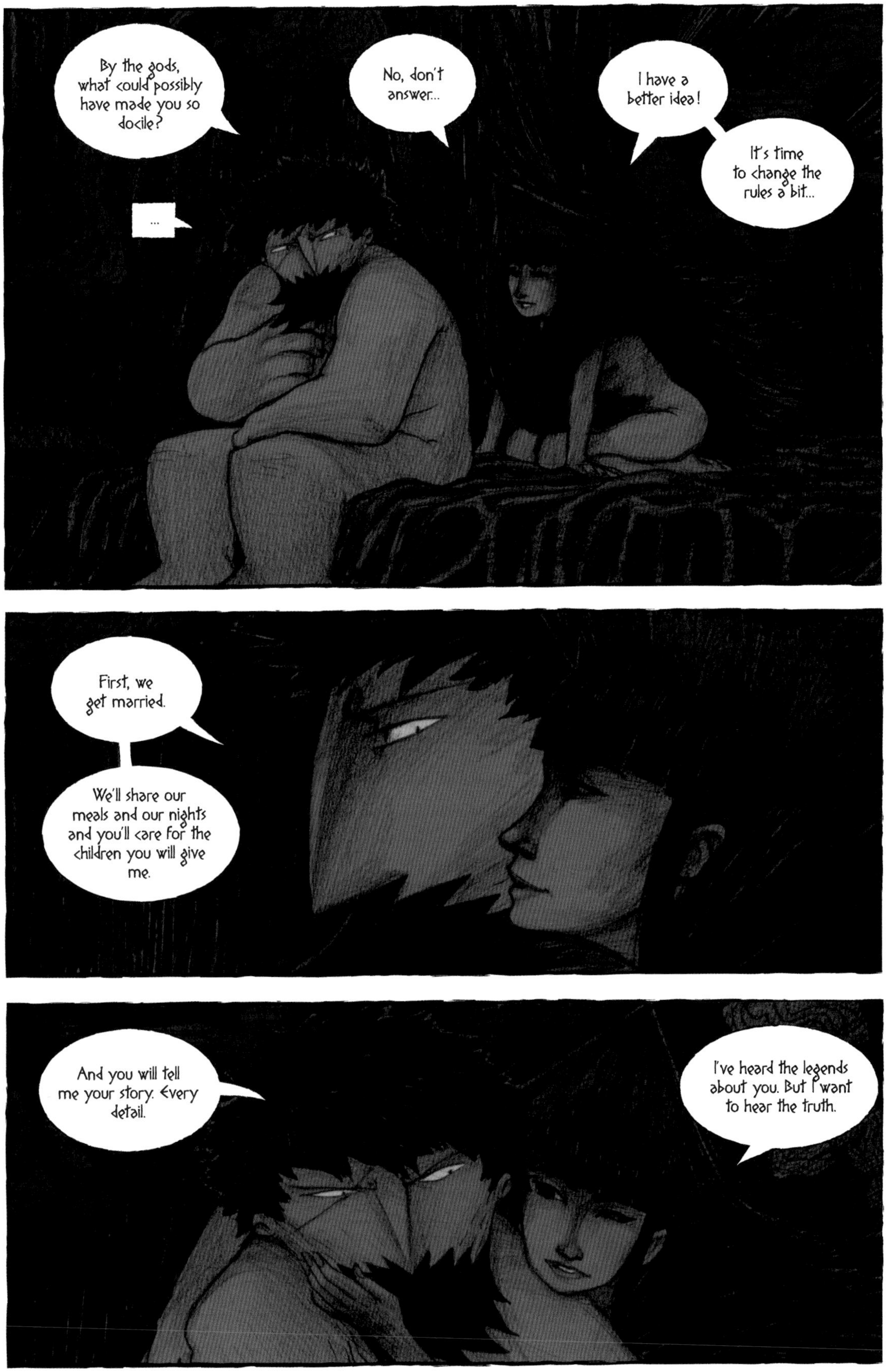
By the gods, what could possibly have made you so docile?
...
No, don't answer...
I have a better idea!
It's time to change the rules a bit...
First, we get married.
We'll share our meals and our nights and you'll care for the children you will give me.
And you will tell me your story. Every detail.
I've heard the legends about you. But I want to hear the truth.

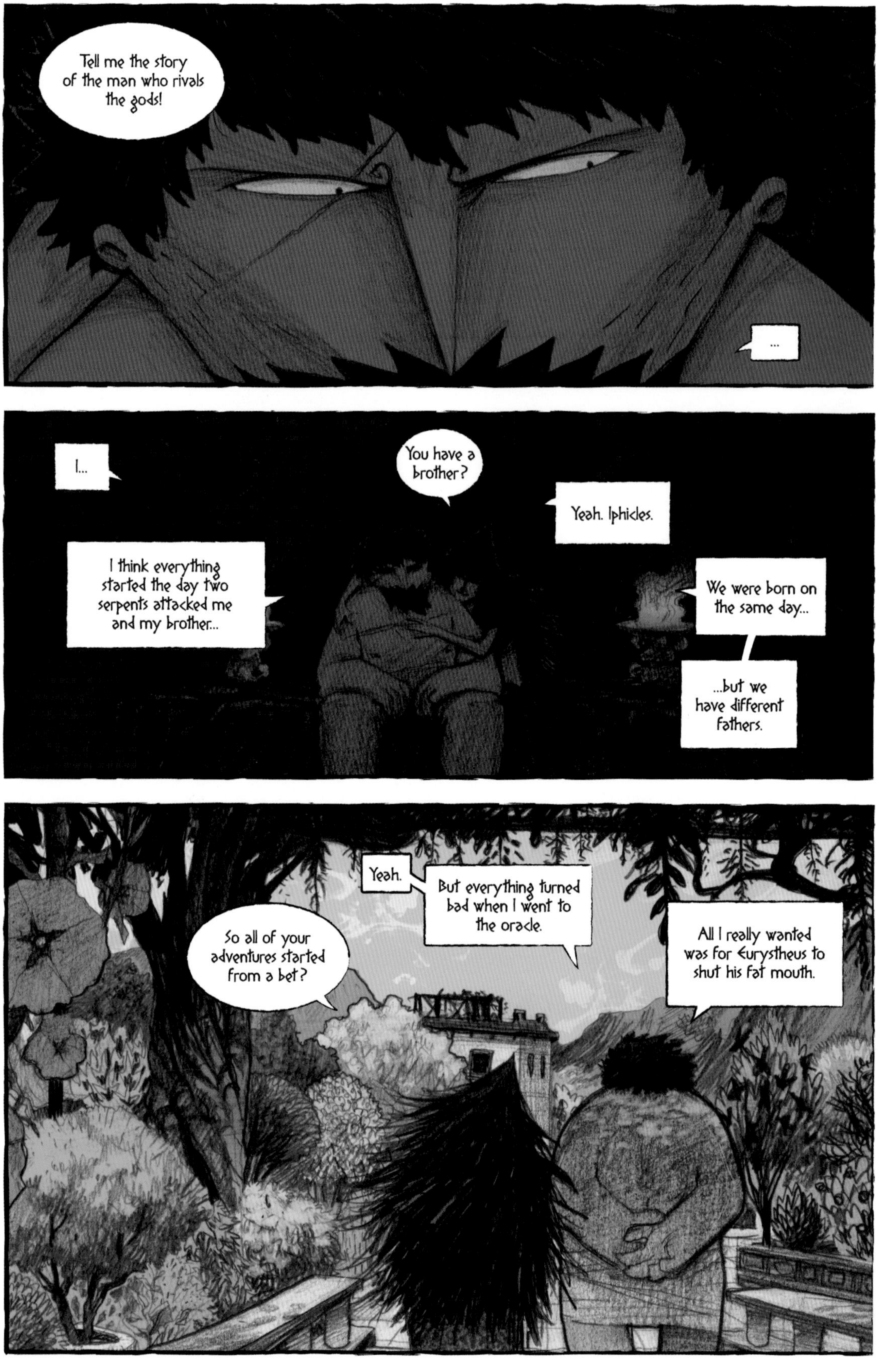
Tell me the story of the man who rivals the gods!
...
I...
You have a brother?
Yeah. Iphicles.
I think everything started the day two serpents attacked me and my brother...
We were born on the same day...
...but we have different fathers.
So all of your adventures started from a bet?
Yeah.
But everything turned bad when I went to the oracle.
All I really wanted was for Eurystheus to shut his fat mouth.

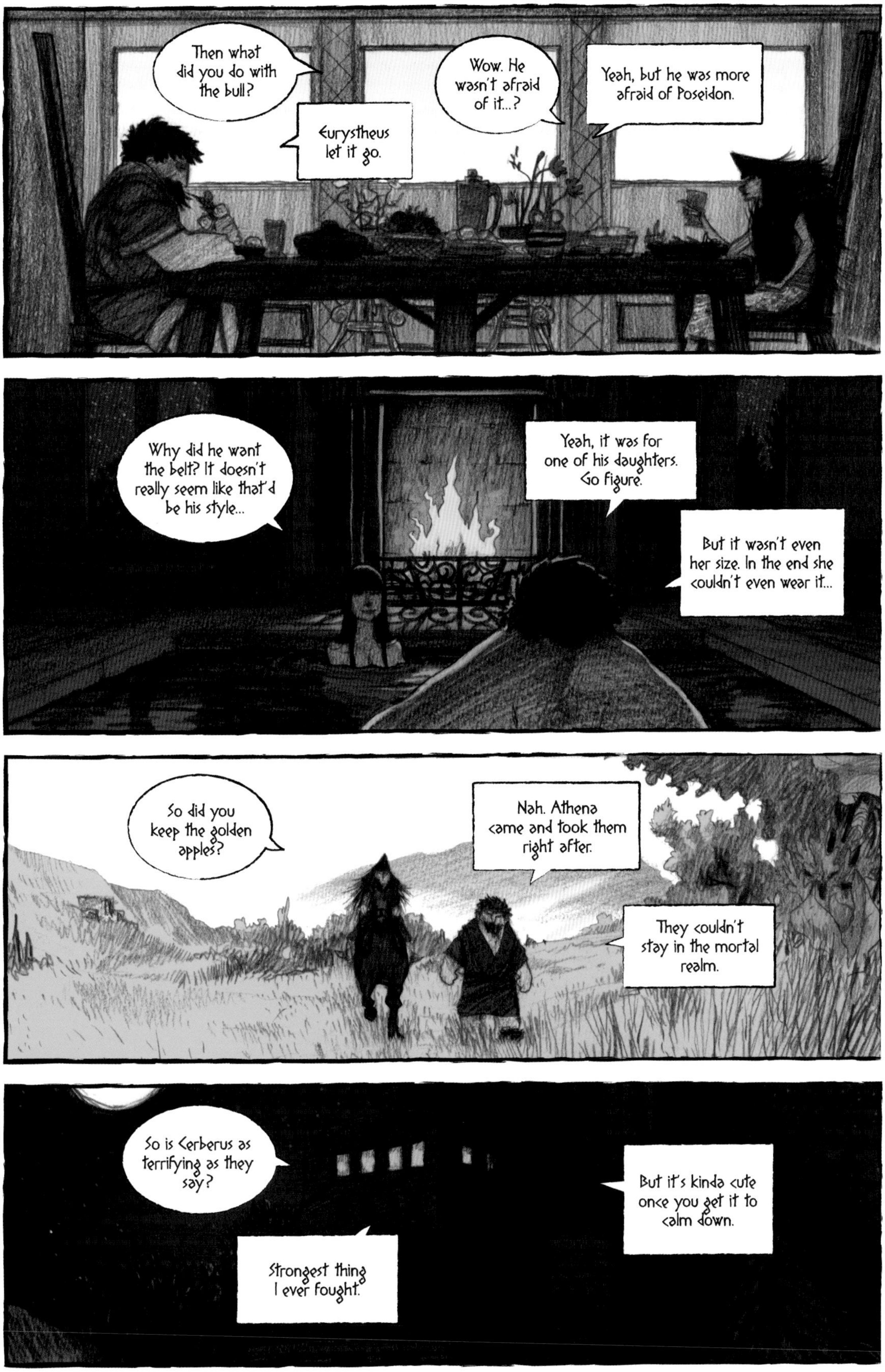
Then what did you do with the bull?
Eurystheus let it go.
Wow. He wasn't afraid of it...?
Yeah, but he was more afraid of Poseidon.
Why did he want the belt? It doesn't really seem like that'd be his style...
Yeah, it was for one of his daughters. Go figure.
But it wasn't even her size. In the end she couldn't even wear it...
So did you keep the golden apples?
Nah. Athena came and took them right after.
They couldn't stay in the mortal realm.
So is Cerberus as terrifying as they say?
Strongest thing I ever fought.
But it's kinda cute once you get it to calm down.

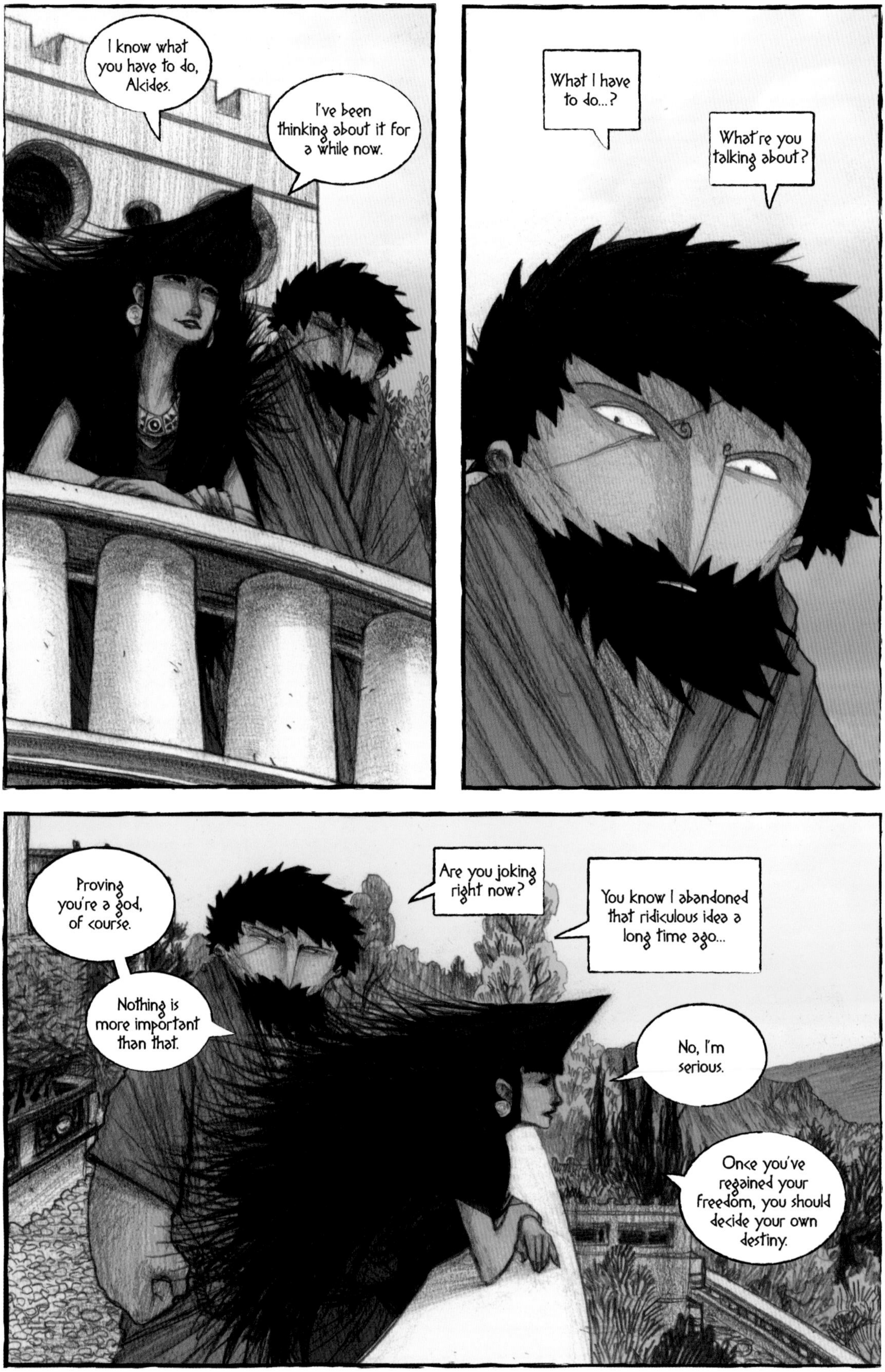
I know what you have to do, Alcides.
I've been thinking about it for a while now.
What I have to do...?
What're you talking about?
Proving you're a god, of course.
Nothing is more important than that.
Are you joking right now?
You know I abandoned that ridiculous idea a long time ago...
No, I'm serious.
Once you've regained your freedom, you should decide your own destiny.

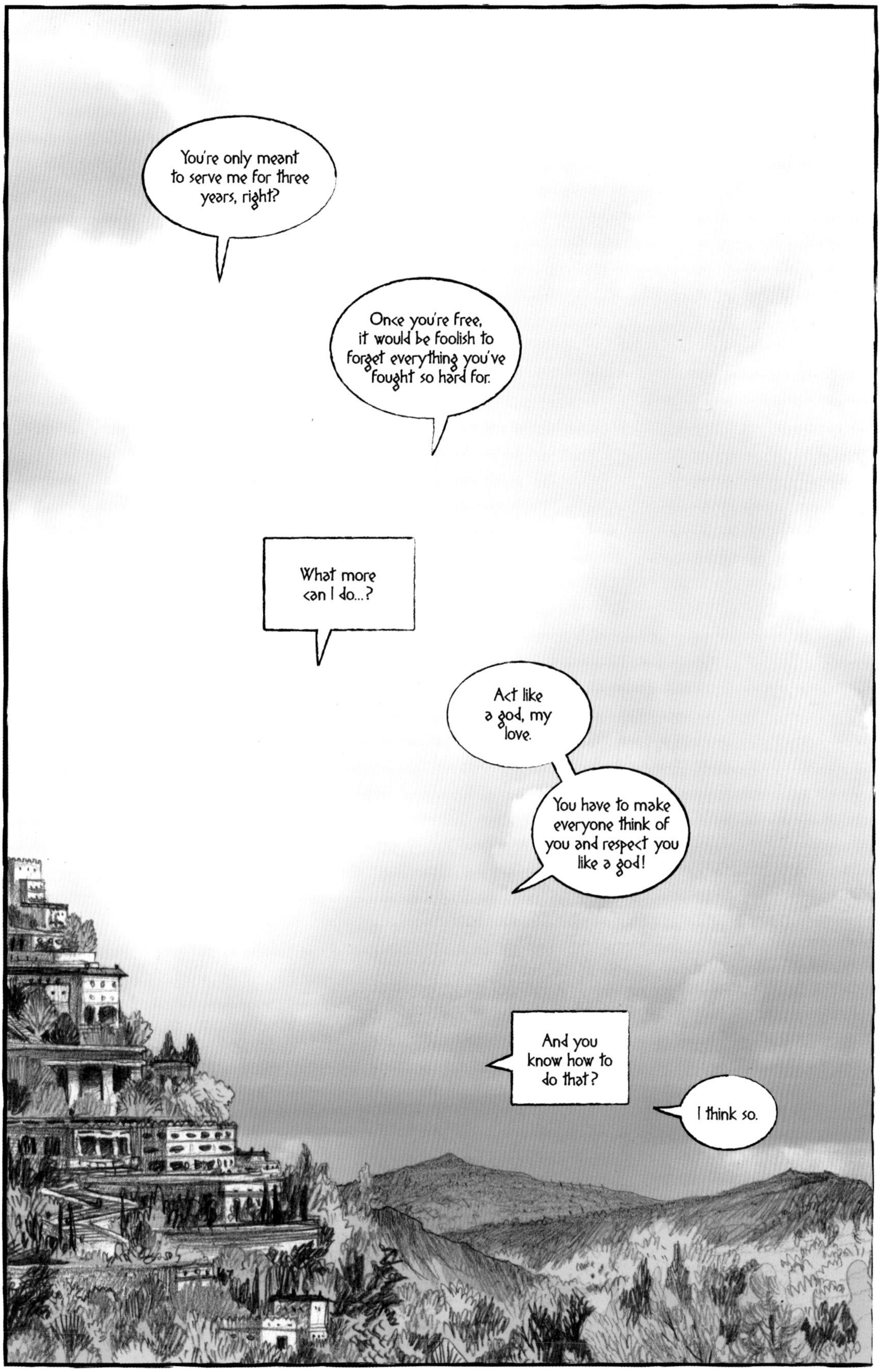
You're only meant to serve me for three years, right?
Once you're free, it would be foolish to forget everything you've fought so hard for.
What more can I do...?
Act like a god, my love.
You have to make everyone think of you and respect you like a god!
And you know how to do that?
I think so.

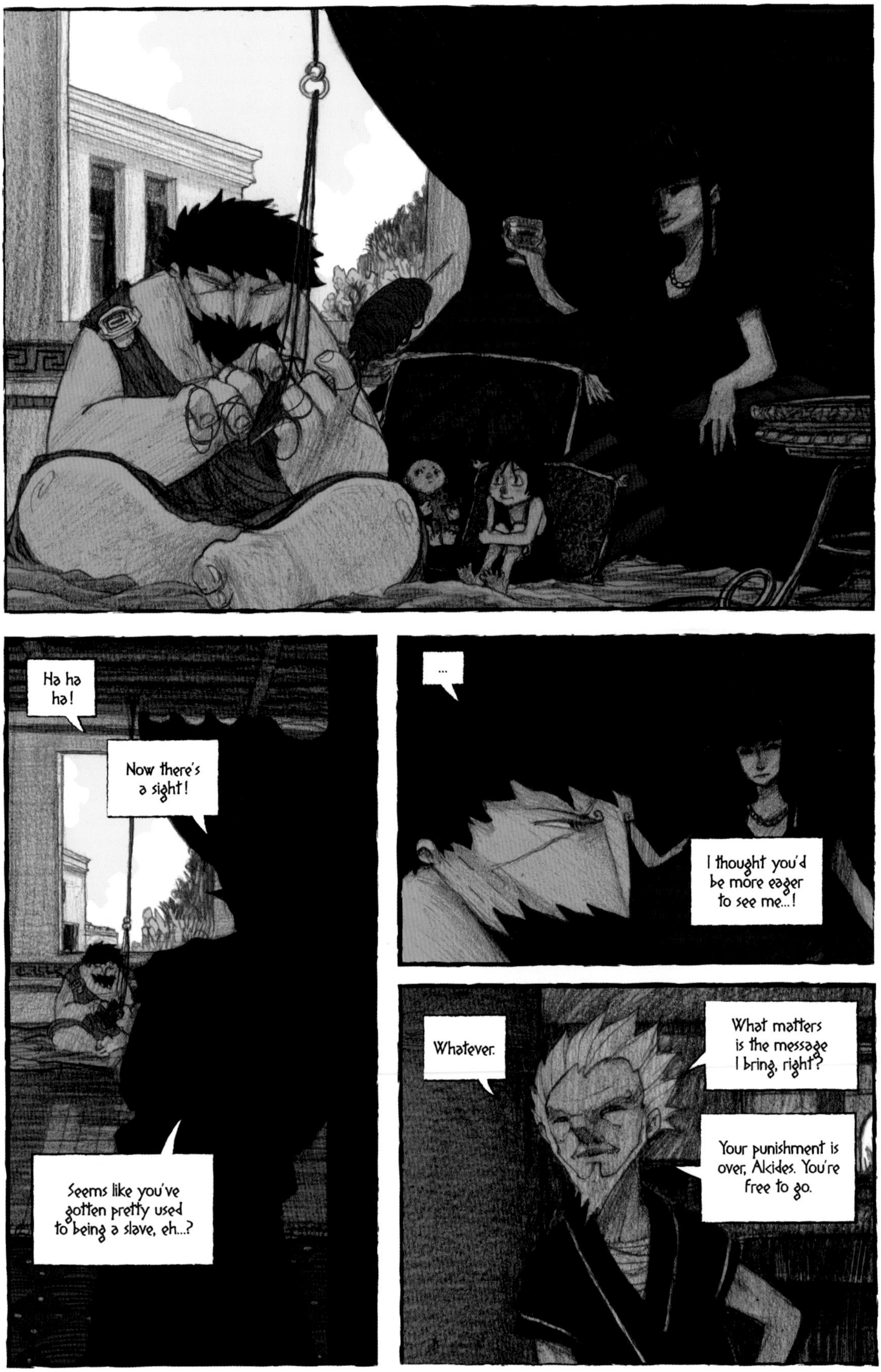

Ha ha ha!
Now there's a sight!
Seems like you've gotten pretty used to being a slave, eh...?
...
I thought you'd be more eager to see me...!
Whatever.
What matters is the message I bring, right?
Your punishment is over, Alcides. You're free to go.

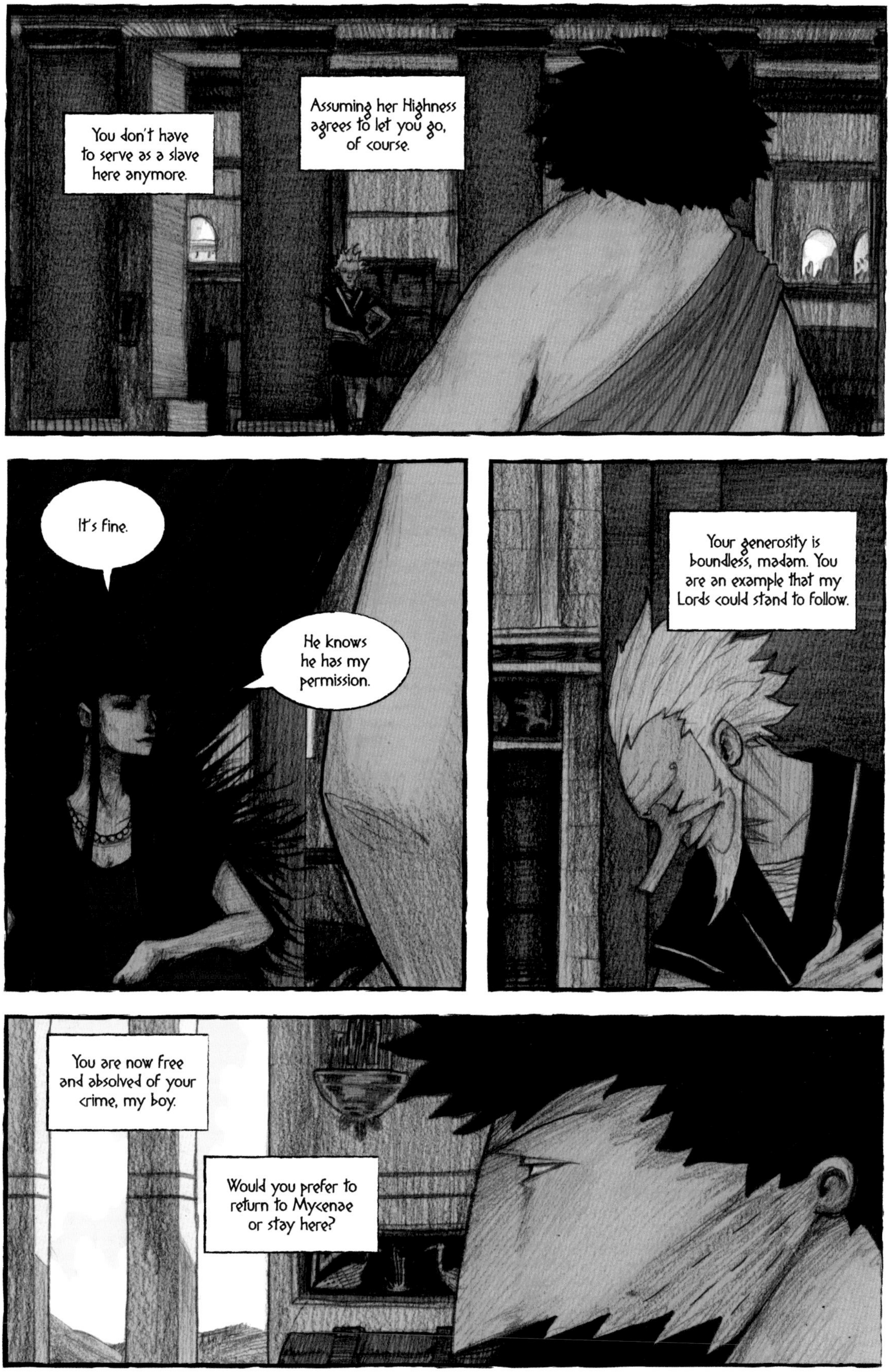
You don't have to serve as a slave here anymore.
Assuming her Highness agrees to let you go, of course.
It's fine.
He knows he has my permission.
Your generosity is boundless, madam. You are an example that my Lords could stand to follow.
You are now free and absolved of your crime, my boy.
Would you prefer to return to Mycenae or stay here?

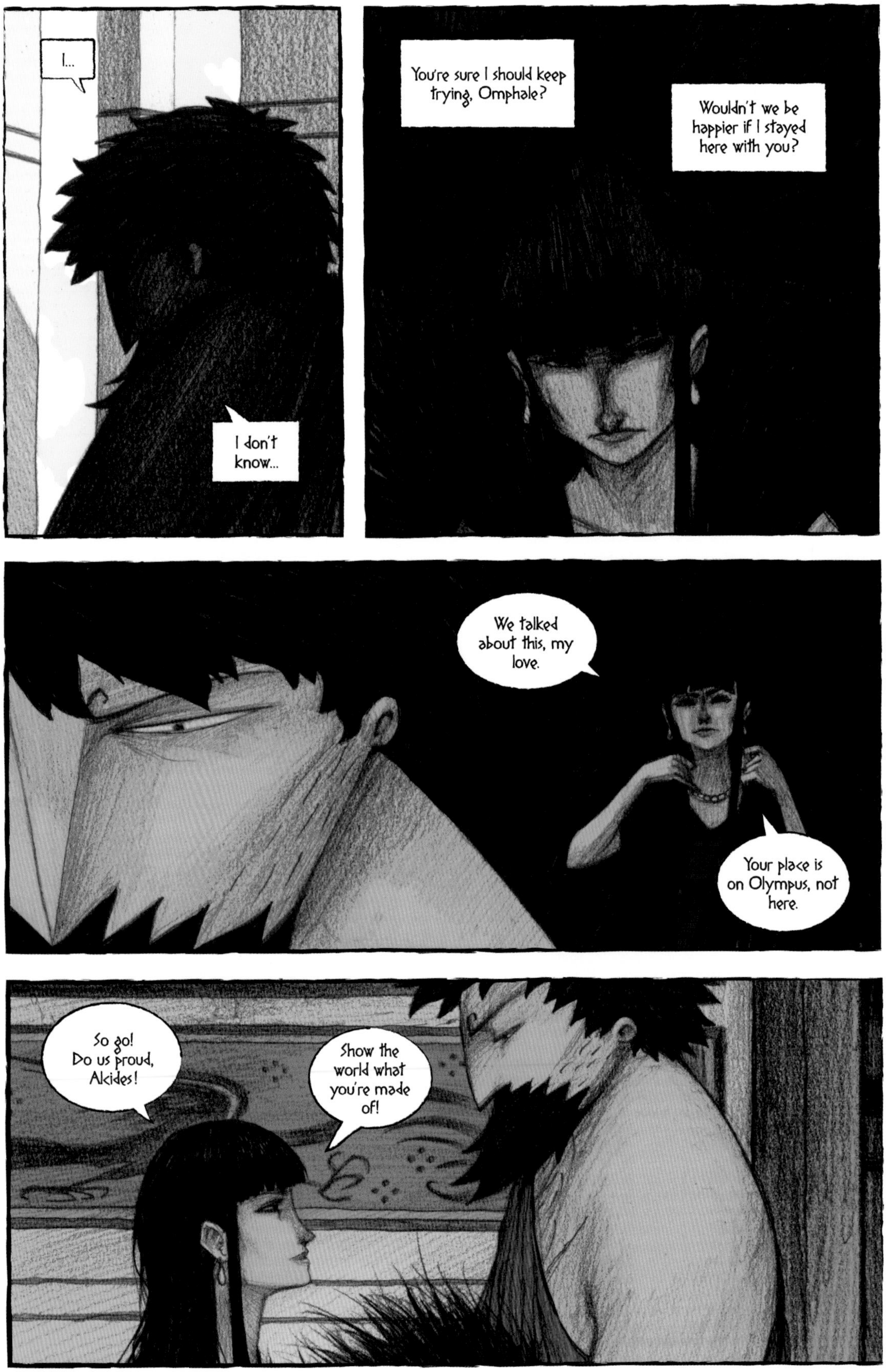
I...
I don't know...
You're sure I should keep trying, Omphale?
Wouldn't we be happier if I stayed here with you?
We talked about this, my love.
Your place is on Olympus, not here.
So go! Do us proud, Alkides!
Show the world what you're made of!

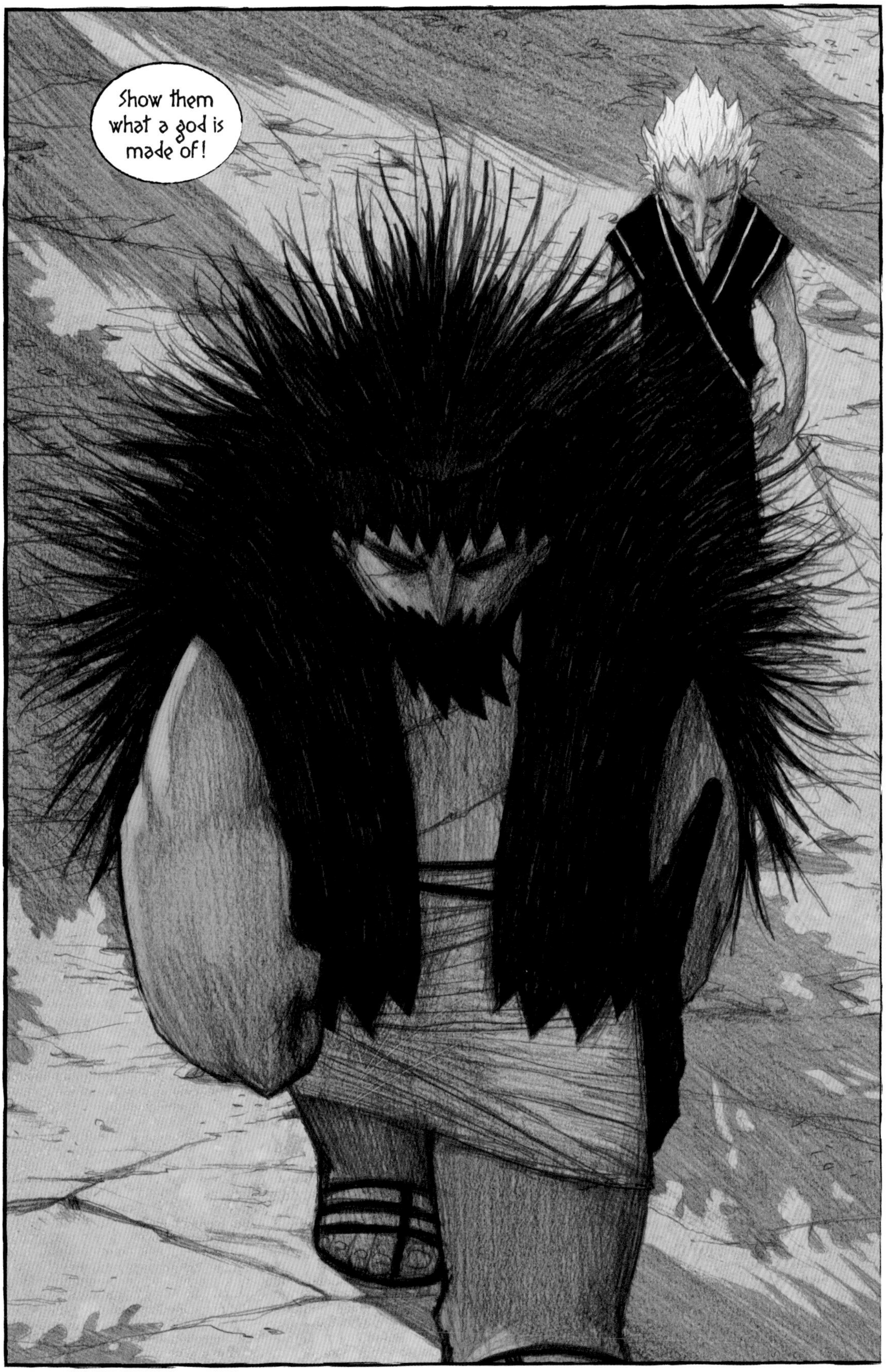
Show them what a god is made of!

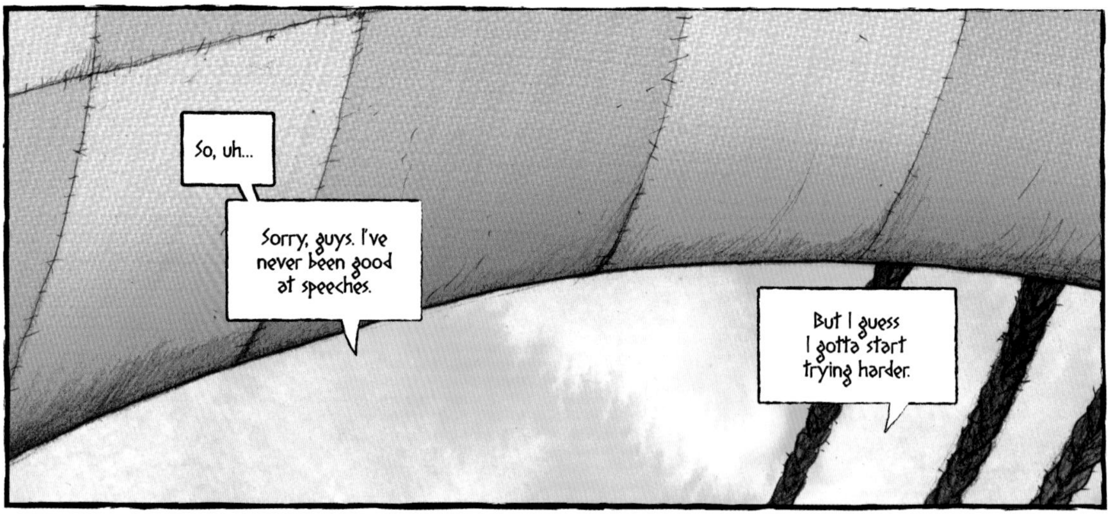
So, uh...
Sorry, guys. I've never been good at speeches.
But I guess I gotta start trying harder.

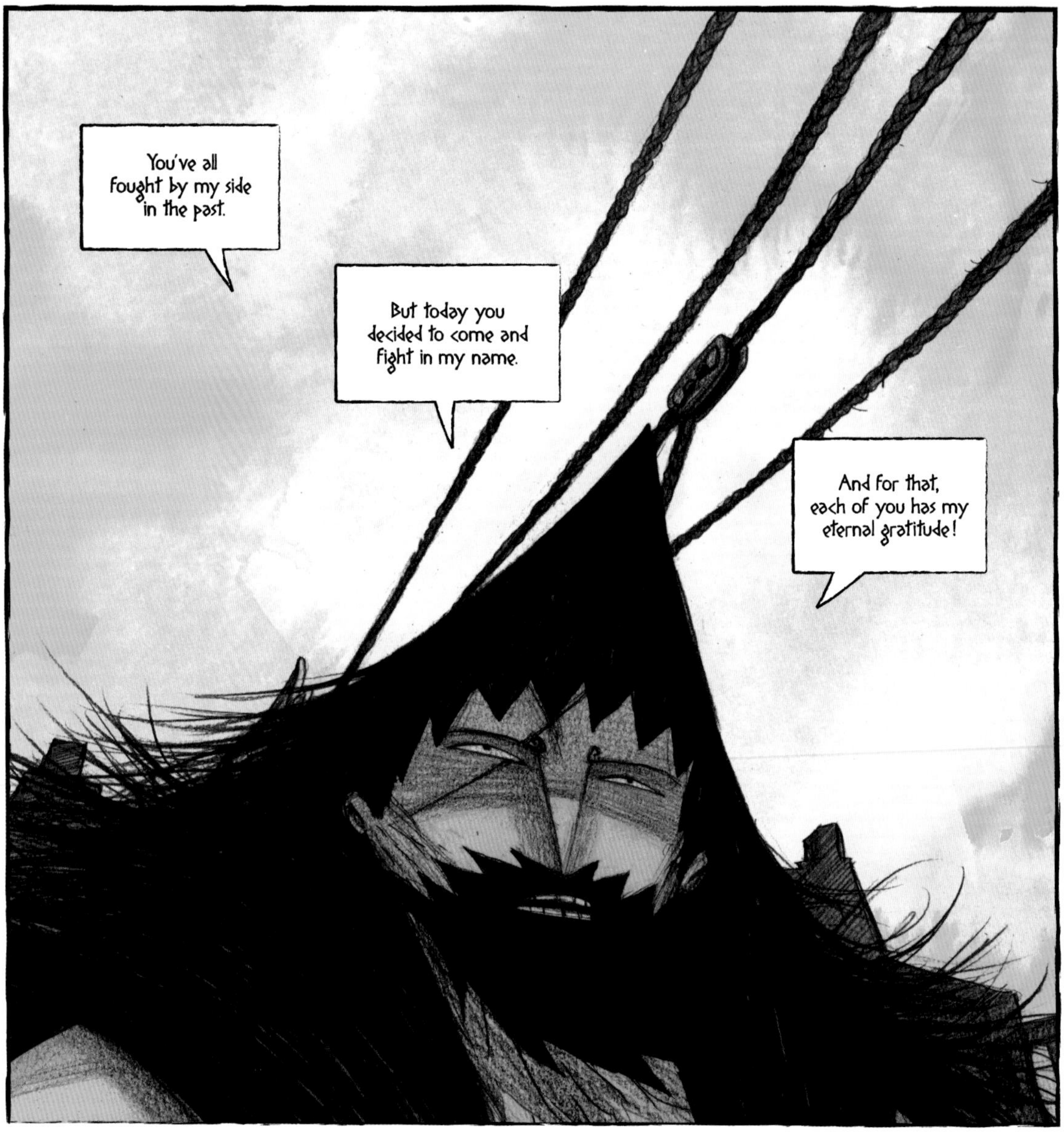
You've all fought by my side in the past.
But today you decided to come and fight in my name.
And for that, each of you has my eternal gratitude!

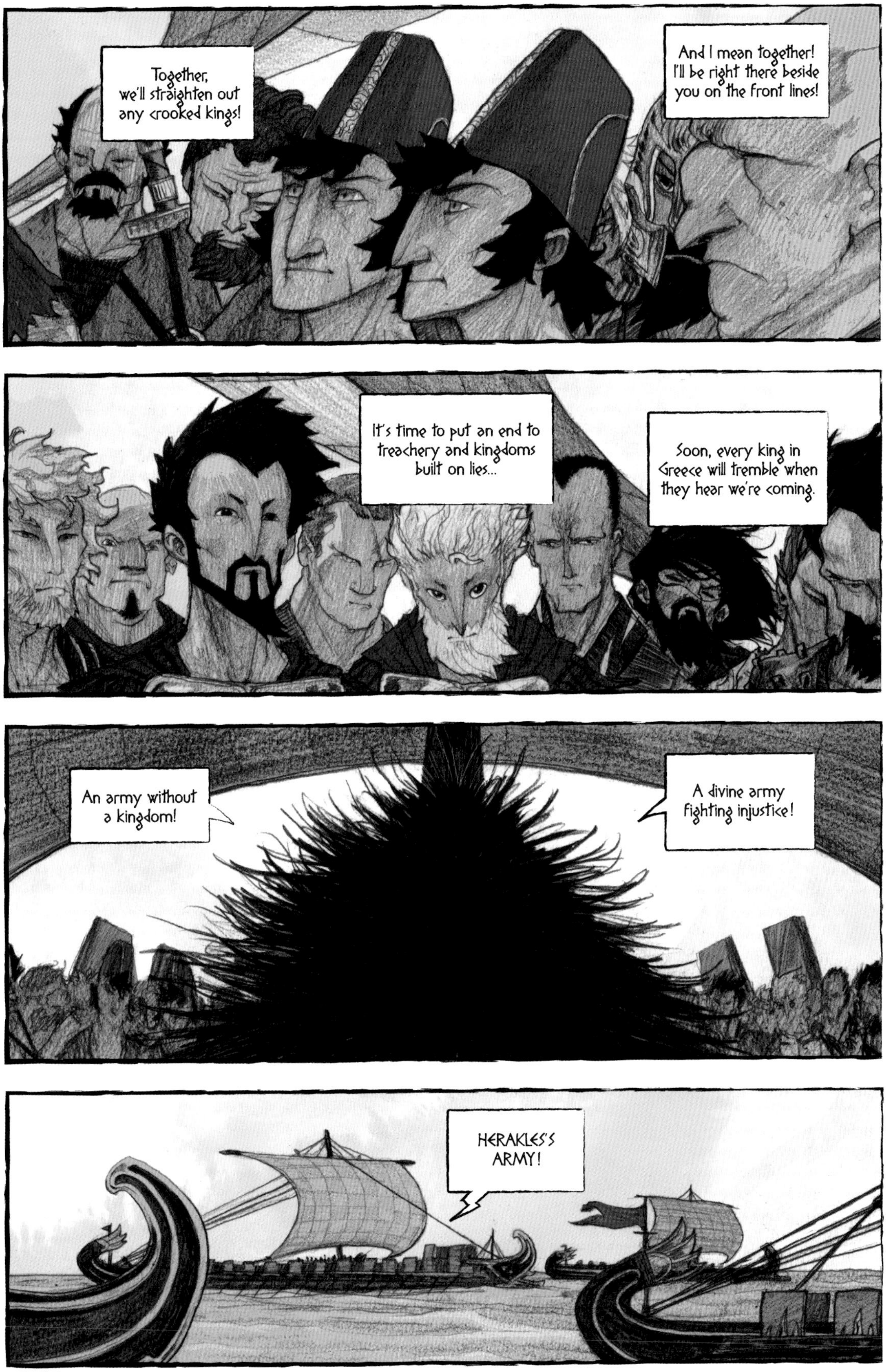
Together, we'll straighten out any crooked kings!
And I mean together! I'll be right there beside you on the front lines!
It's time to put an end to treachery and kingdoms built on lies...
Soon, every king in Greece will tremble when they hear we're coming.
An army without a kingdom!
A divine army fighting injustice!
HERAKLES'S ARMY!

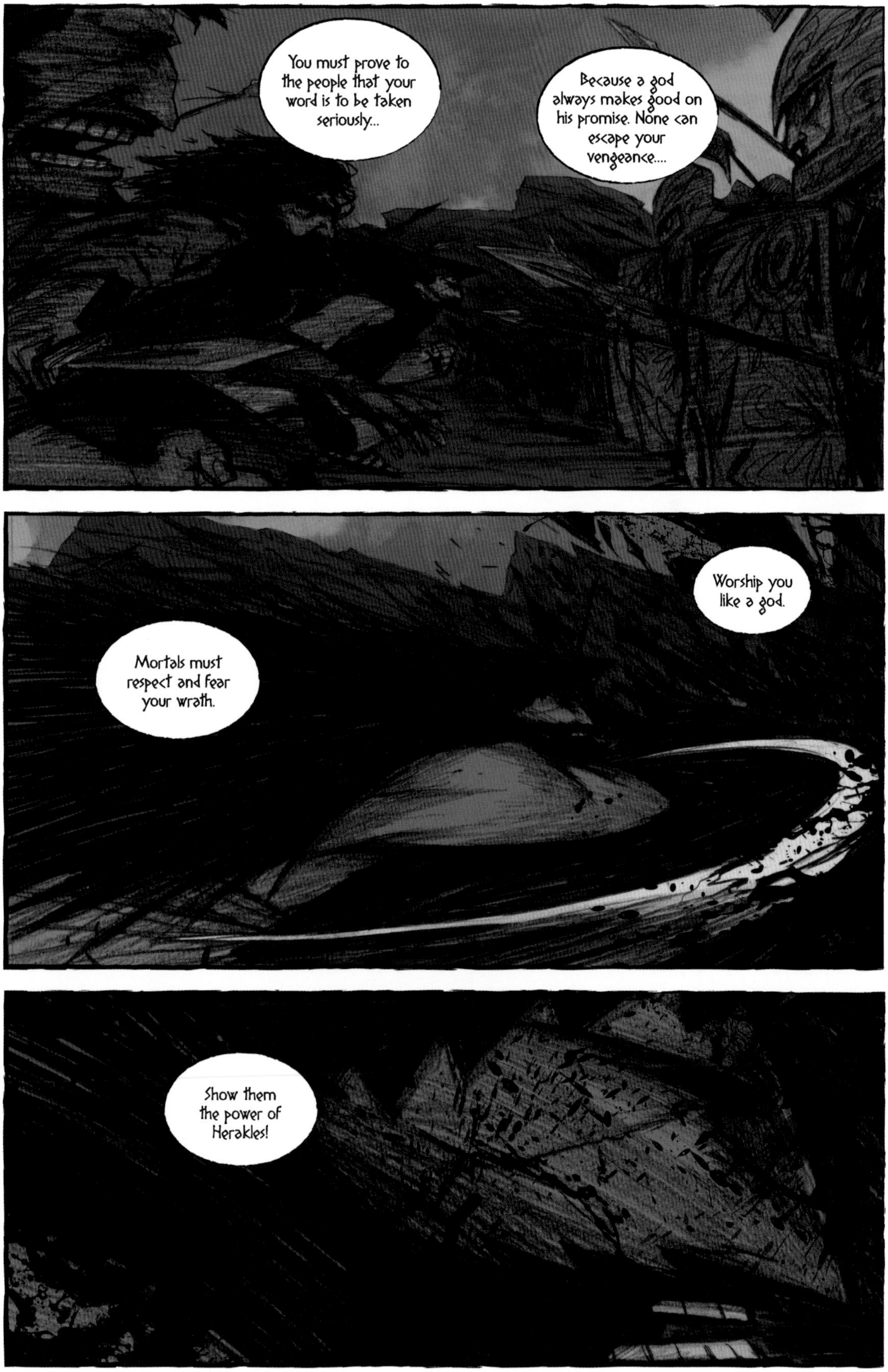
You must prove to the people that your word is to be taken seriously...
Because a god always makes good on his promise. None can escape your vengeance....
Worship you like a god.
Mortals must respect and fear your wrath.
Show them the power of Herakles!

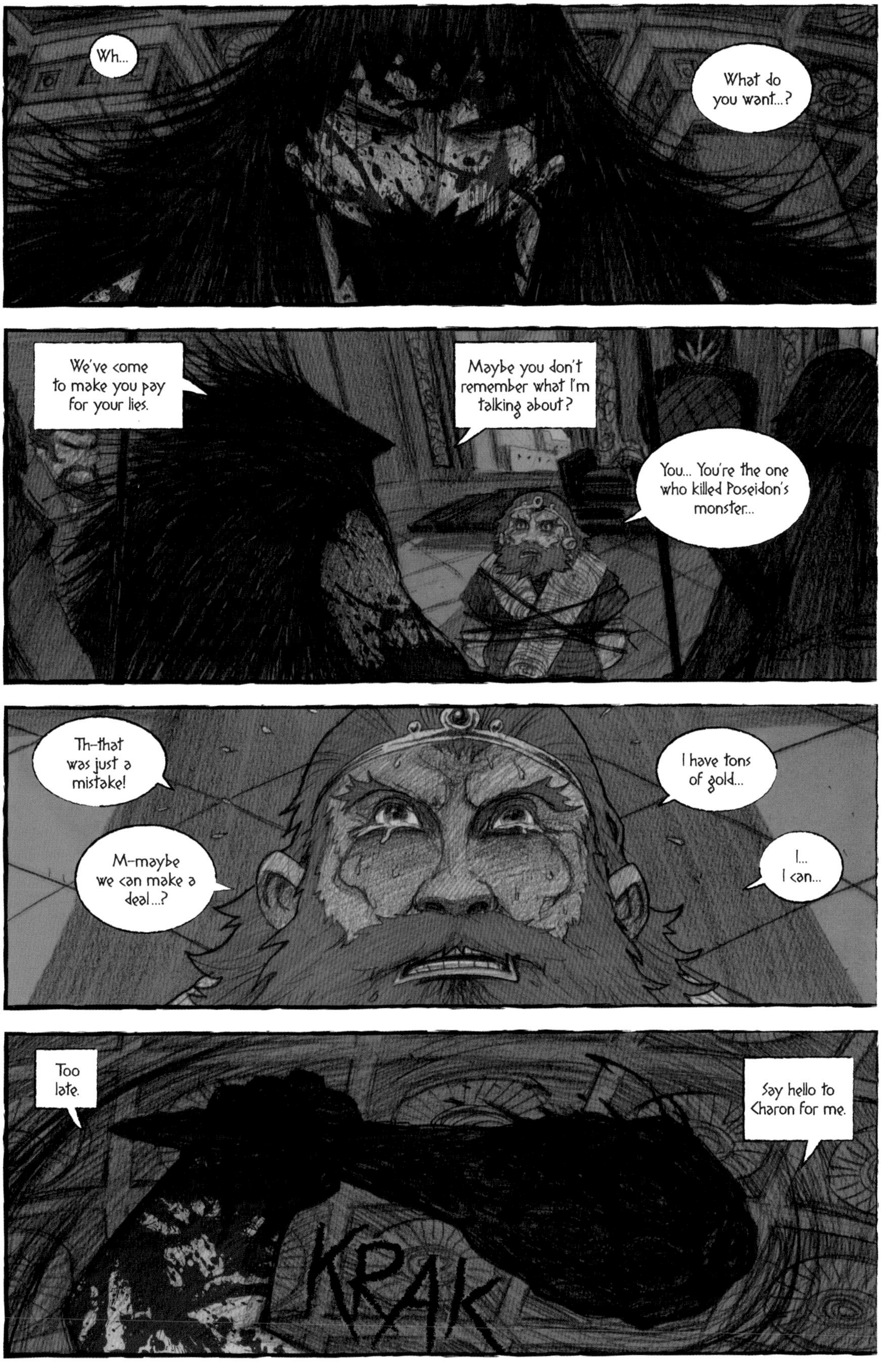
Wh...
What do you want...?
We've come to make you pay for your lies.
Maybe you don't remember what I'm talking about?
You... You're the one who killed Poseidon's monster...
Th-that was just a mistake!
M-maybe we can make a deal...?
I have tons of gold...
I... I can...
Too late.
Say hello to Charon for me.
KRAK

ALCIDES?!
HEY!
Alcides...?
Can you hear me?
...?
Ha!
He's awake!
You okay, brother?
I was starting to get worried...!
What the...?
What happened?
Where are we?

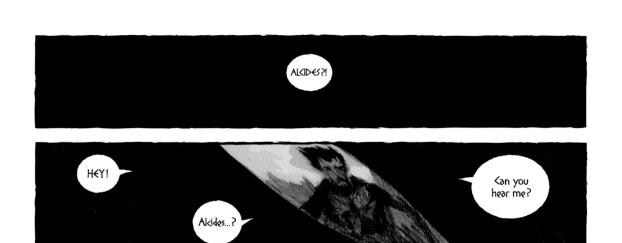

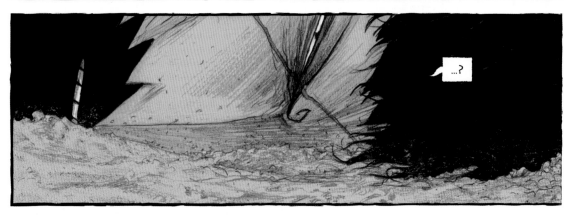

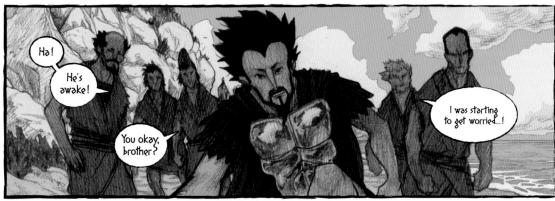

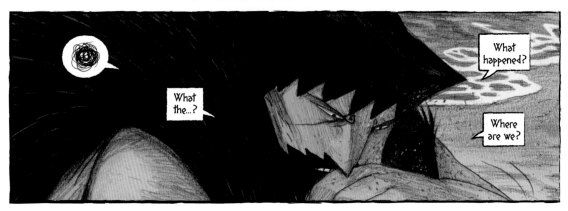

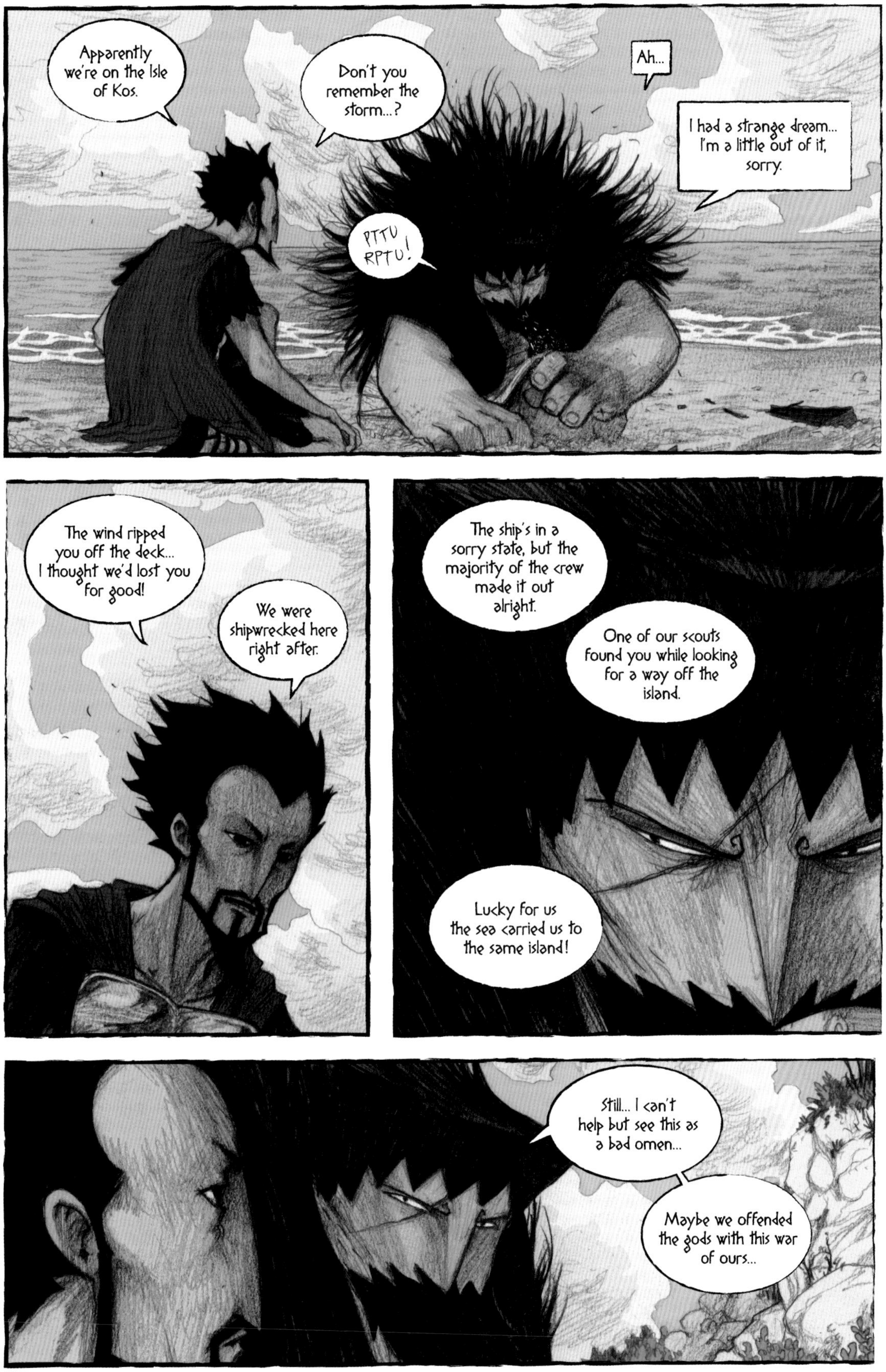
Apparently we're on the Isle of Kos.
Don't you remember the storm...?
Ah...
I had a strange dream... I'm a little out of it, sorry.
PTTU RPTU!
The wind ripped you off the deck... I thought we'd lost you for good!
We were shipwrecked here right after.
The ship's in a sorry state, but the majority of the crew made it out alright.
One of our scouts found you while looking for a way off the island.
Lucky for us the sea carried us to the same island!
Still... I can't help but see this as a bad omen...
Maybe we offended the gods with this war of ours...

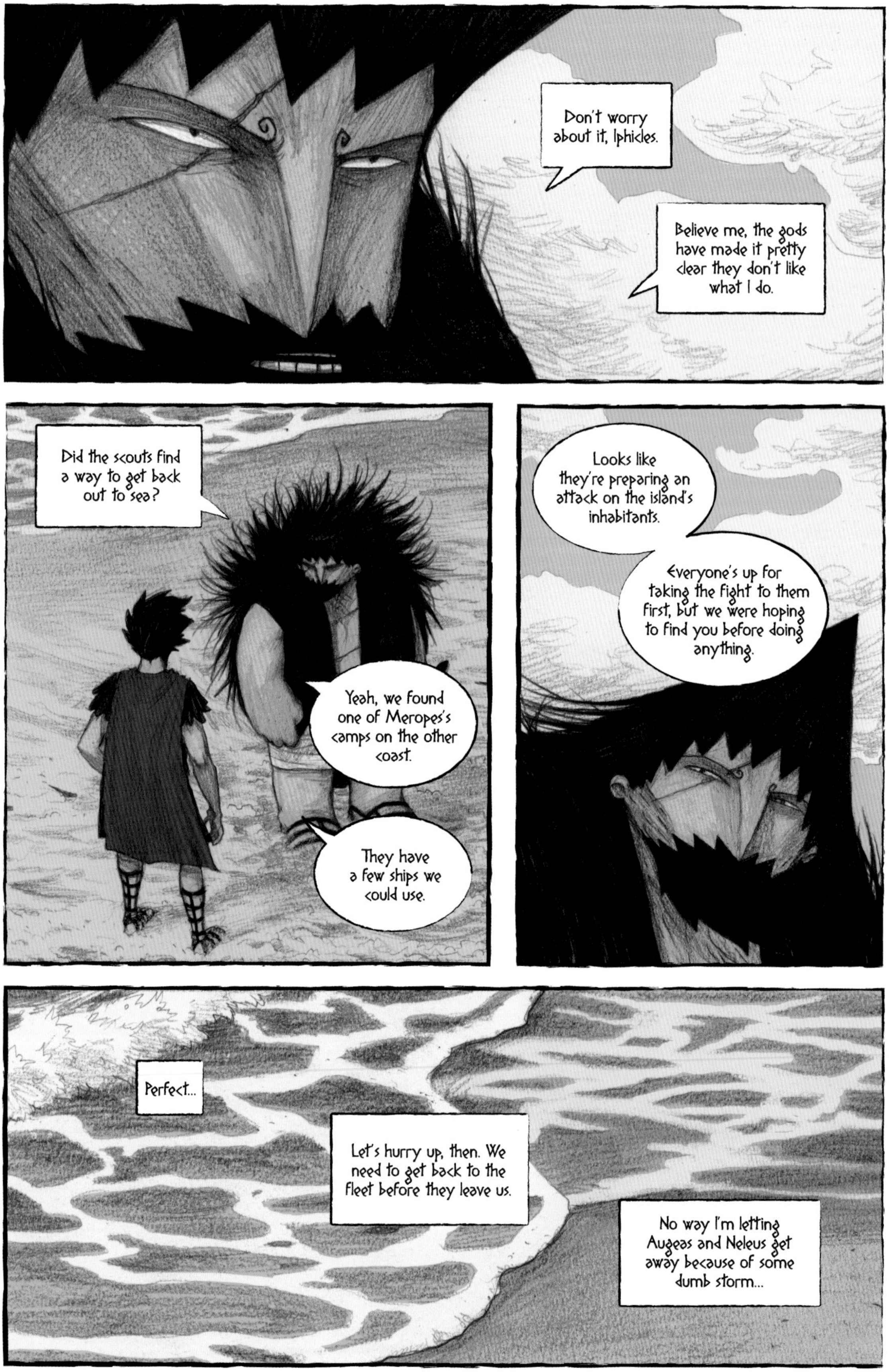
Don't worry about it, Iphicles.
Believe me, the gods have made it pretty clear they don't like what I do.
Did the scouts find a way to get back out to sea?
Yeah, we found one of Meropes's camps on the other coast.
They have a few ships we could use.
Looks like they're preparing an attack on the island's inhabitants.
Everyone's up for taking the fight to them first, but we were hoping to find you before doing anything.
Perfect...
Let's hurry up, then. We need to get back to the fleet before they leave us.
No way I'm letting Augeas and Neleus get away because of some dumb storm...

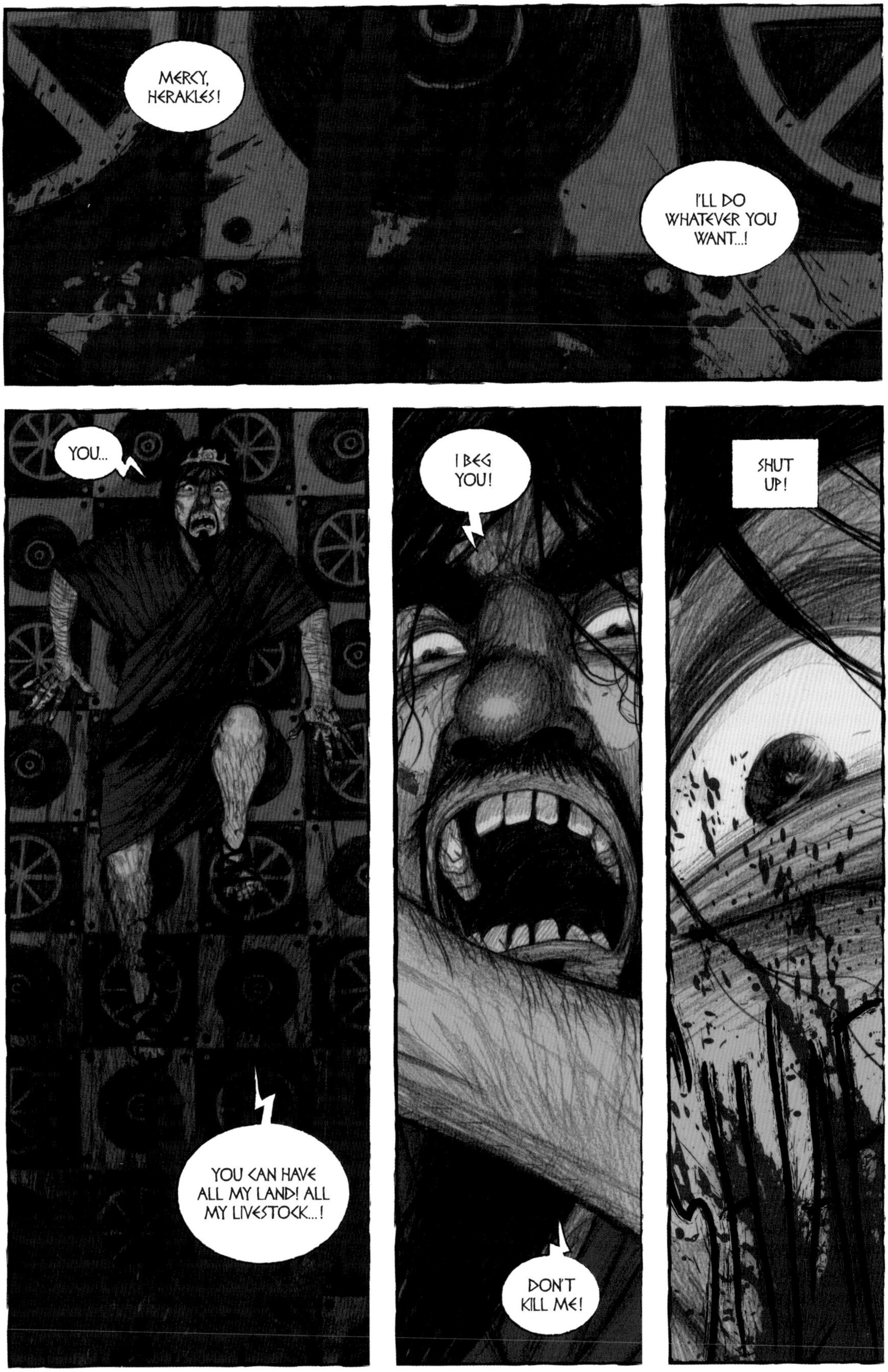
MERCY, HERAKLES!
I'LL DO WHATEVER YOU WANT...!
YOU...
YOU CAN HAVE ALL MY LAND! ALL MY LIVESTOCK...!
I BEG YOU!
DON'T KILL ME!
SHUT UP!

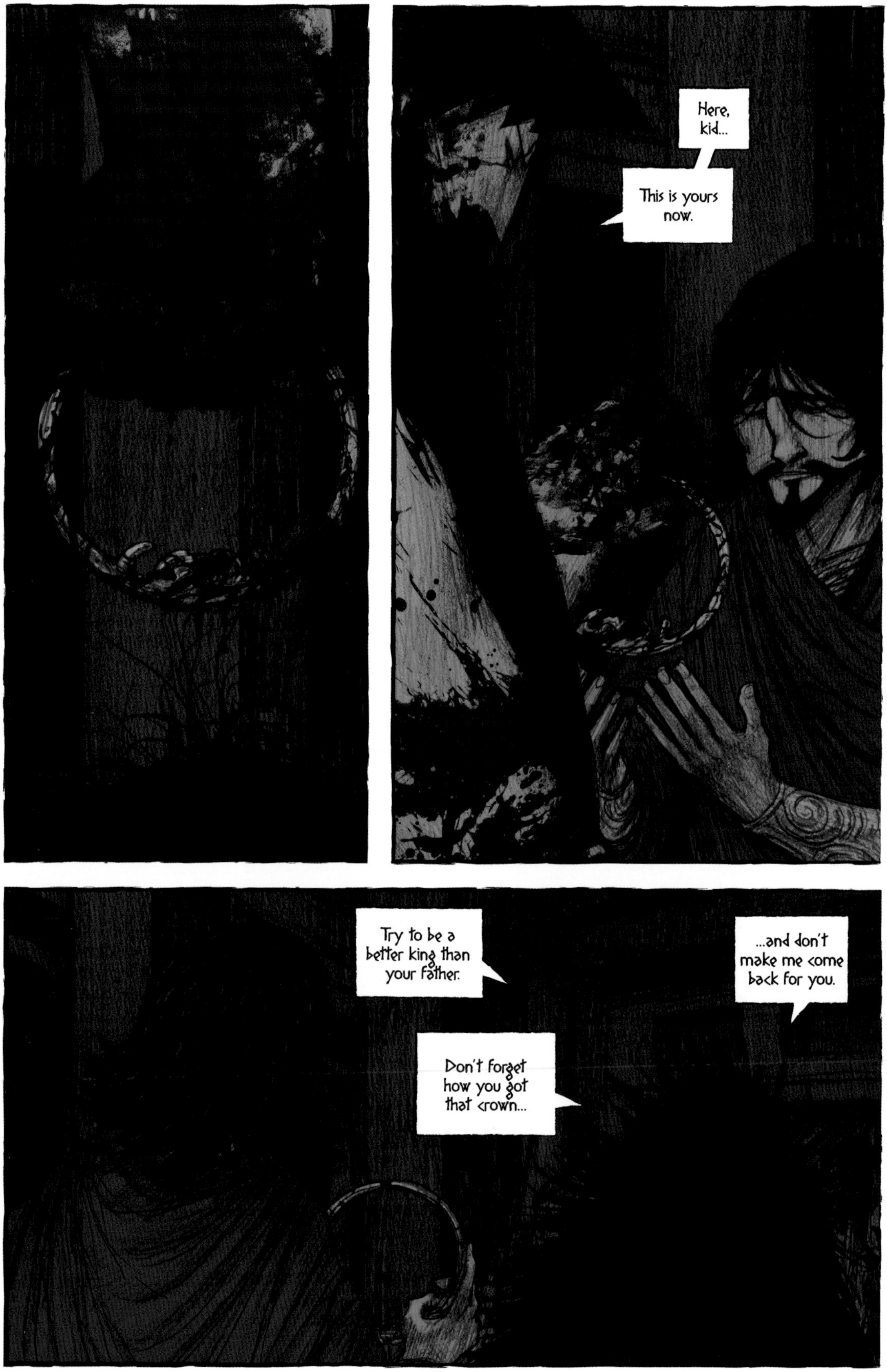
Here, kid...
This is yours now.
Try to be a better king than your father.
...and don't make me come back for you.
Don't forget how you got that crown...

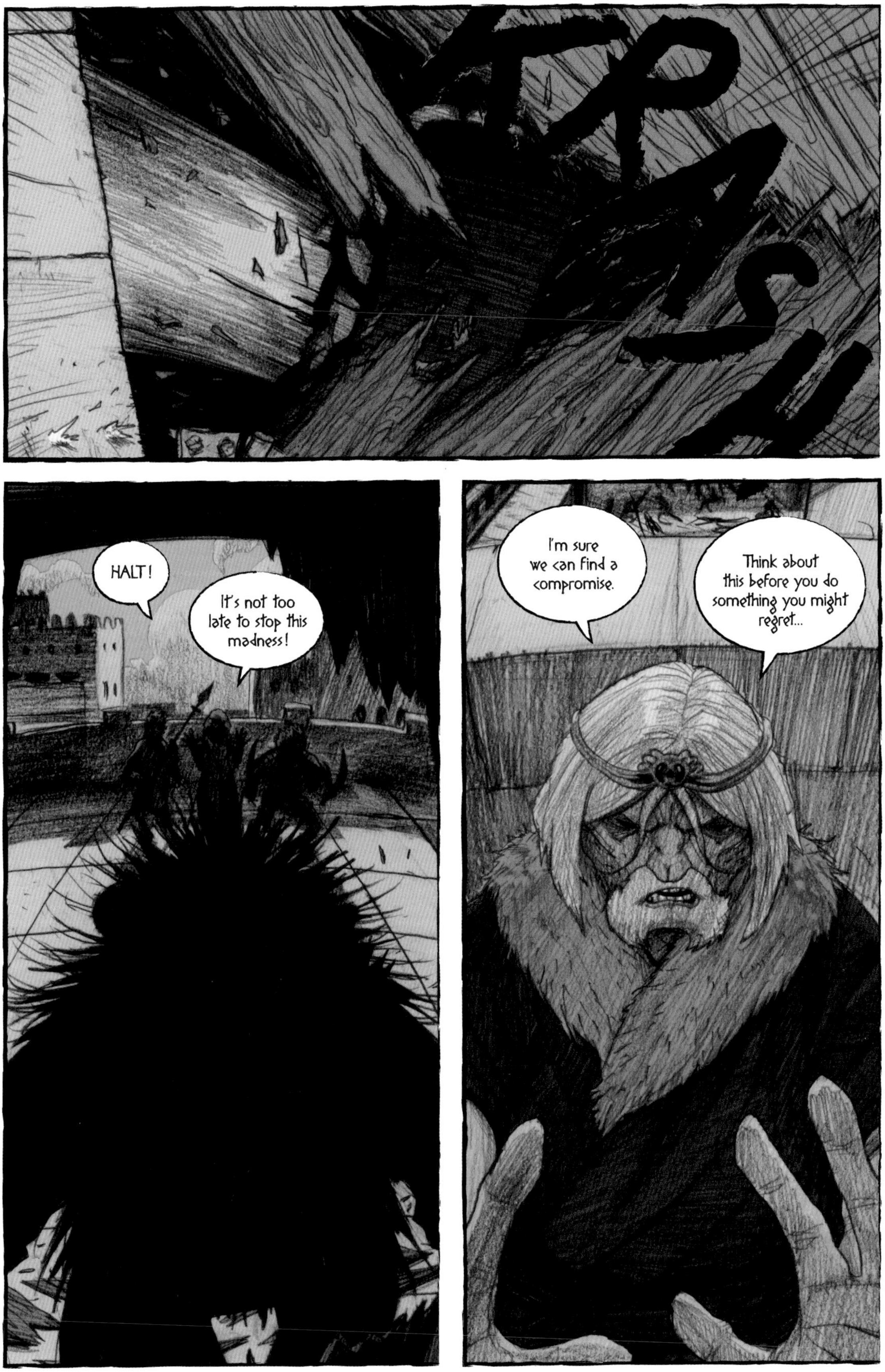
KRASH
HALT!
It's not too late to stop this madness!
I'm sure we can find a compromise.
Think about this before you do something you might regret...

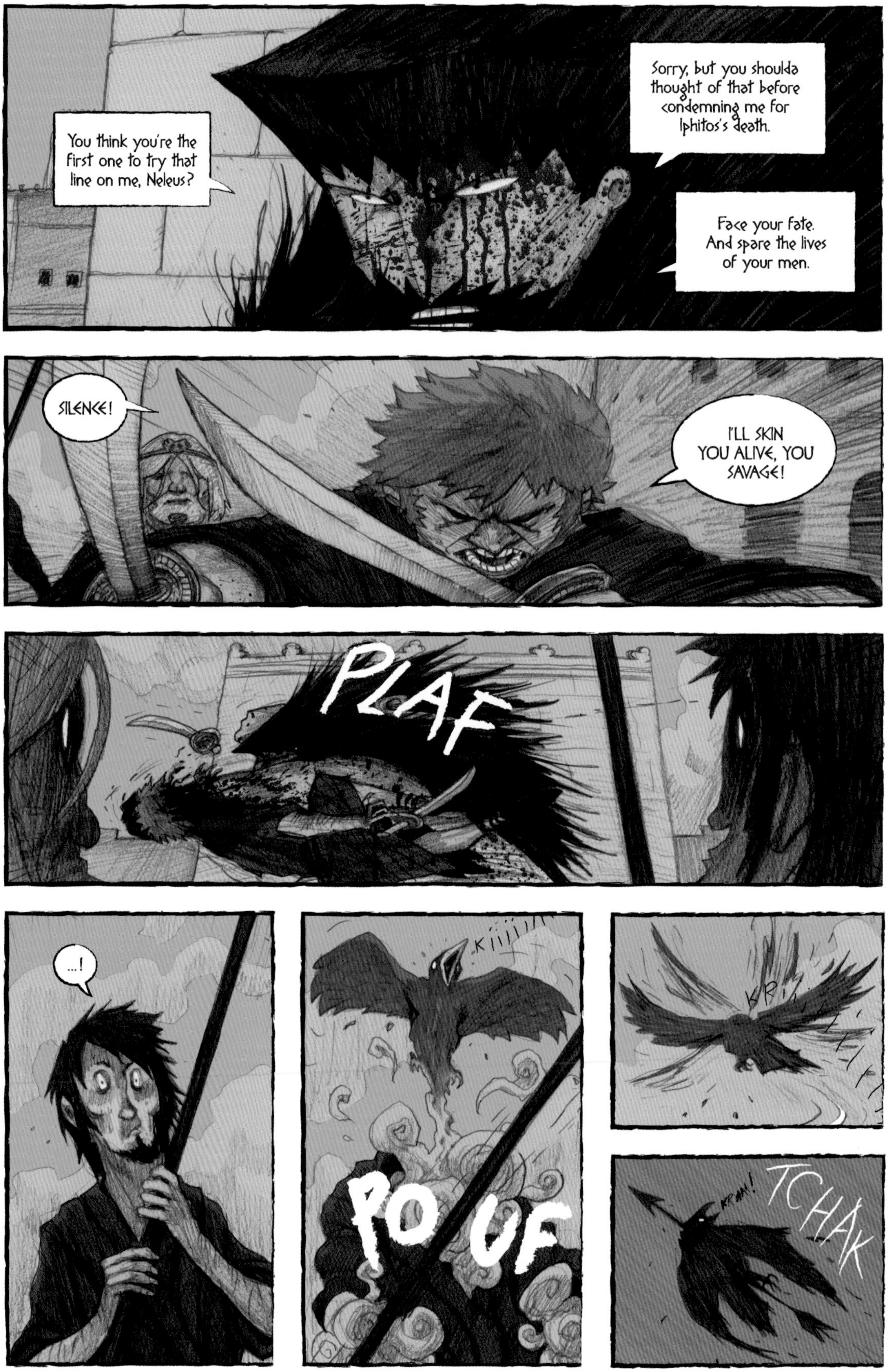
You think you're the first one to try that line on me, Neleus?
Sorry, but you shoulda thought of that before condemning me for Iphitos's death.
Face your fate. And spare the lives of your men.
SILENCE!
I'LL SKIN YOU ALIVE, YOU SAVAGE!
PLAF
...!
POUF
TCHAK

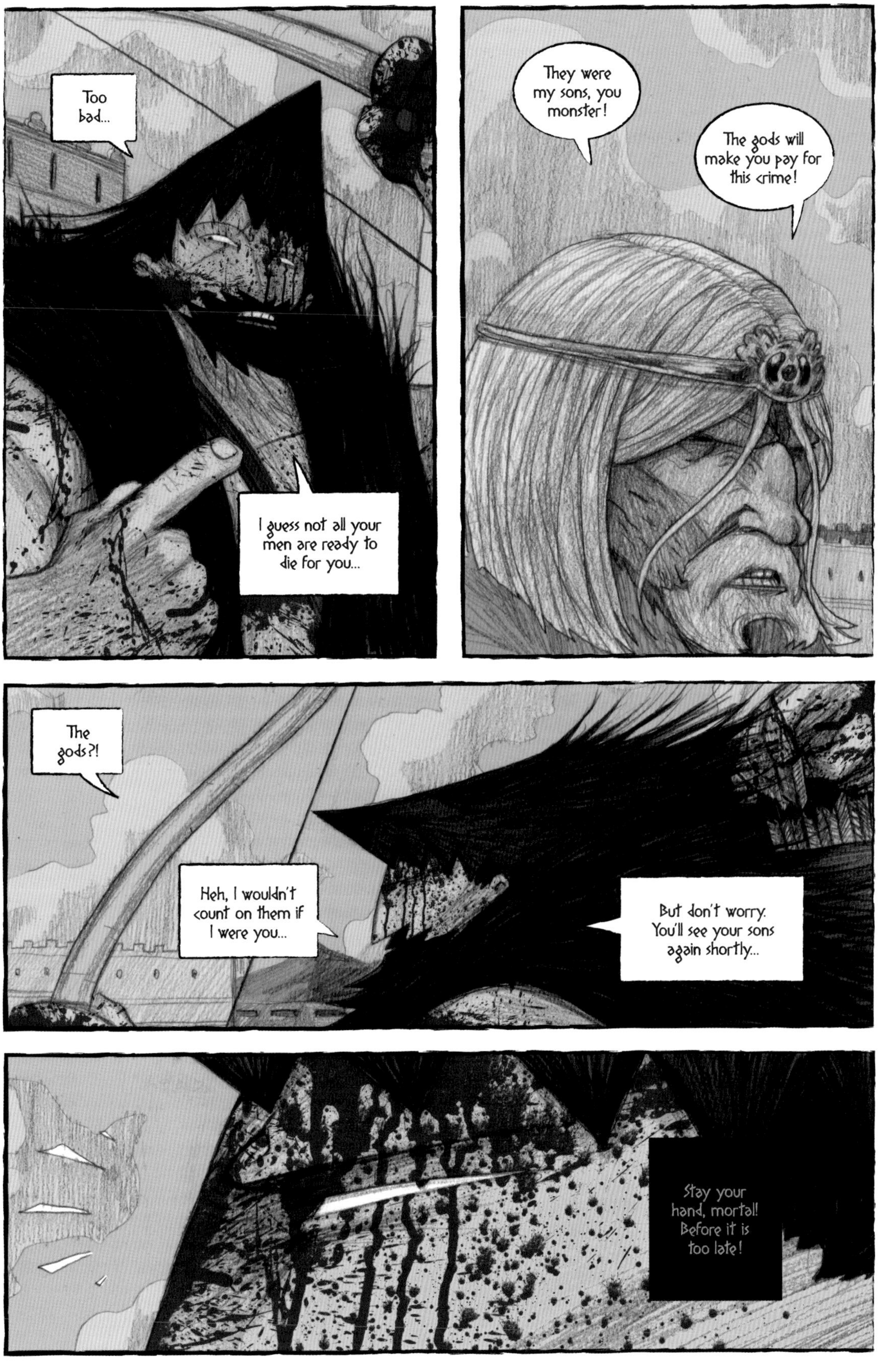
Too bad...
I guess not all your men are ready to die for you...
They were my sons, you monster!
The gods will make you pay for this crime!
The gods?!
Heh, I wouldn't count on them if I were you...
But don't worry. You'll see your sons again shortly...
Stay your hand, mortal! Before it is too late!

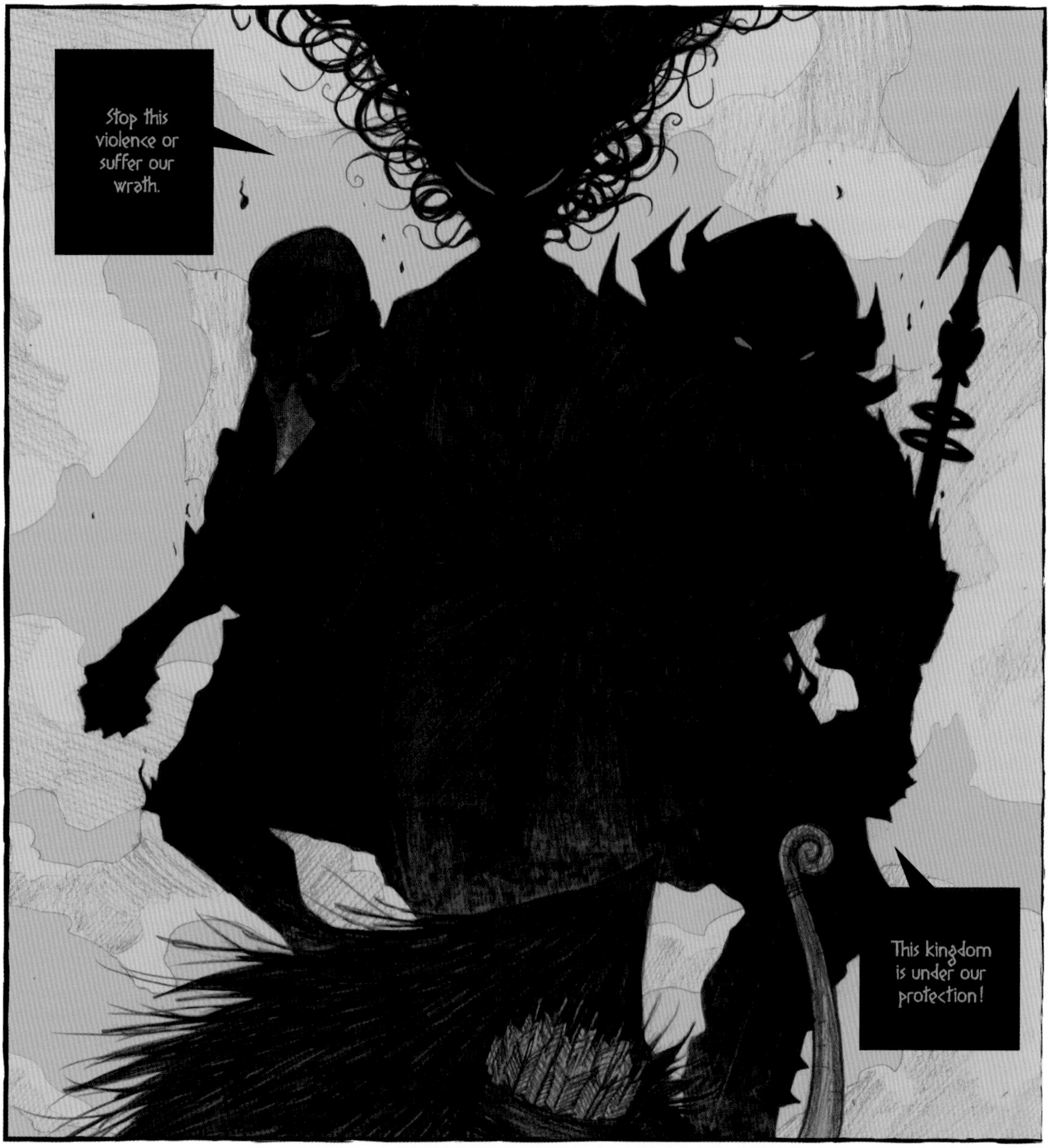
Stop this violence or suffer our wrath.
This kingdom is under our protection!

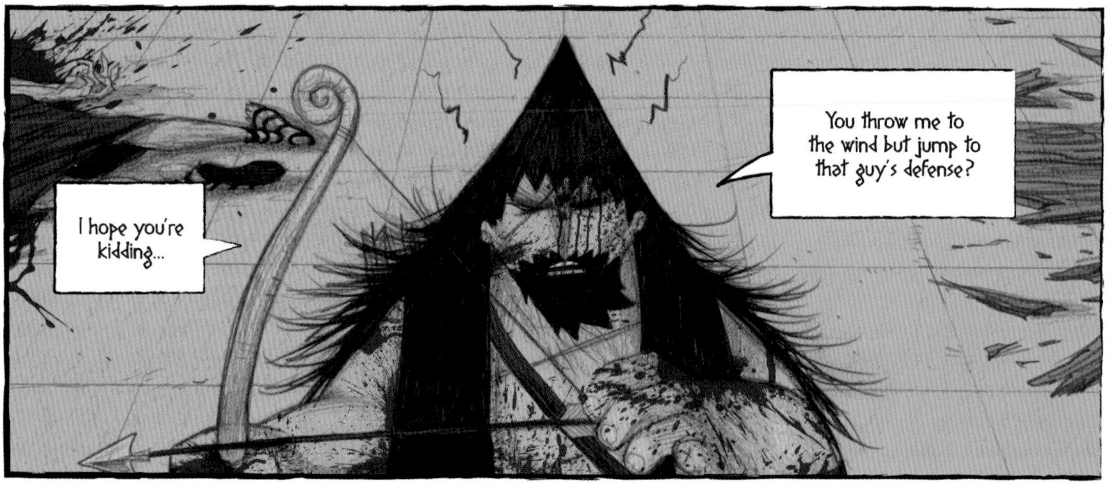
You throw me to the wind but jump to that guy's defense?
I hope you're kidding...

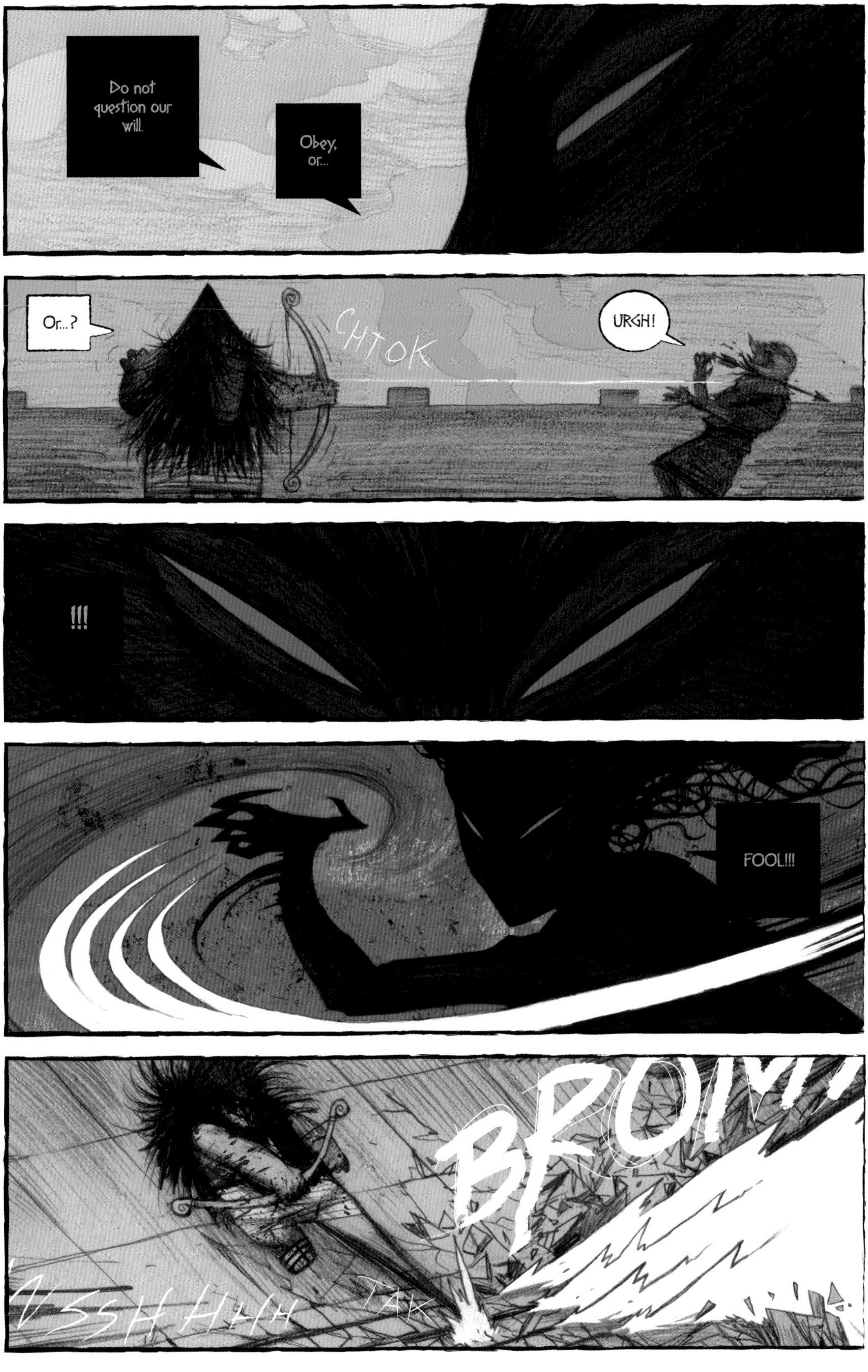
Do not question our will.
Obey, or...
Or...?
CHTOK
URGH!
!!!
FOOL!!!
BROM
VSSHHHH
TAK

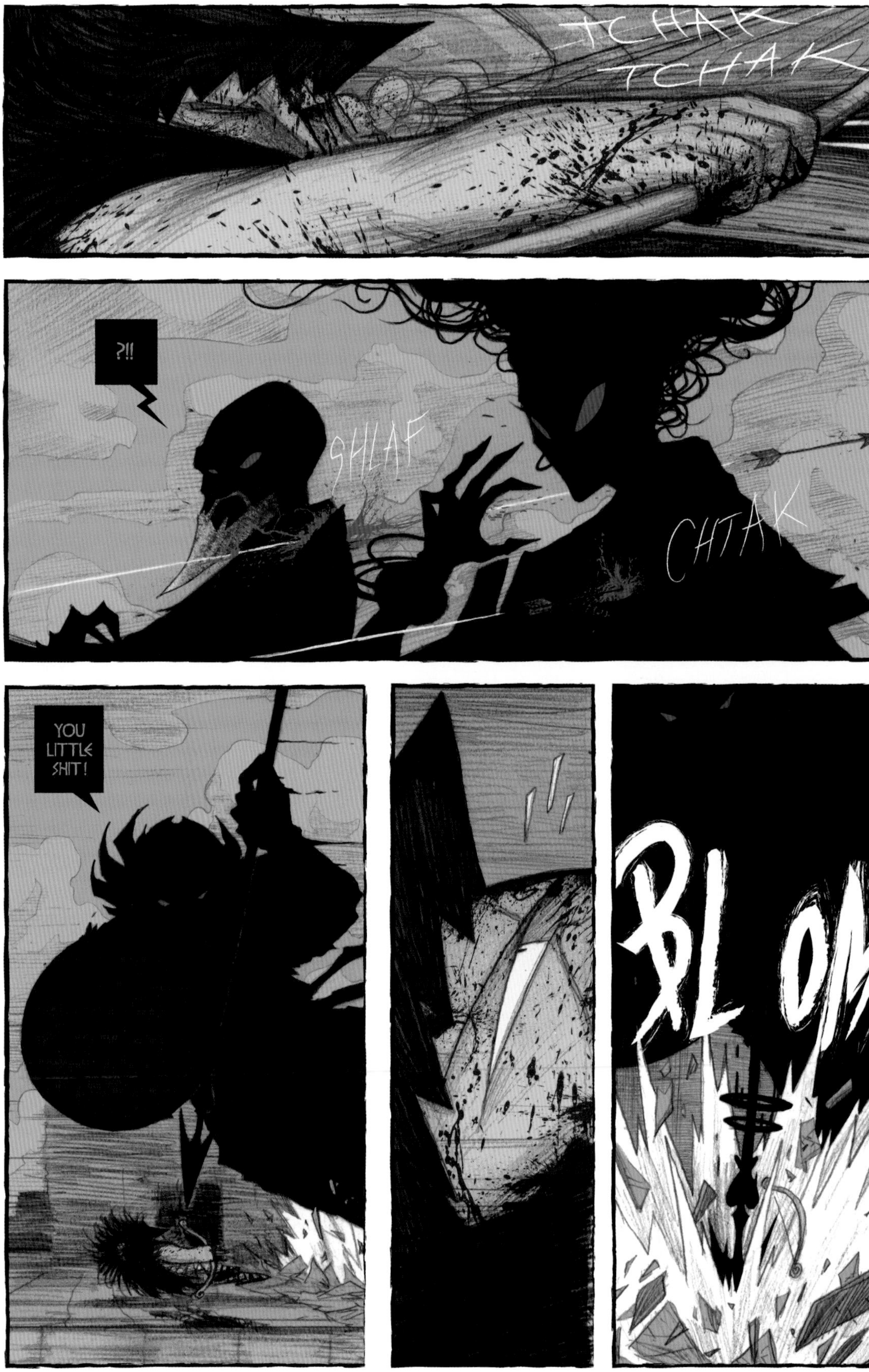
TCHAK
TCHAK
?!!
SHLAF
CHTAK
YOU LITTLE SHIT!
BLOM

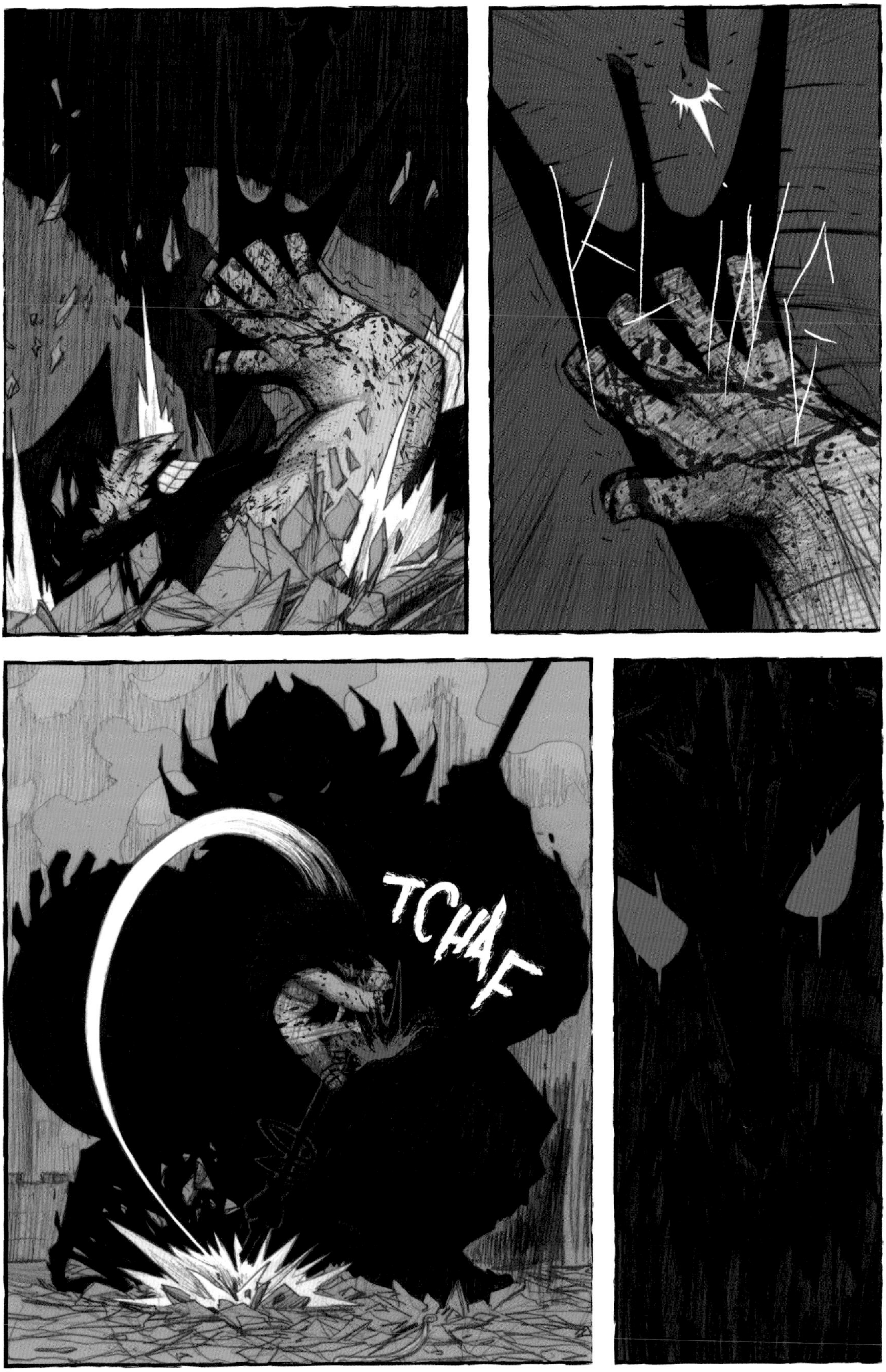
KLING
TCHAF

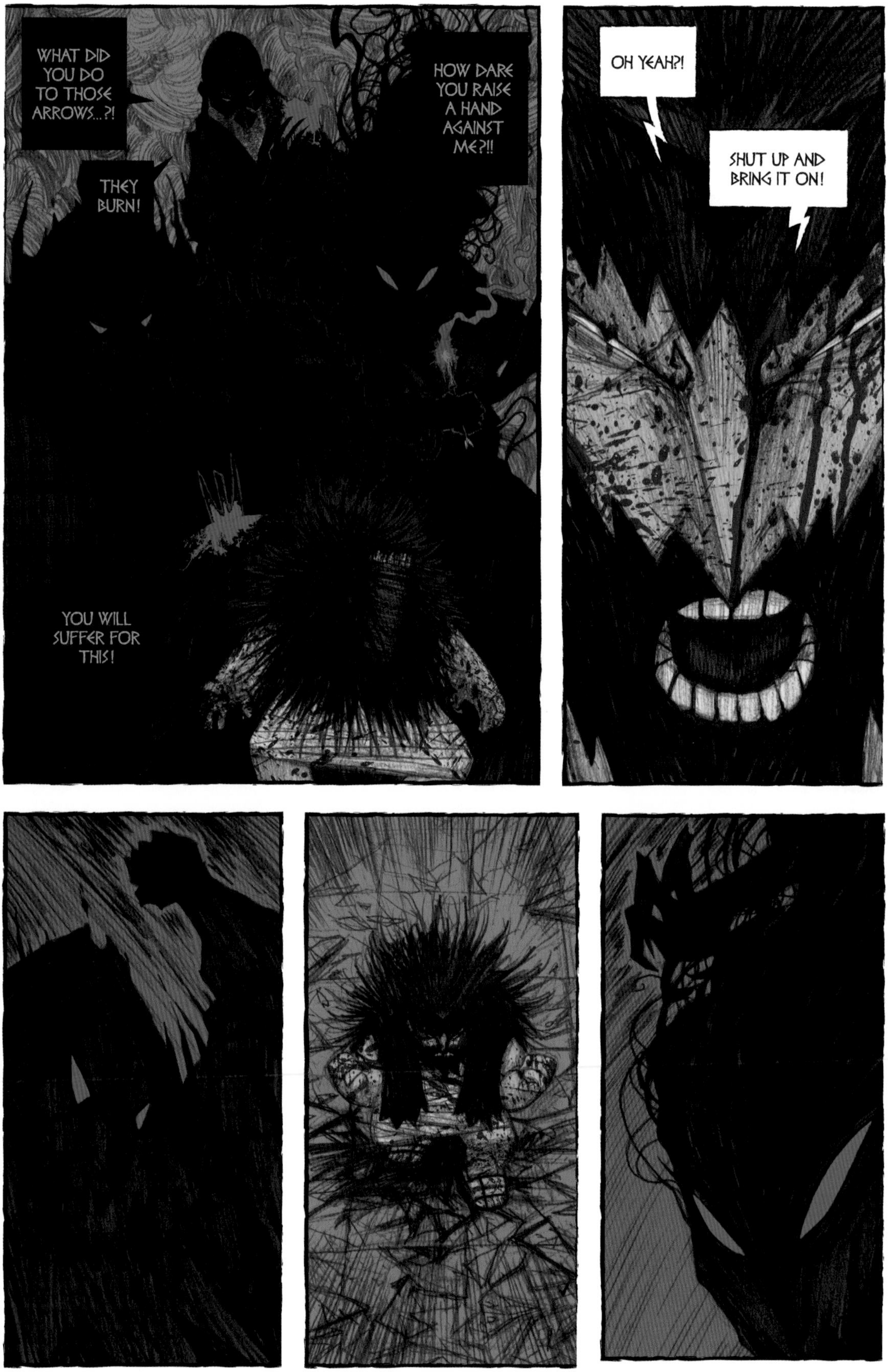
WHAT DID YOU DO TO THOSE ARROWS...?!
THEY BURN!
HOW DARE YOU RAISE A HAND AGAINST ME?!!
YOU WILL SUFFER FOR THIS!
OH YEAH?!
SHUT UP AND BRING IT ON!

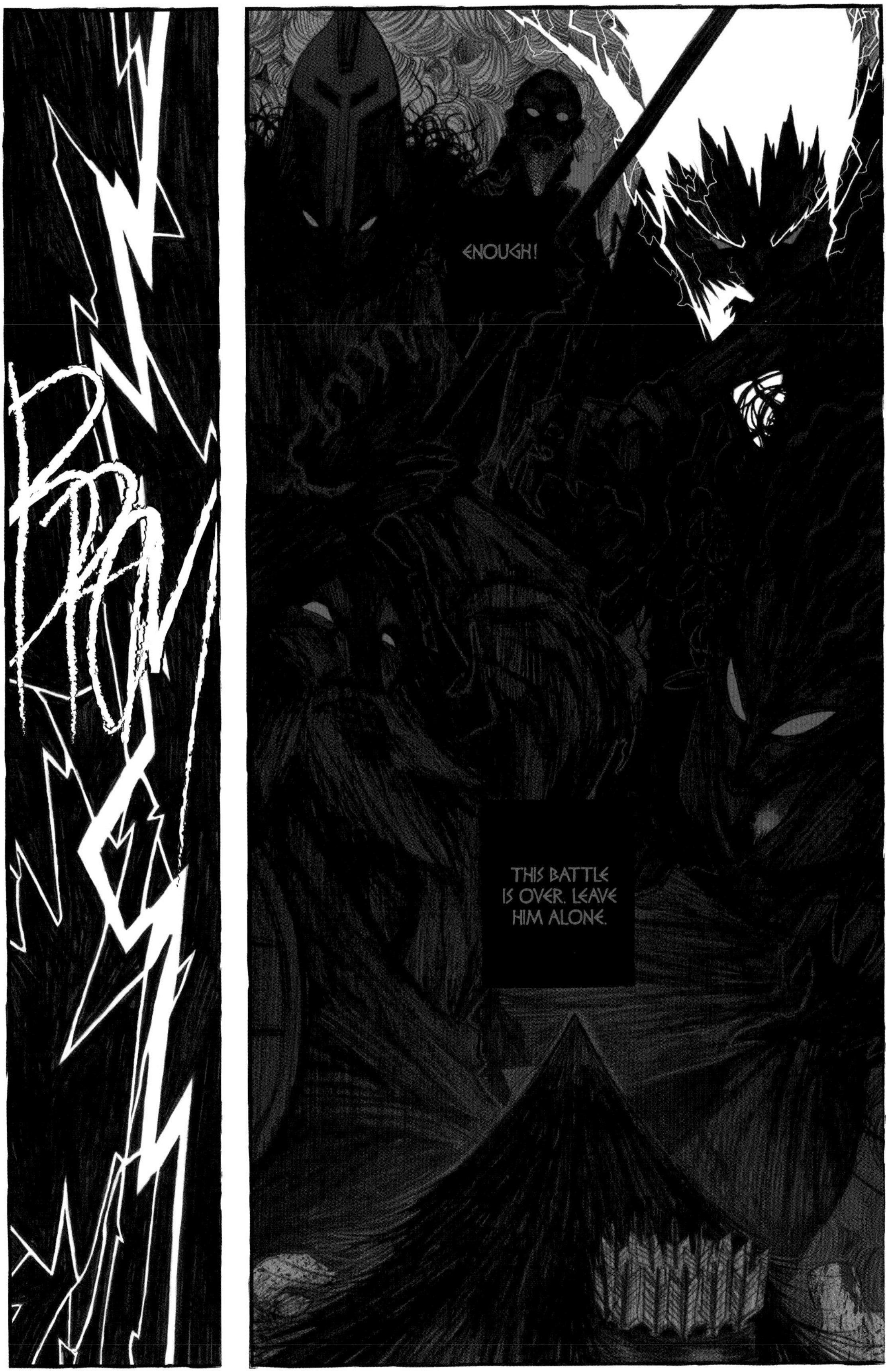
ENOUGH!
THIS BATTLE IS OVER. LEAVE HIM ALONE.

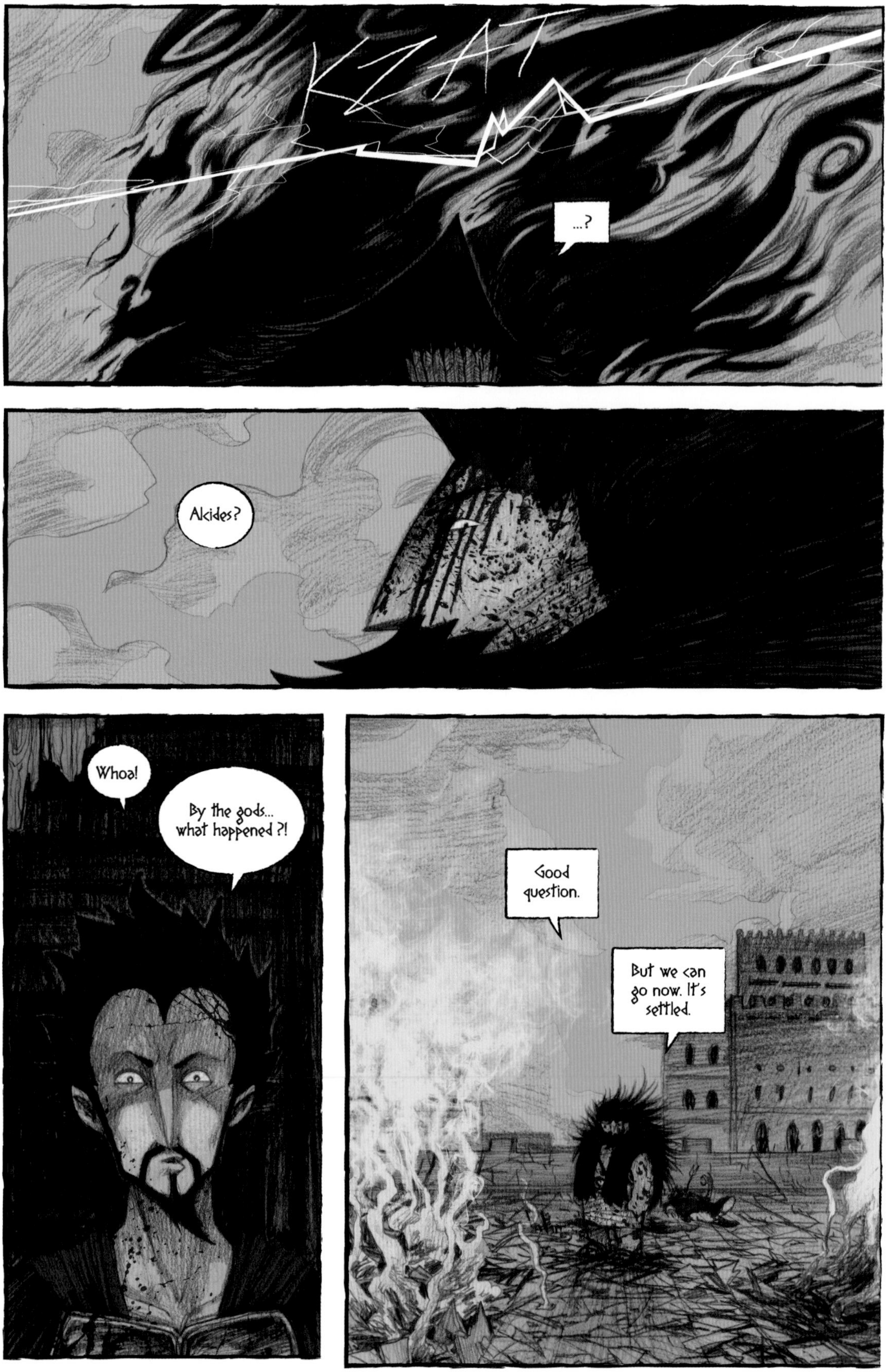
KZAT
...?
Alcides?
Whoa!
By the gods... what happened ?!
Good question.
But we can go now. It's settled.

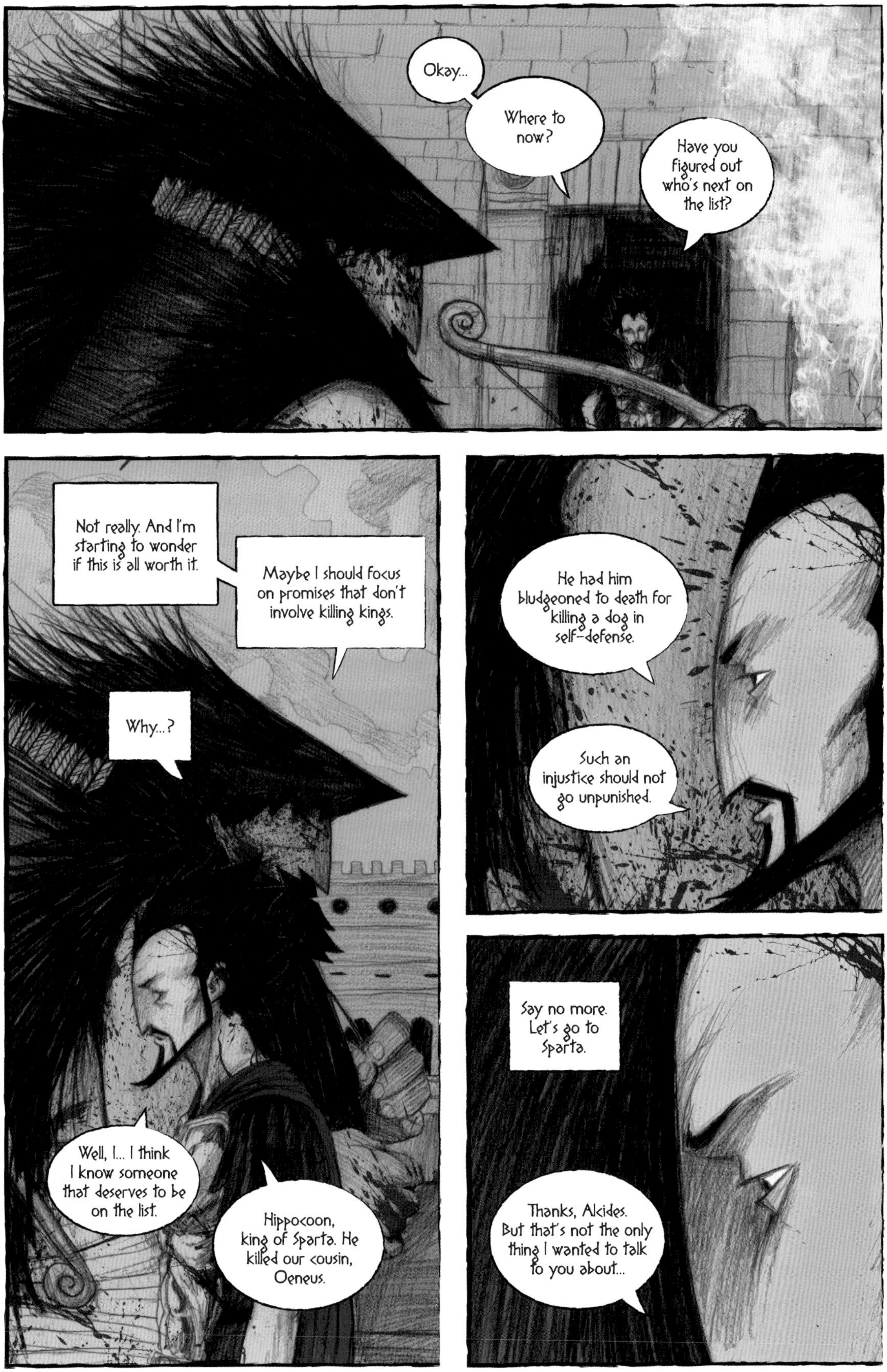
Okay...
Where to now?
Have you figured out who's next on the list?
Not really. And I'm starting to wonder if this is all worth it.
Maybe I should focus on promises that don't involve killing kings.
Why...?
Well, I... I think I know someone that deserves to be on the list.
Hippocoon, king of Sparta. He killed our cousin, Oeneus.
He had him bludgeoned to death for killing a dog in self-defense.
Such an injustice should not go unpunished.
Say no more. Let's go to Sparta.
Thanks, Alcides. But that's not the only thing I wanted to talk to you about...

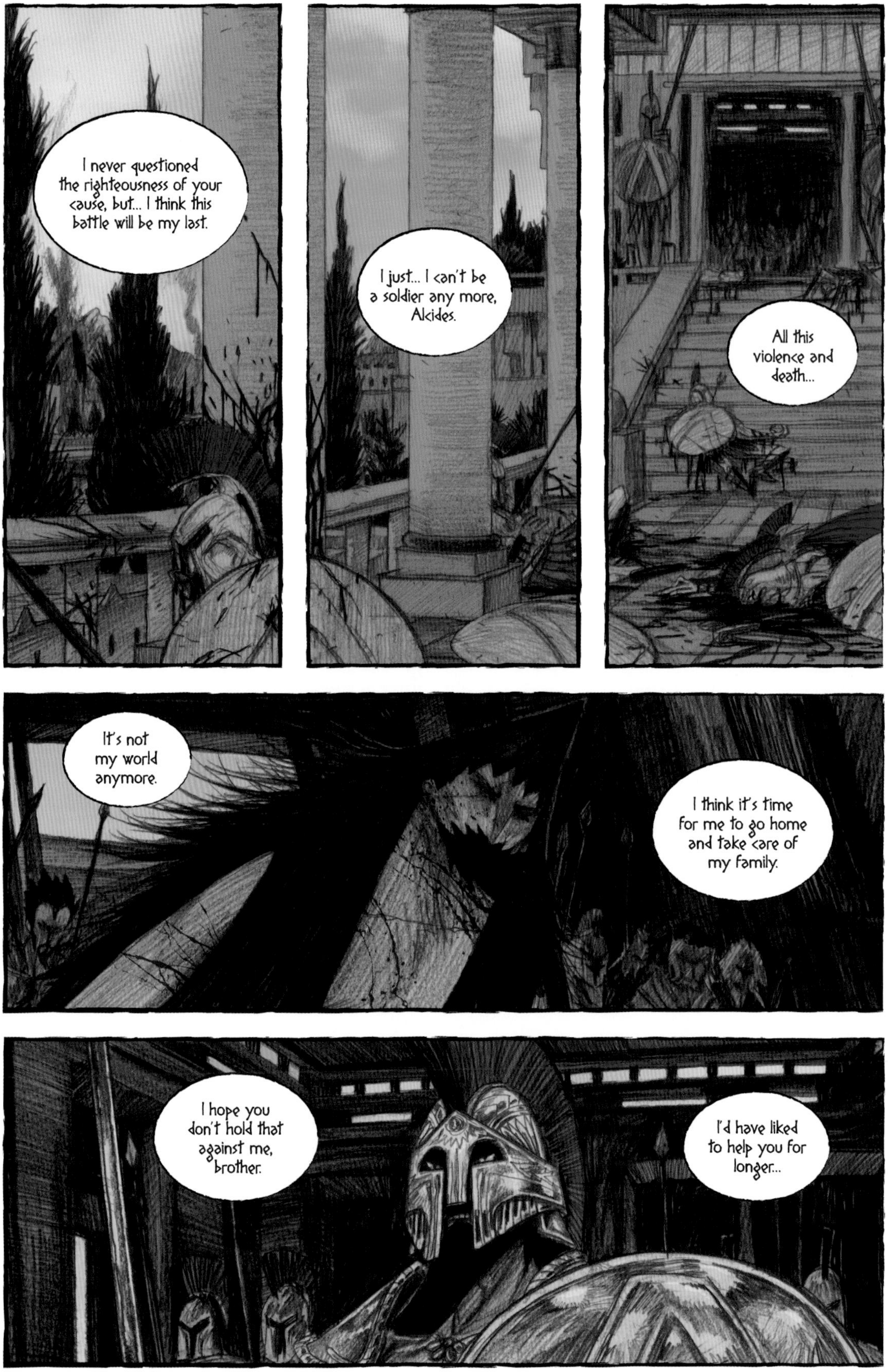
I never questioned the righteousness of your cause, but... I think this battle will be my last.
I just... I can't be a soldier any more, Alcides.
All this violence and death...
It's not my world anymore.
I think it's time for me to go home and take care of my family.
I hope you don't hold that against me, brother.
I'd have liked to help you for longer...

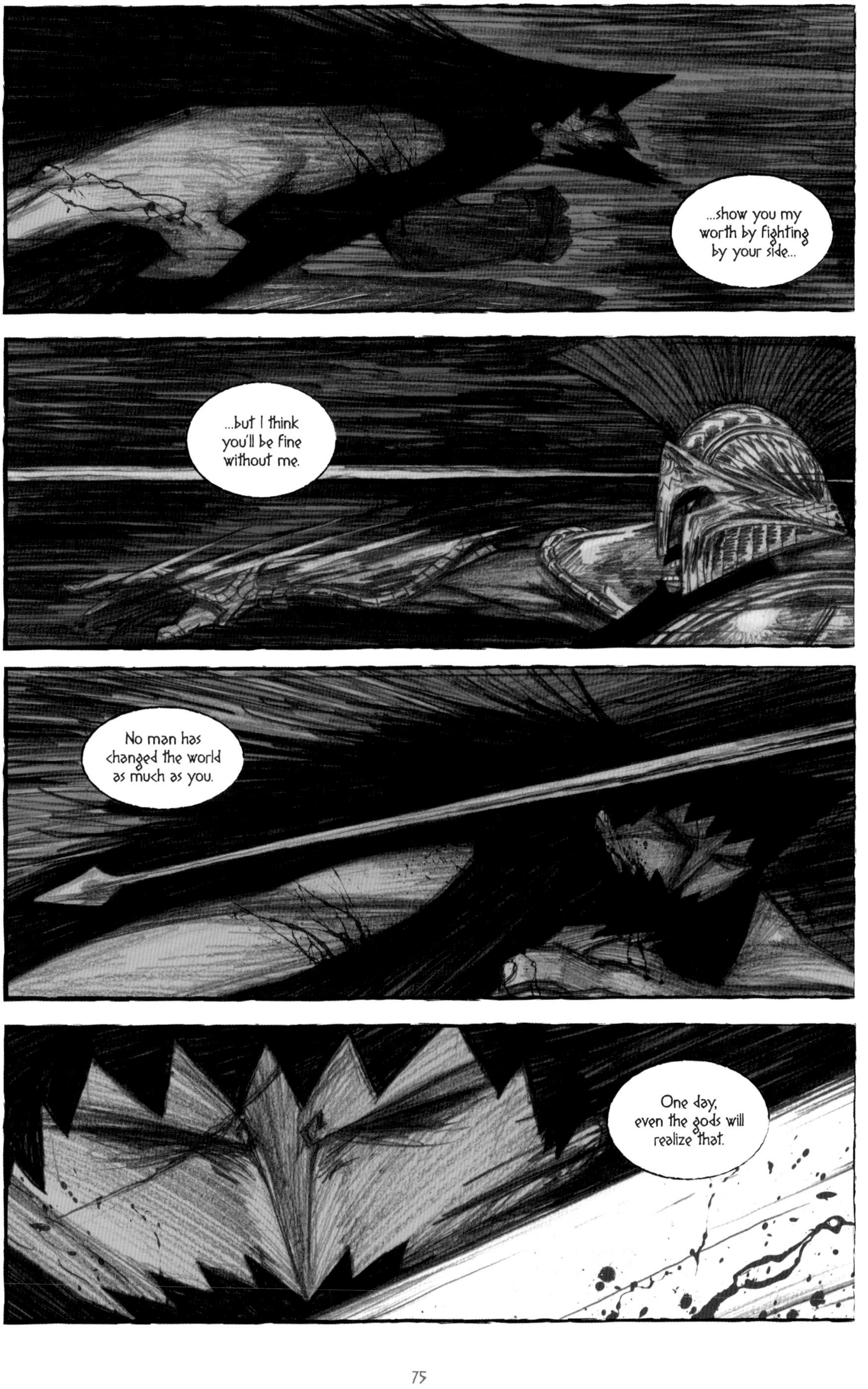
...show you my worth by fighting by your side...
...but I think you'll be fine without me.
No man has changed the world as much as you.
One day, even the gods will realize that.

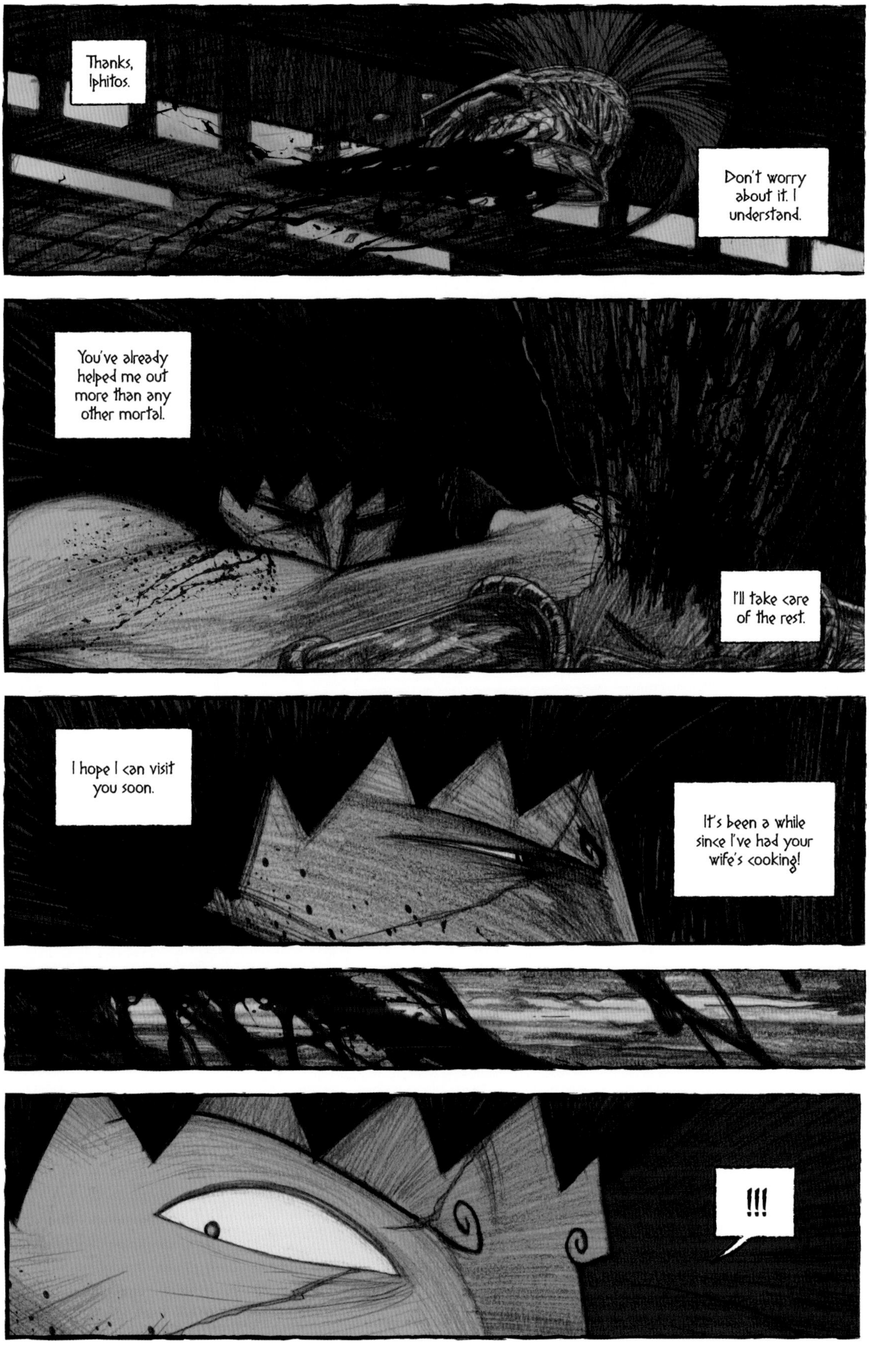
Thanks, Iphitos.
Don't worry about it. I understand.
You've already helped me out more than any other mortal.
I'll take care of the rest.
I hope I can visit you soon.
It's been a while since I've had your wife's cooking!
!!!

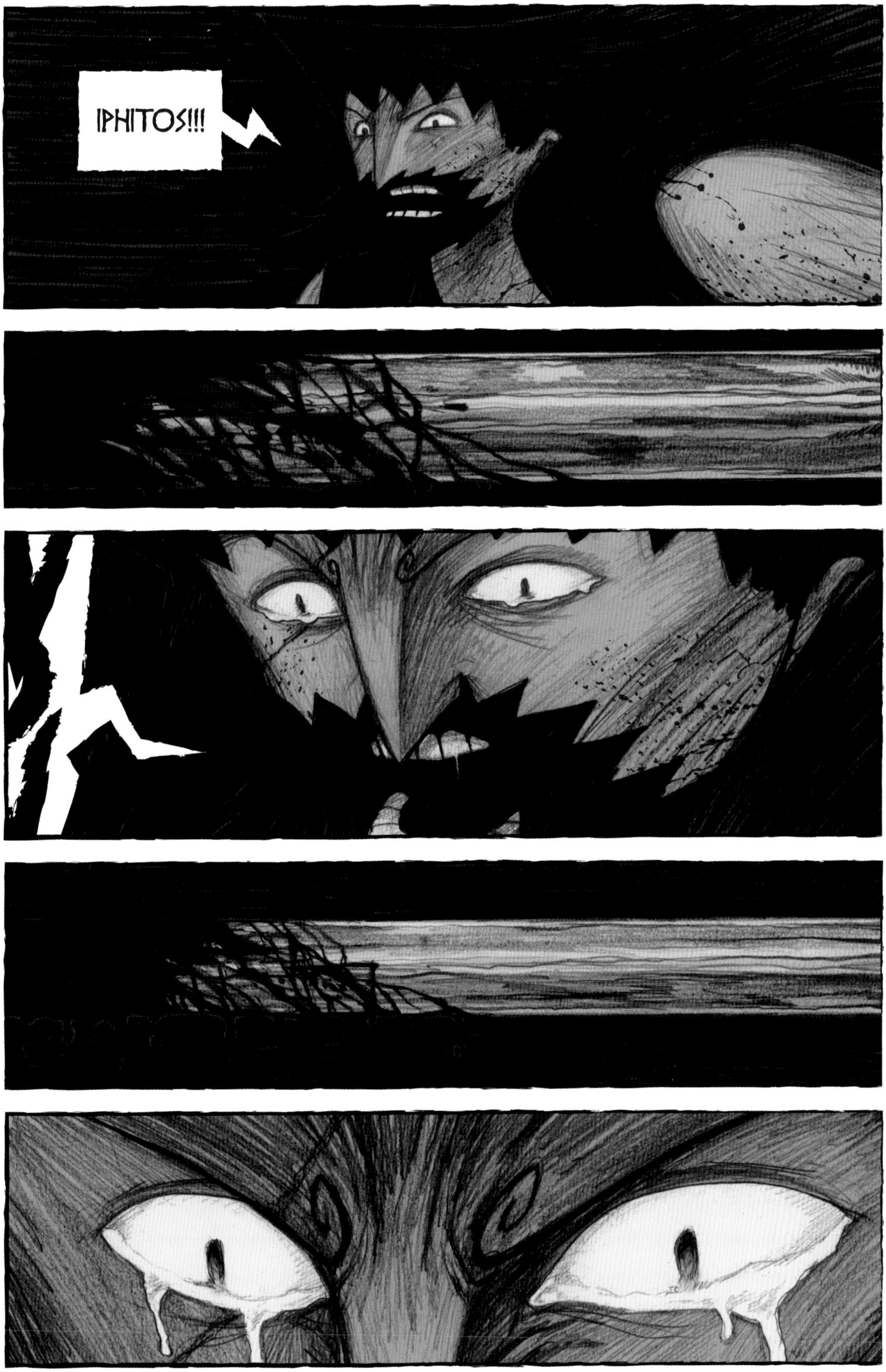
IPHITOS!!!

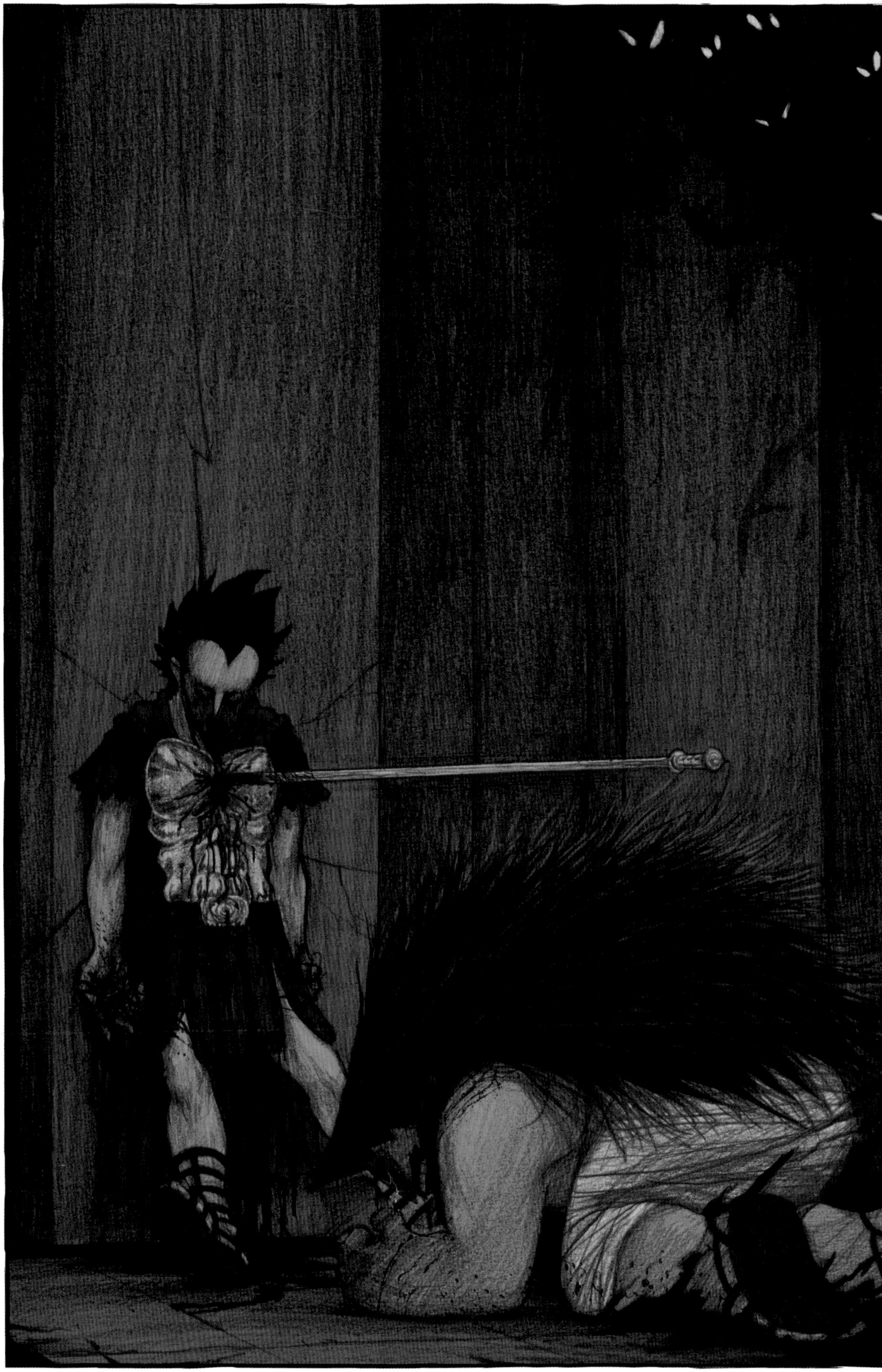

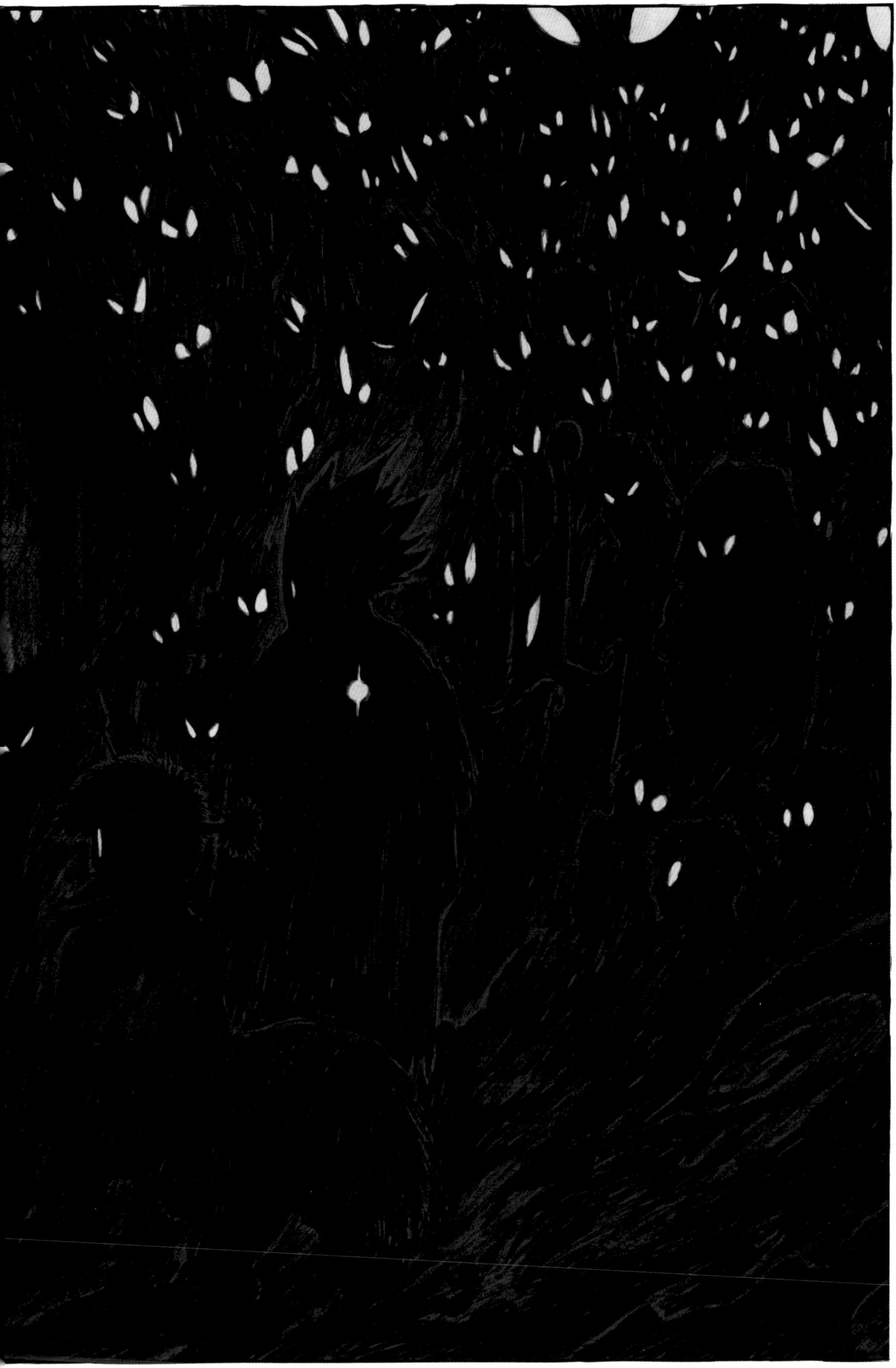

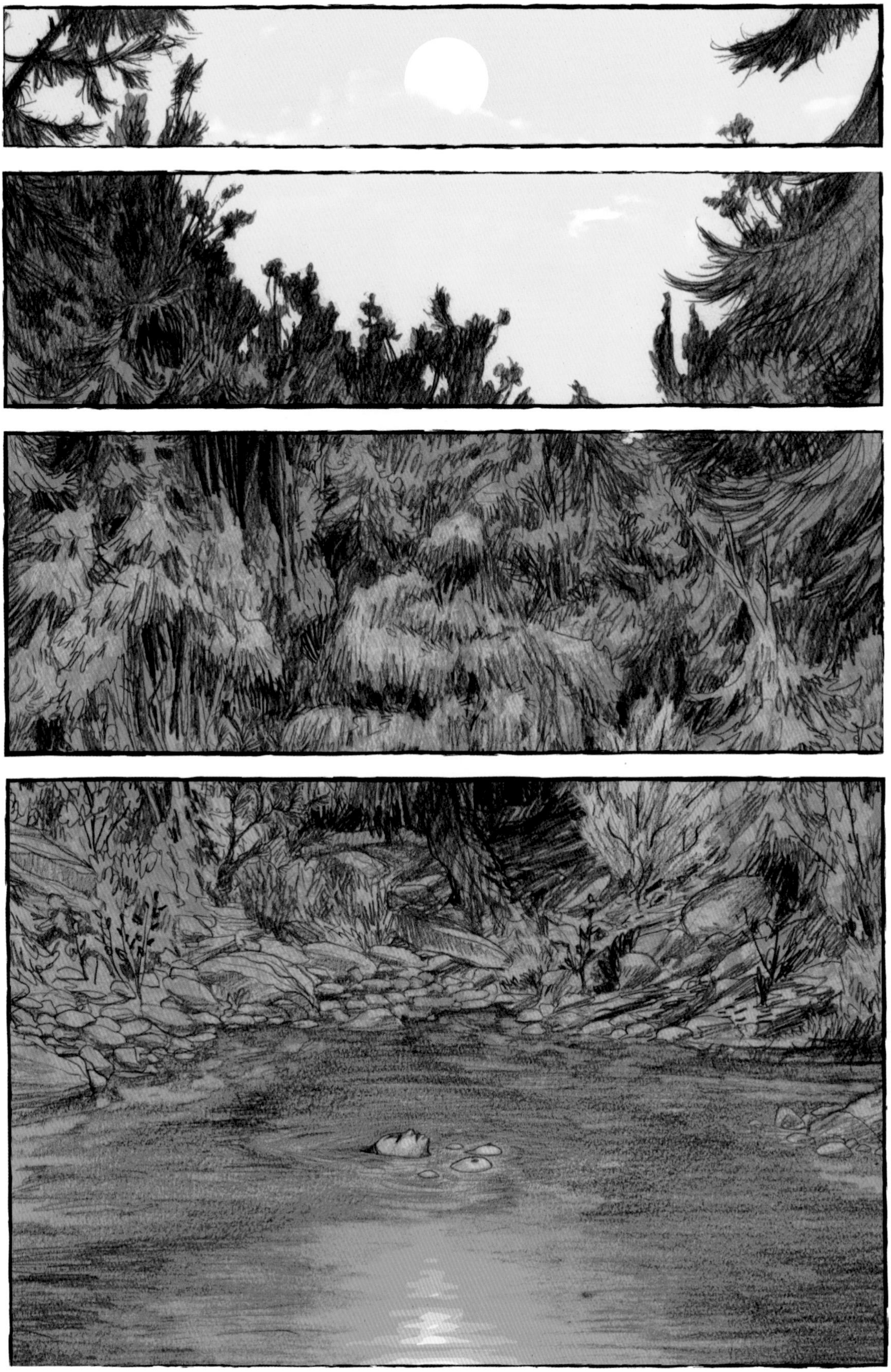

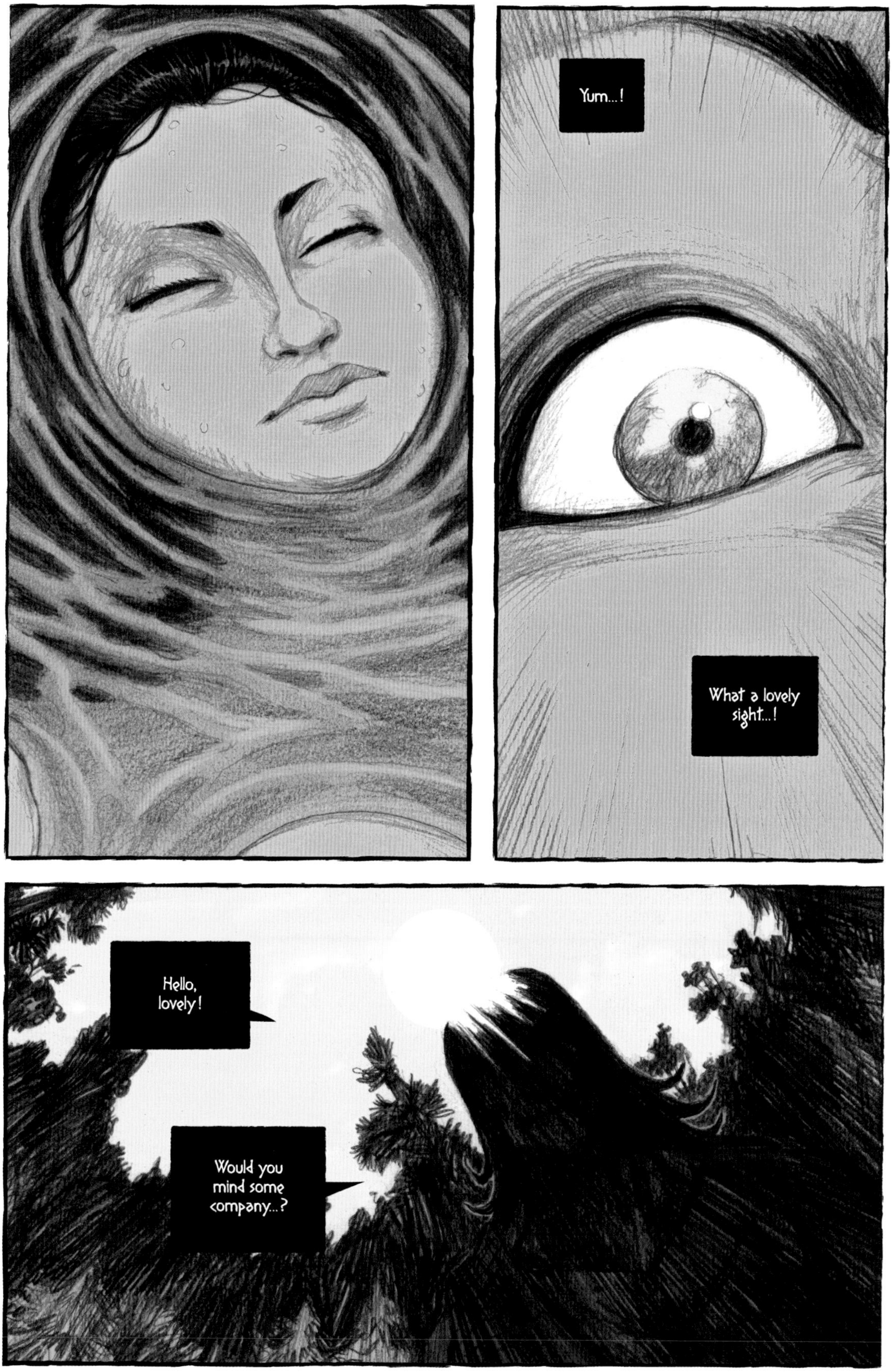
Yum...!
What a lovely sight...!
Hello, lovely!
Would you mind some company...?

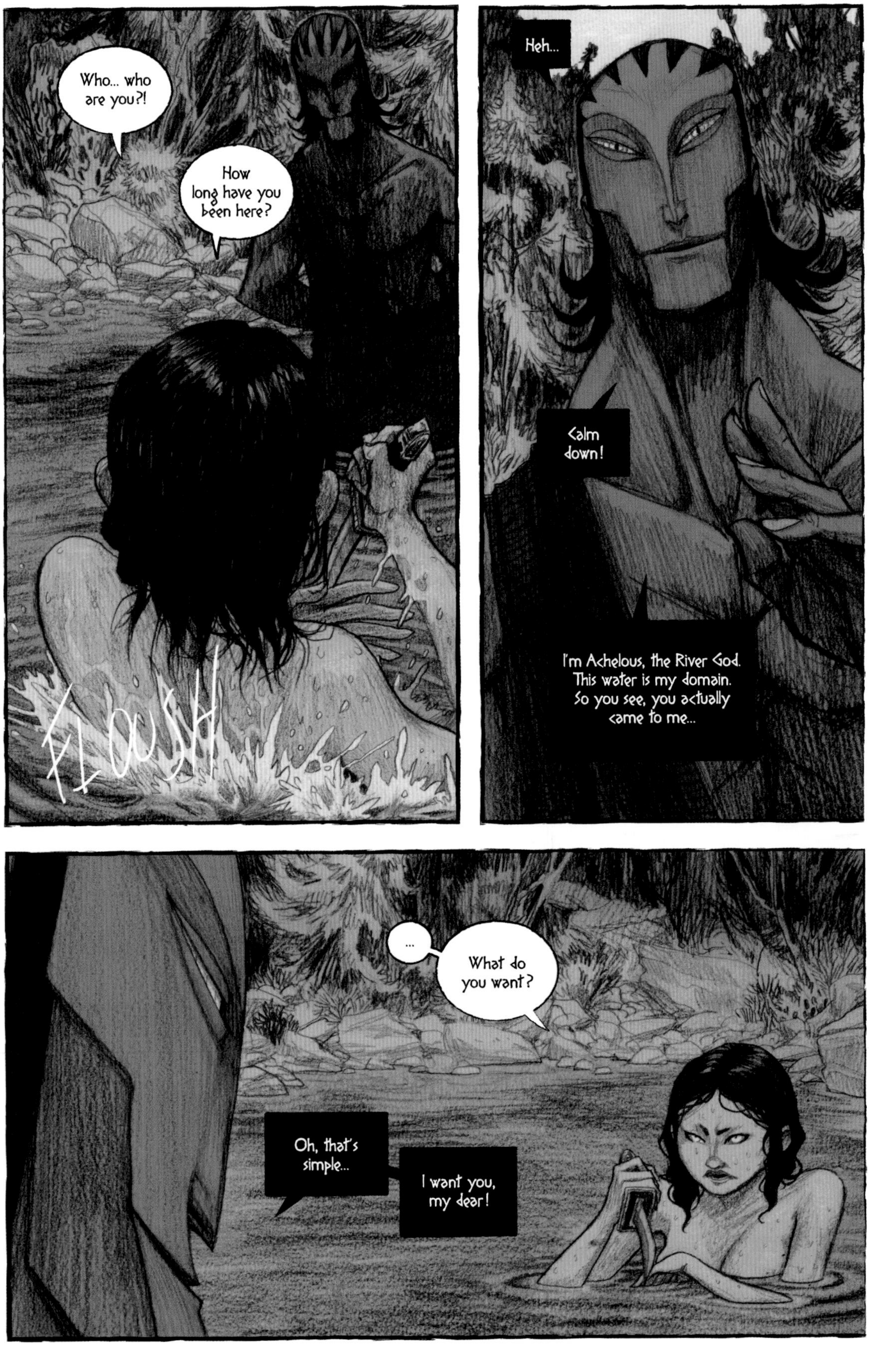
Who... who are you?!
How long have you been here?
FLOUSH
Heh...
Calm down!
I'm Achelous, the River God. This water is my domain. So you see, you actually came to me...
...
What do you want?
Oh, that's simple...
I want you, my dear!

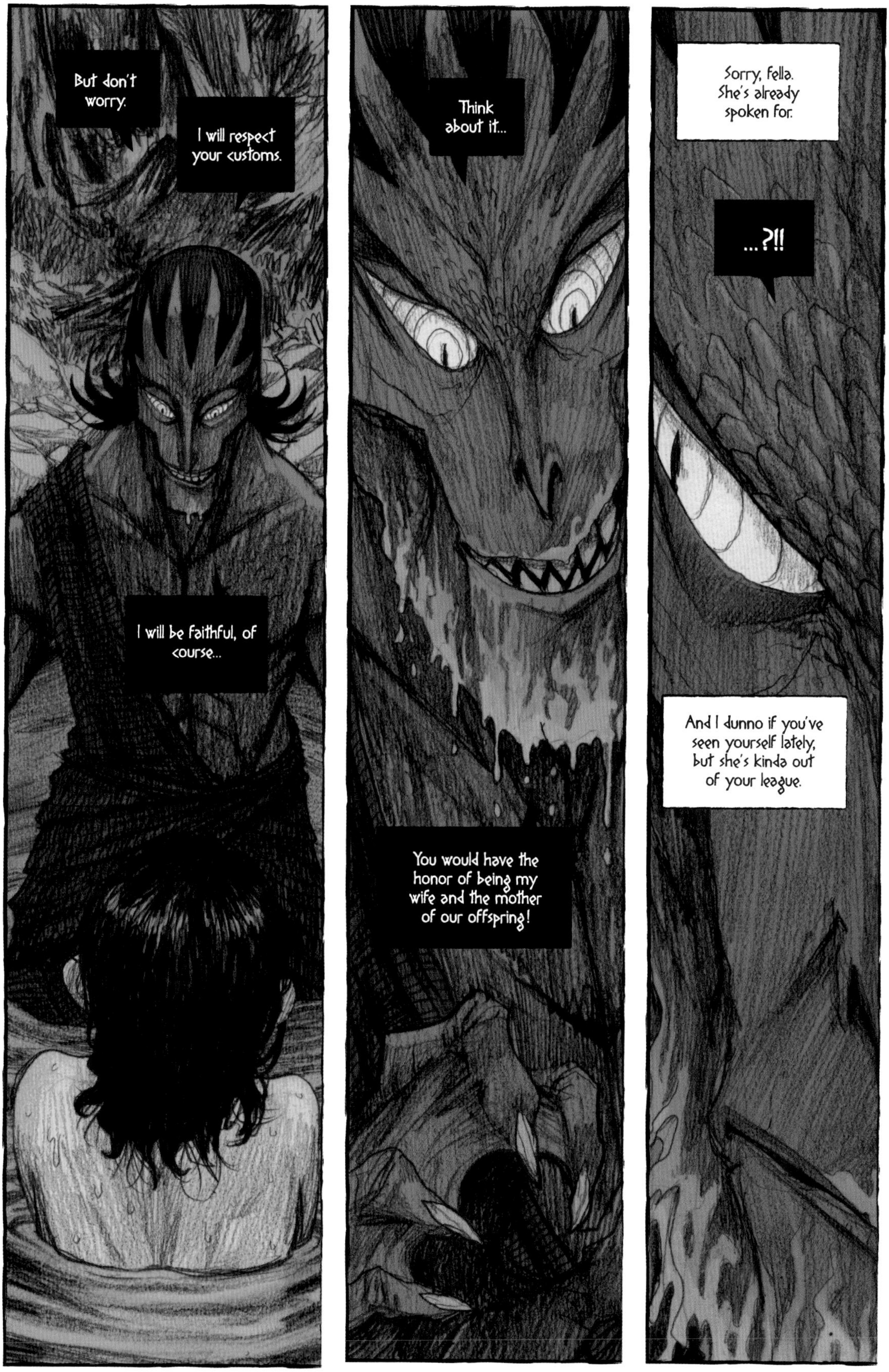
But don't worry.
I will respect your customs.
I will be faithful, of course...
Think about it...
You would have the honor of being my wife and the mother of our offspring!
Sorry, fella. She's already spoken for.
...?!!
And I dunno if you've seen yourself lately, but she's kinda out of your league.

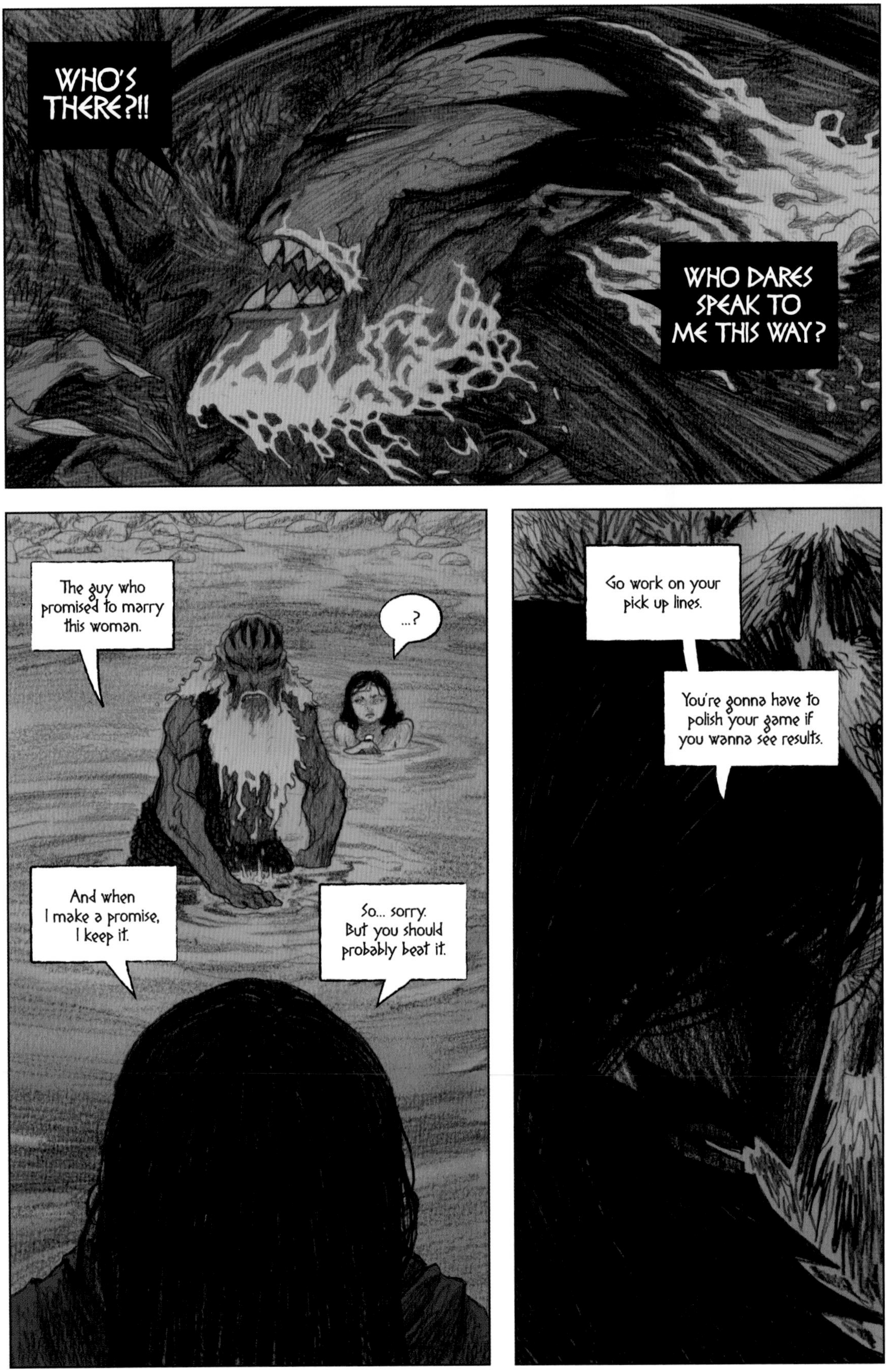
WHO'S THERE?!!
WHO DARES SPEAK TO ME THIS WAY?
The guy who promised to marry this woman.
...?
And when I make a promise, I keep it.
So... sorry. But you should probably beat it.
Go work on your pick up lines.
You're gonna have to polish your game if you wanna see results.

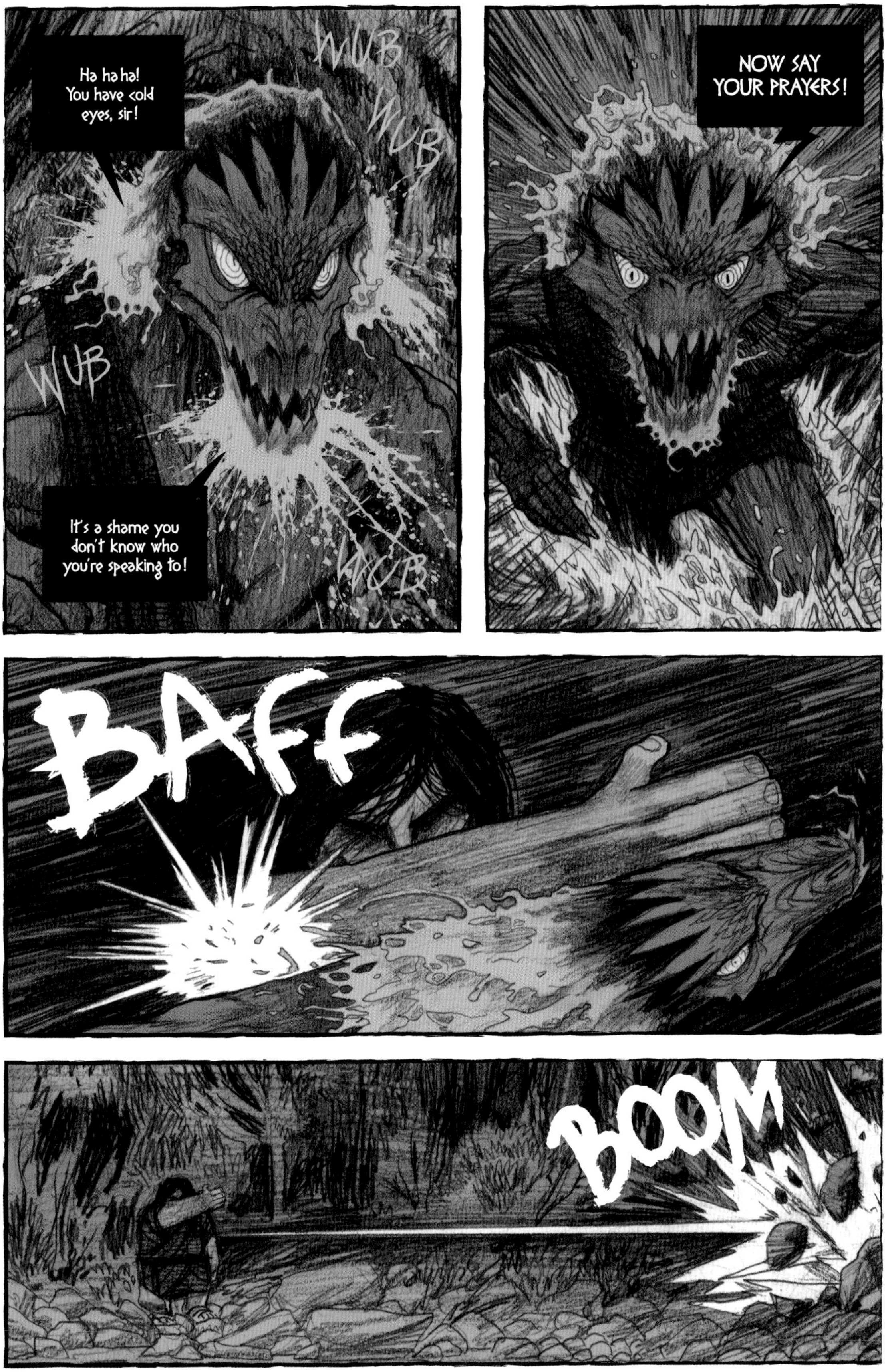

Ha ha ha! You have cold eyes, sir!
WUB
WUB
WUB
It's a shame you don't know who you're speaking to!
WUB
NOW SAY YOUR PRAYERS!
BAFF
BOOM

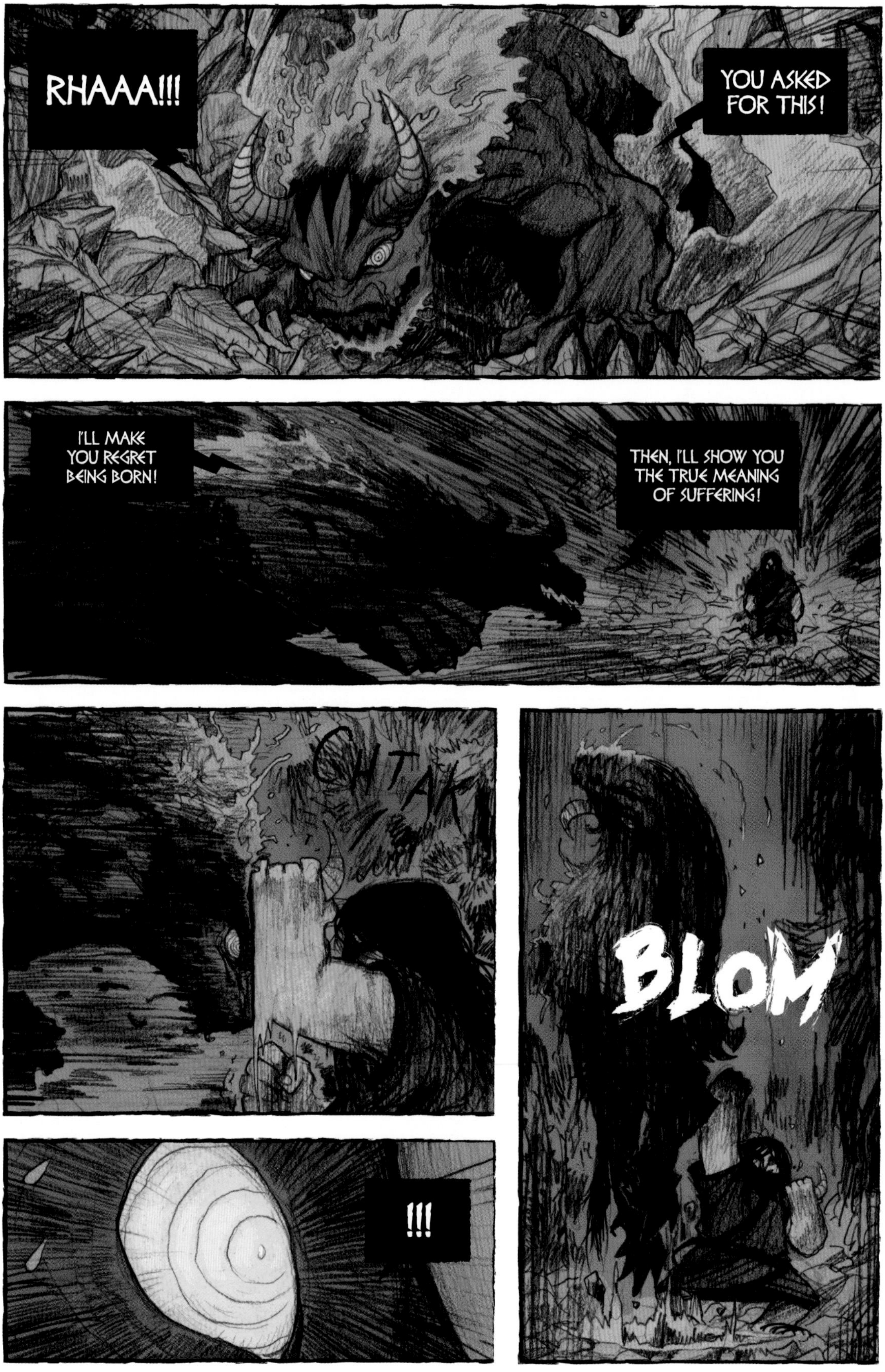
RHAAA!!!
YOU ASKED FOR THIS!
I'LL MAKE YOU REGRET BEING BORN!
THEN, I'LL SHOW YOU THE TRUE MEANING OF SUFFERING!
CHTAK
BLOM
!!!

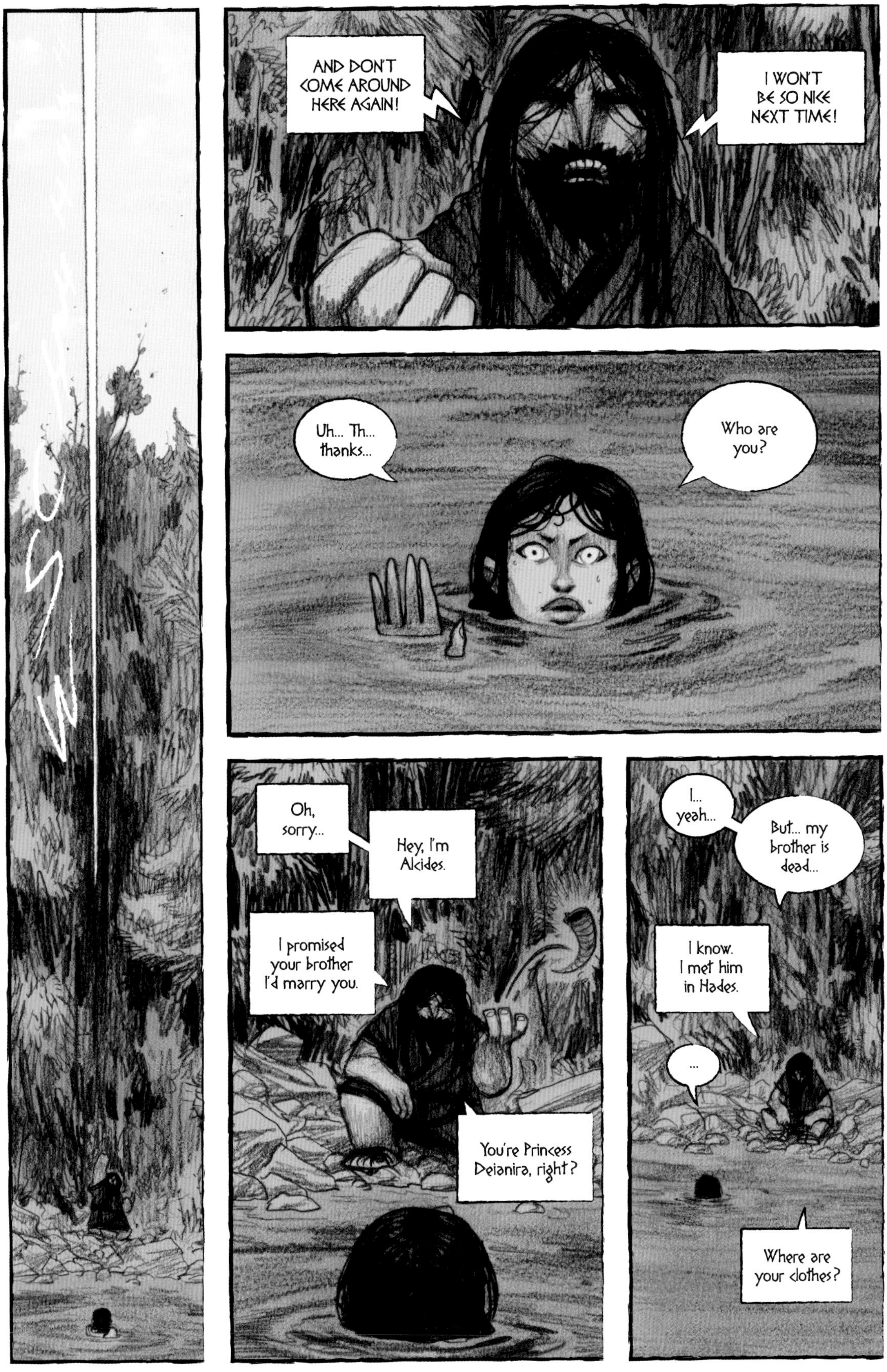
AND DON'T COME AROUND HERE AGAIN!
I WON'T BE SO NICE NEXT TIME!
Uh... Th... thanks...
Who are you?
Oh, sorry...
Hey, I'm Alcides.
I promised your brother I'd marry you.
You're Princess Deianira, right?
I... yeah...
But... my brother is dead...
I know. I met him in Hades.
...
Where are your clothes?

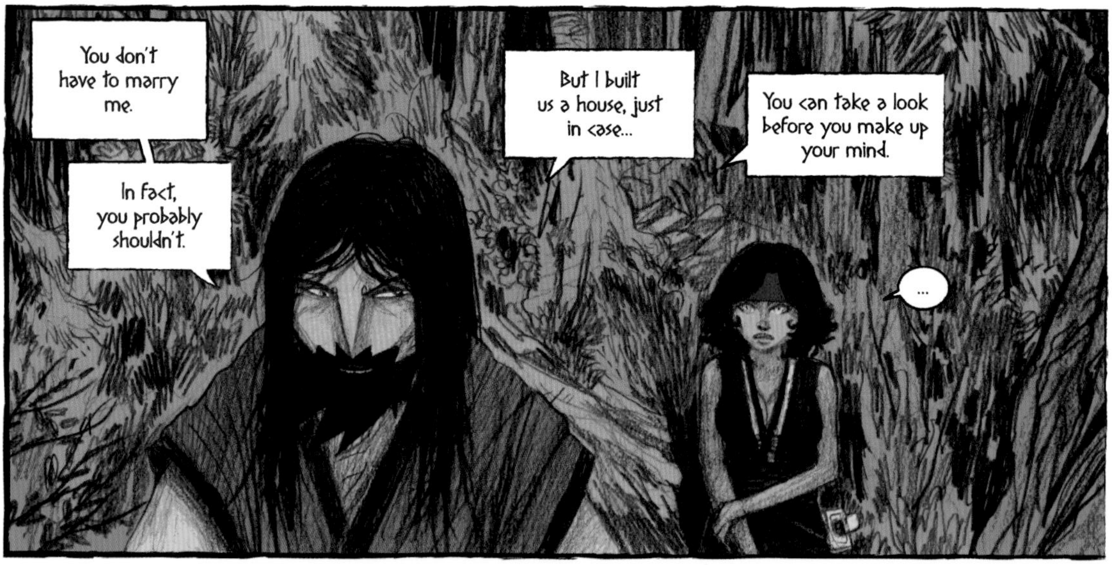
You don't have to marry me.
In fact, you probably shouldn't.
But I built us a house, just in case...
You can take a look before you make up your mind.
...

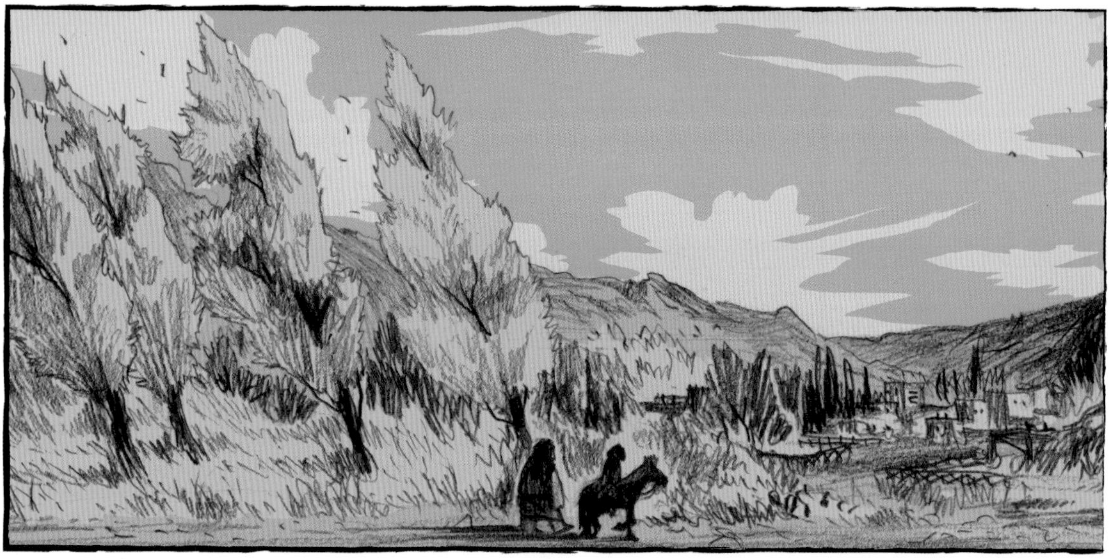

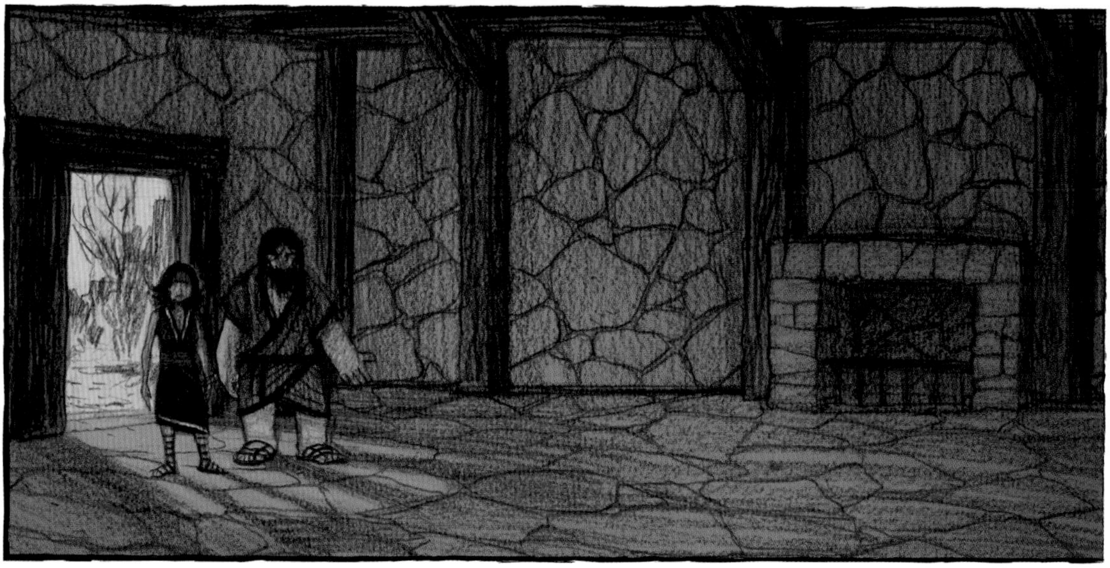

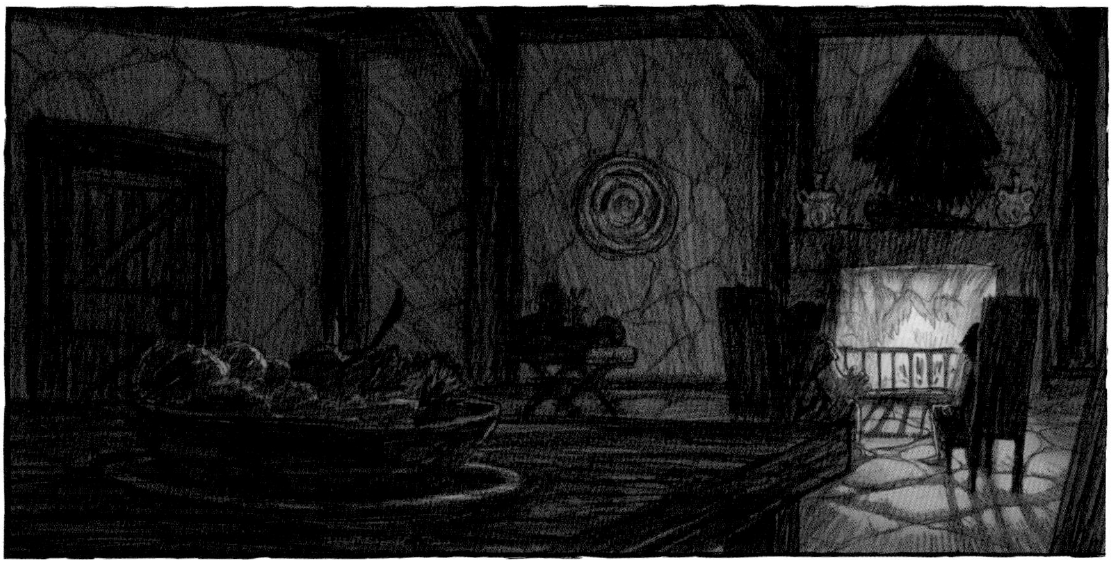

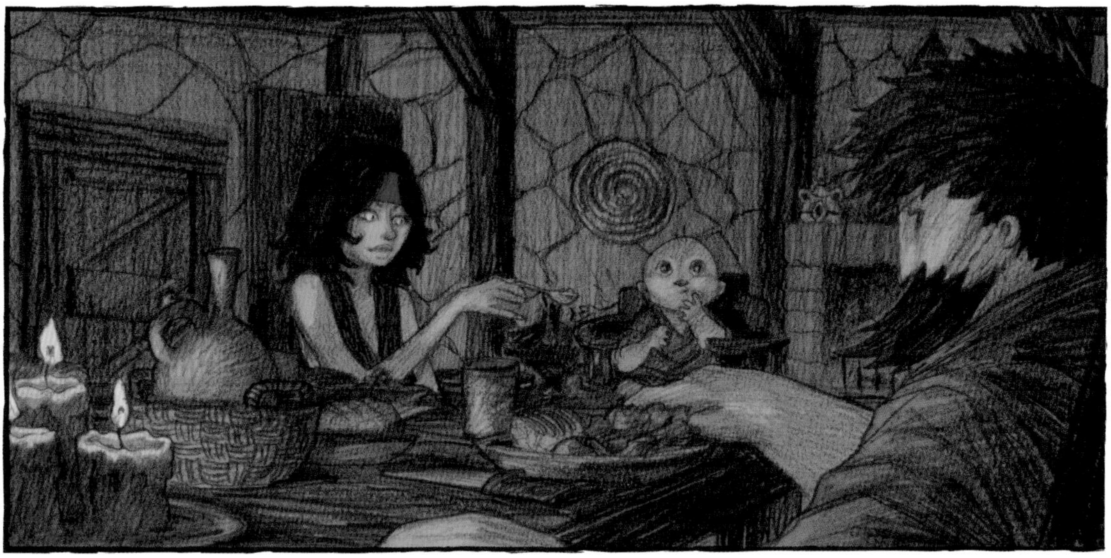

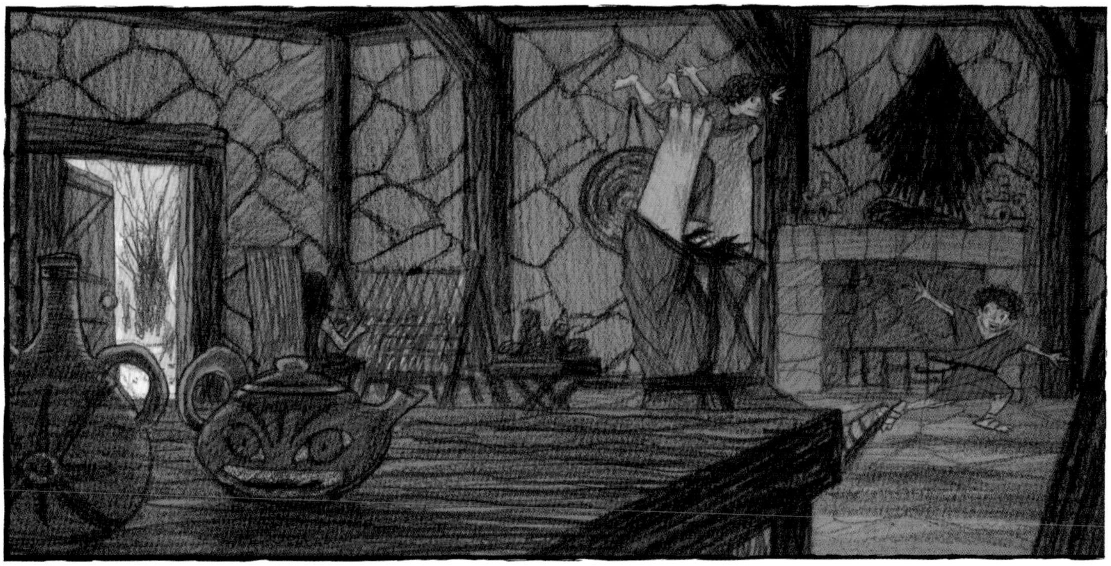

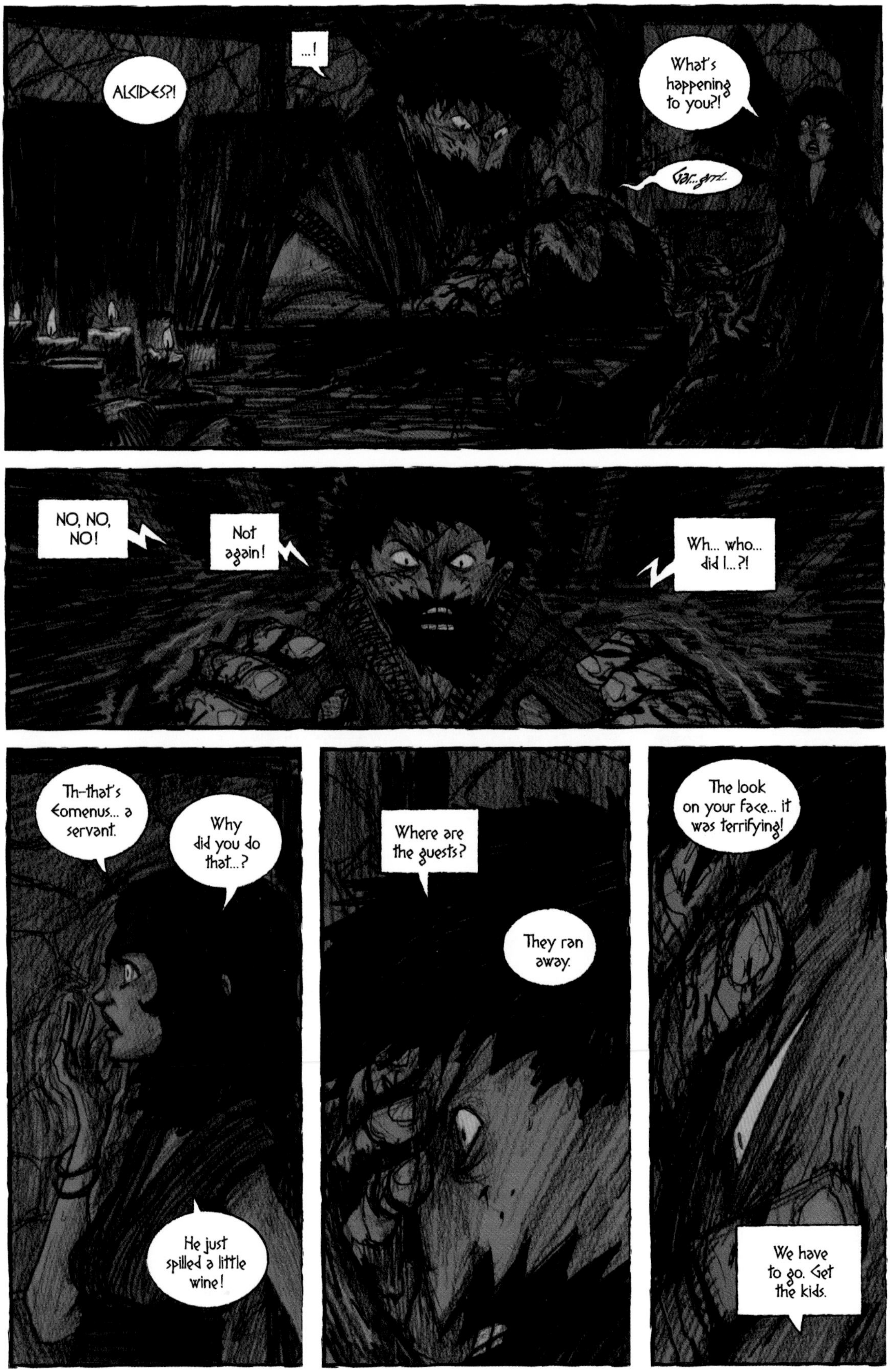
ALCIDES?!
...!
What's happening to you?!
NO, NO, NO!
Not again!
Wh... who... did I...?!
Th-that's Eomenus... a servant.
Why did you do that...?
He just spilled a little wine!
Where are the guests?
They ran away.
The look on your face... it was terrifying!
We have to go. Get the kids.

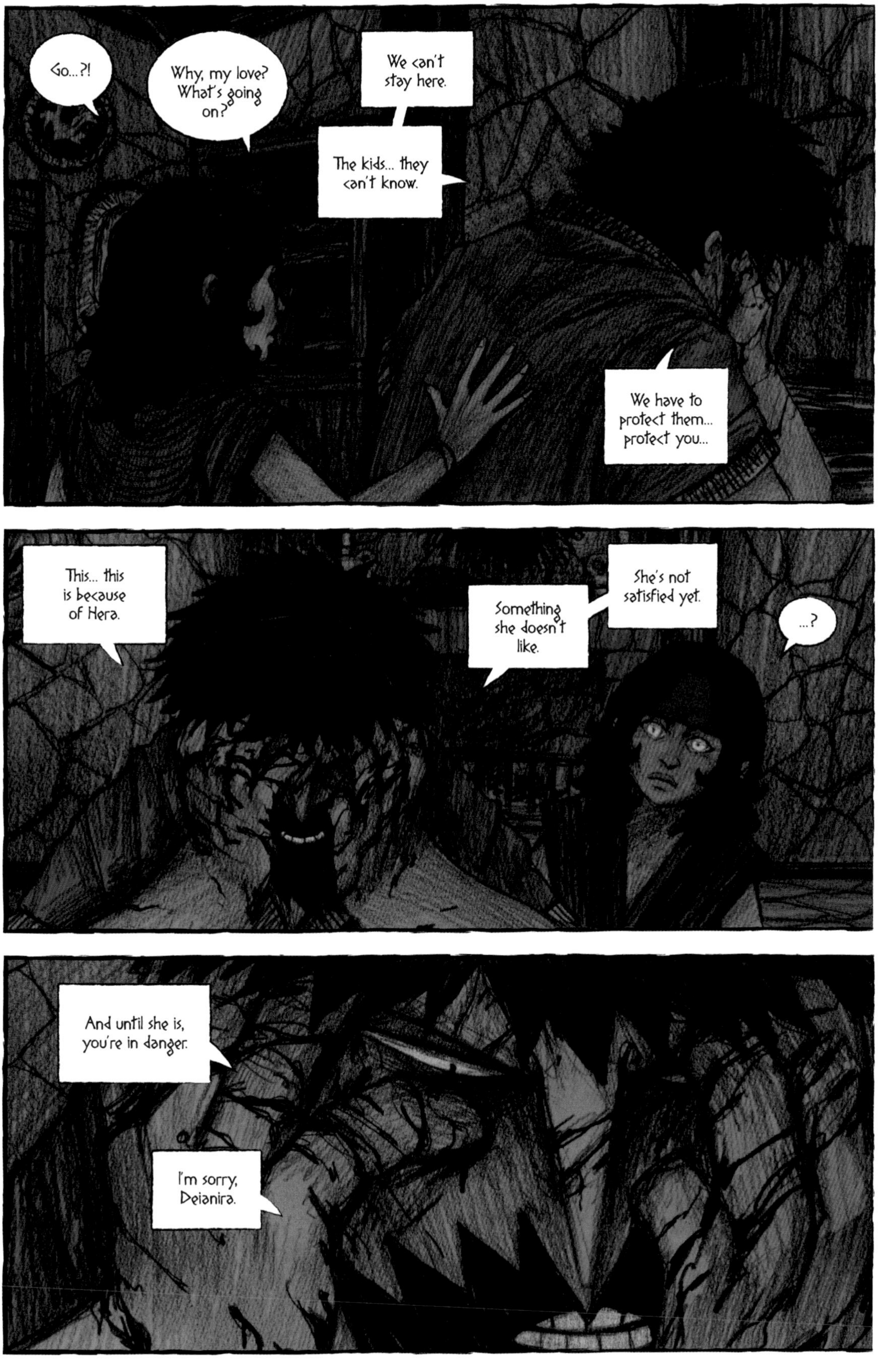
Go...?!
Why, my love? What's going on?
We can't stay here.
The kids... they can't know.
We have to protect them... protect you...
This... this is because of Hera.
Something she doesn't like.
She's not satisfied yet.
...?
And until she is, you're in danger.
I'm sorry, Deianira.

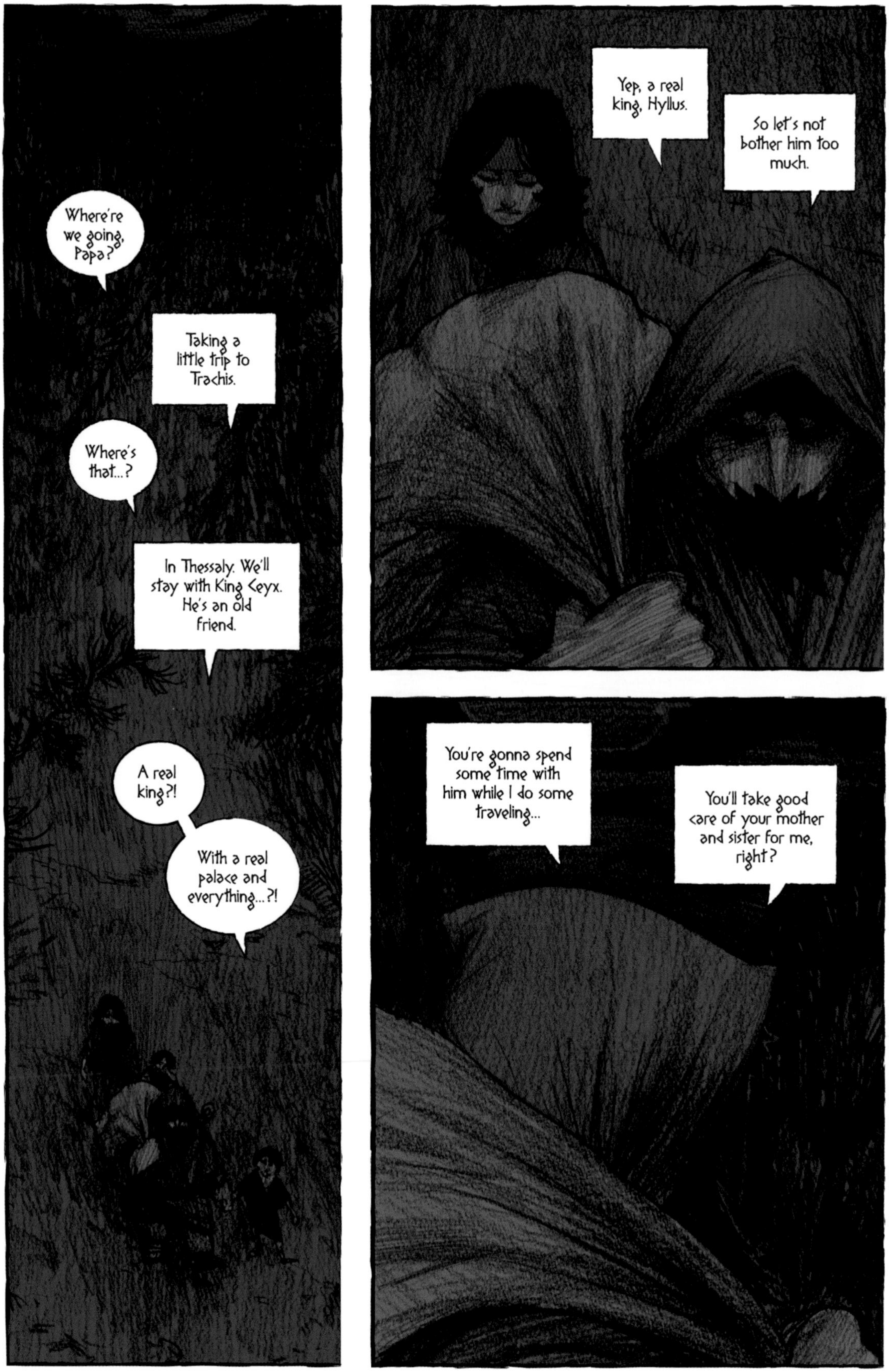
Where're we going, Papa?
Taking a little trip to Trachis.
Where's that...?
In Thessaly. We'll stay with King Ceyx. He's an old friend.
A real king?!
With a real palace and everything...?!
Yep, a real king, Hyllus.
So let's not bother him too much.
You're gonna spend some time with him while I do some traveling...
You'll take good care of your mother and sister for me, right?

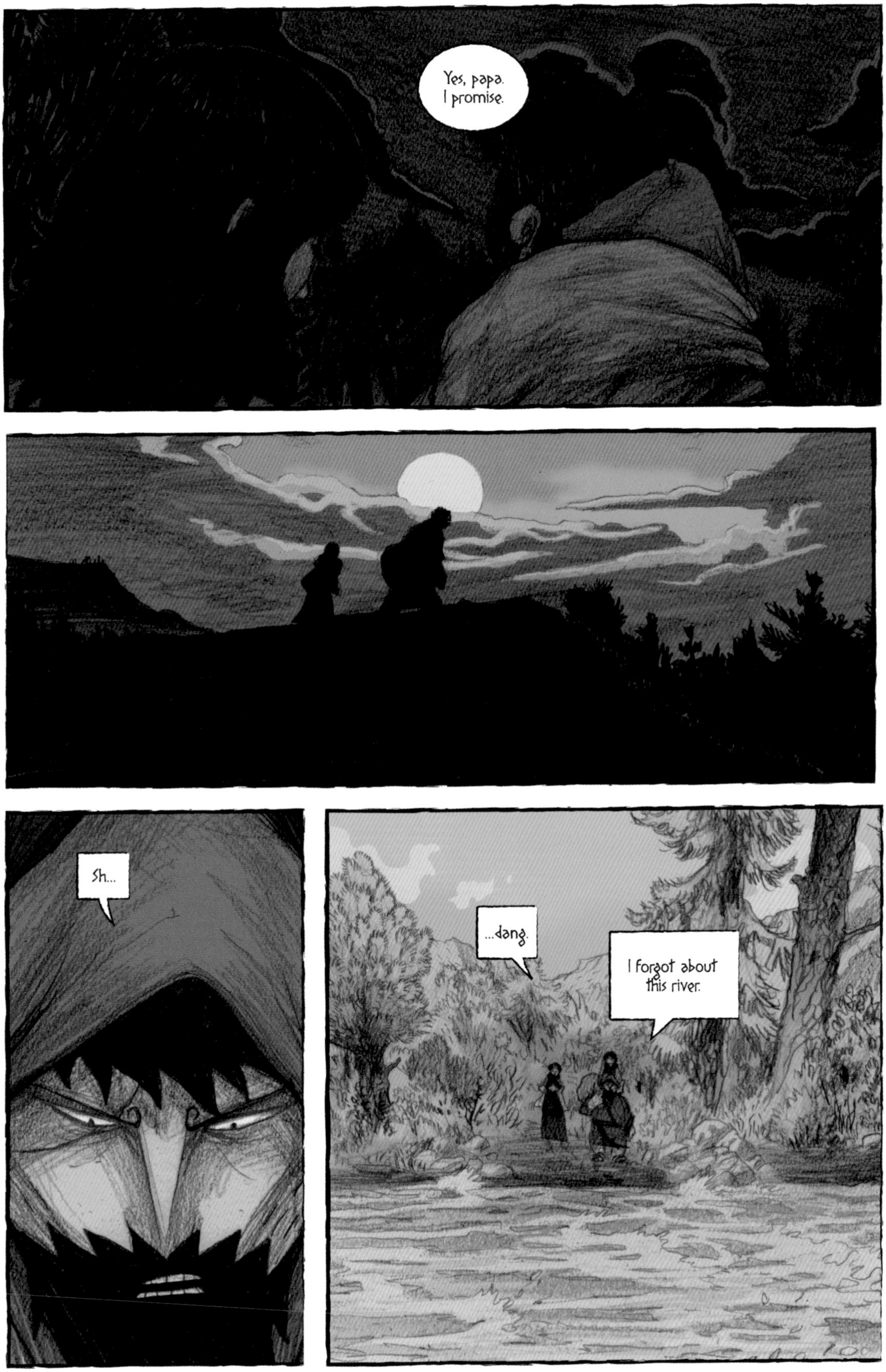
Yes, papa. I promise.
Sh...
...dang.
I forgot about this river.

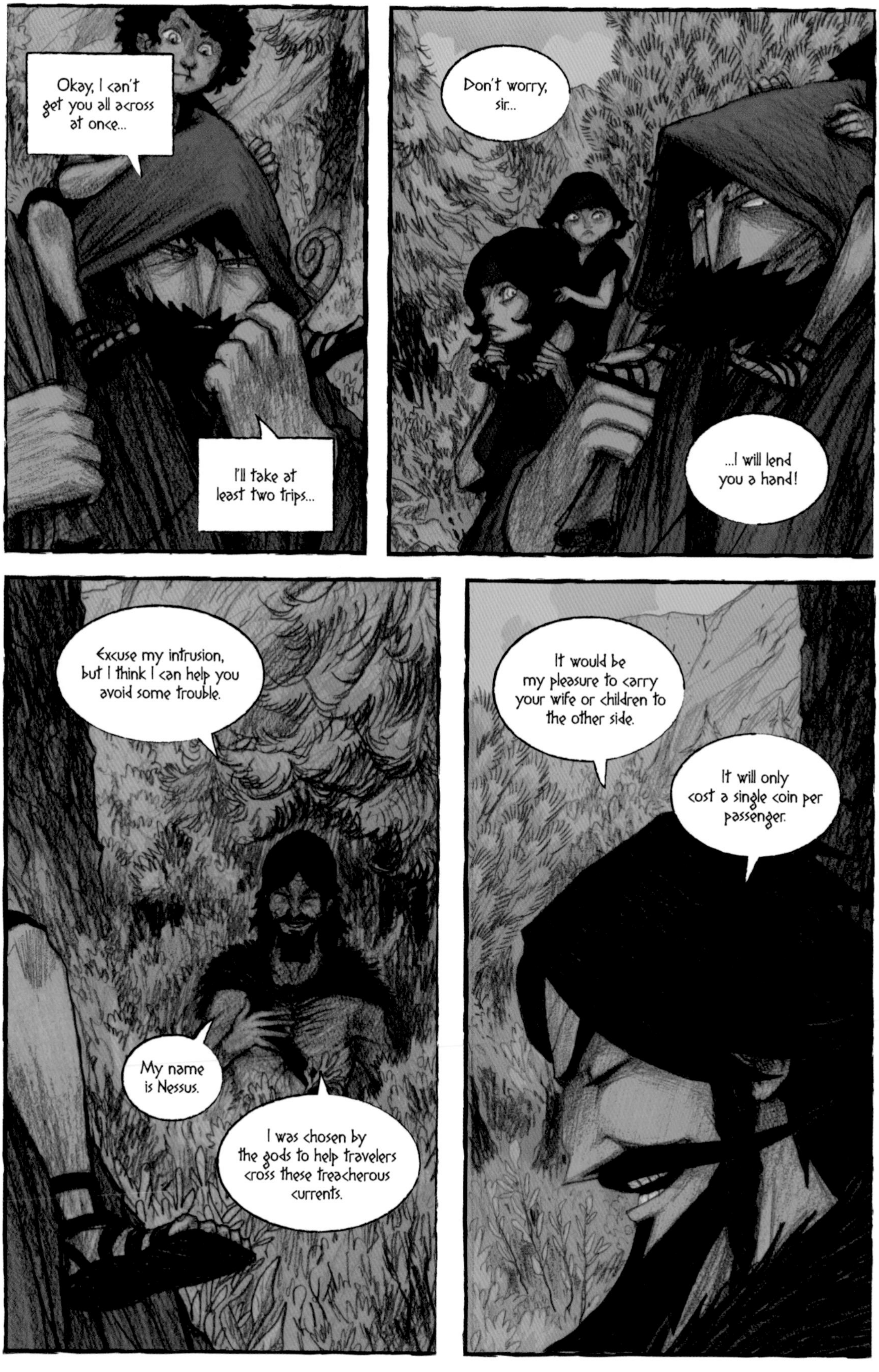
Okay, I can't get you all across at once...
I'll take at least two trips...
Don't worry, sir...
...I will lend you a hand!
Excuse my intrusion, but I think I can help you avoid some trouble.
My name is Nessus.
I was chosen by the gods to help travelers cross these treacherous currents.
It would be my pleasure to carry your wife or children to the other side.
It will only cost a single coin per passenger.

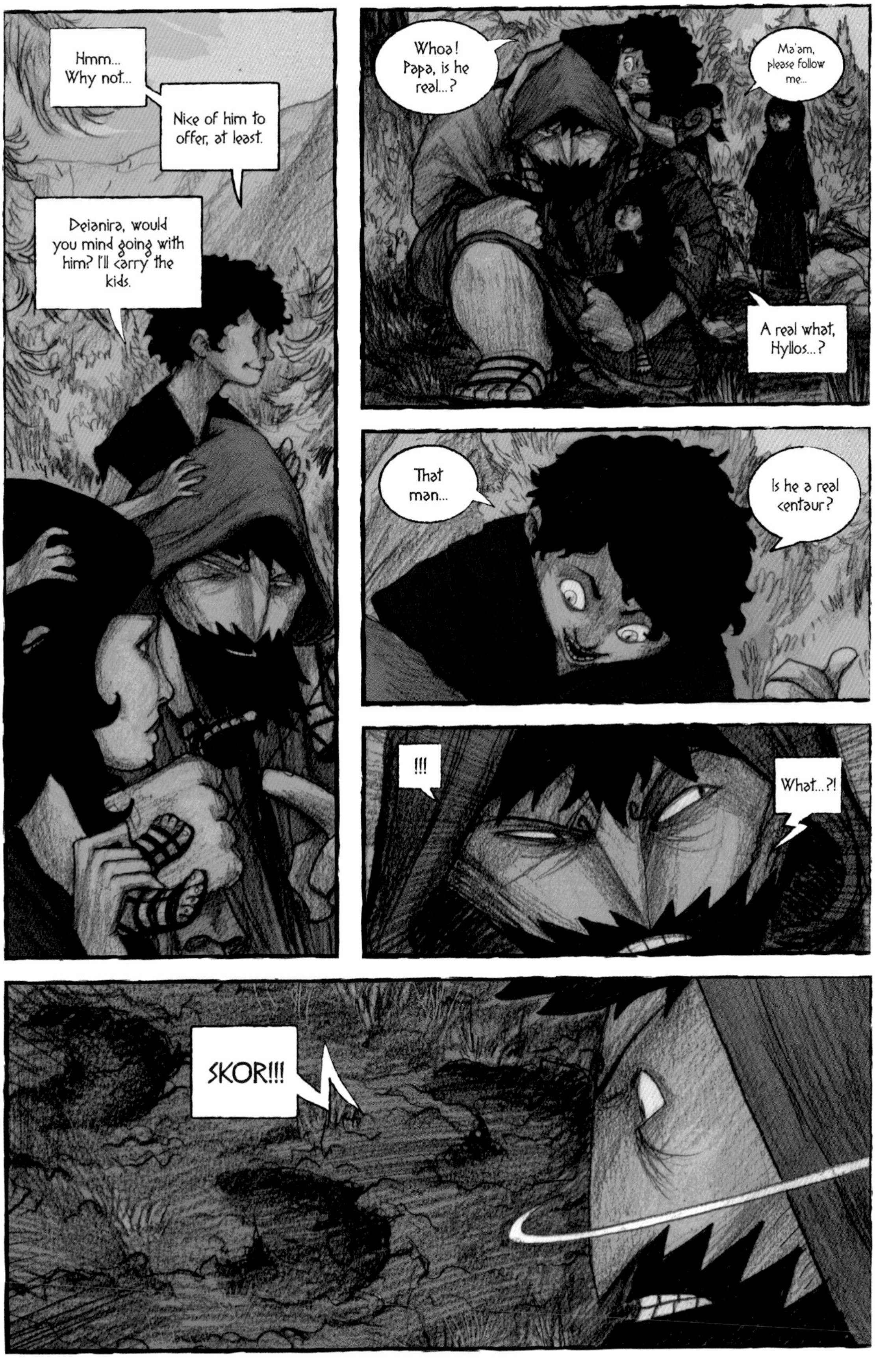

Hmm... Why not...
Nice of him to offer, at least.
Deianira, would you mind going with him? I'll carry the kids.
Whoa! Papa, is he real...?
Ma'am, please follow me...
A real what, Hyllos...?
That man...
Is he a real centaur?
!!!
What...?!
SKOR!!!

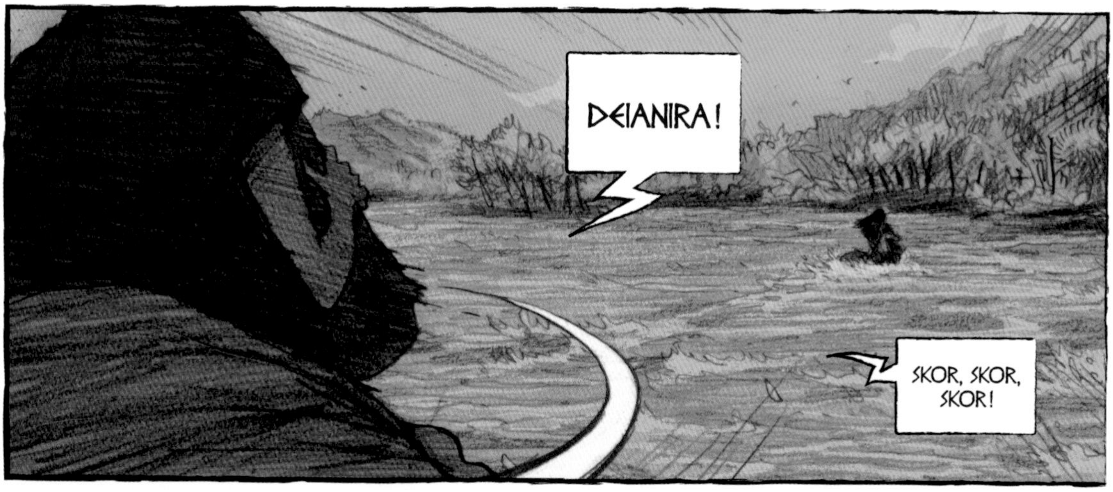
DEIANIRA!
SKOR, SKOR, SKOR!

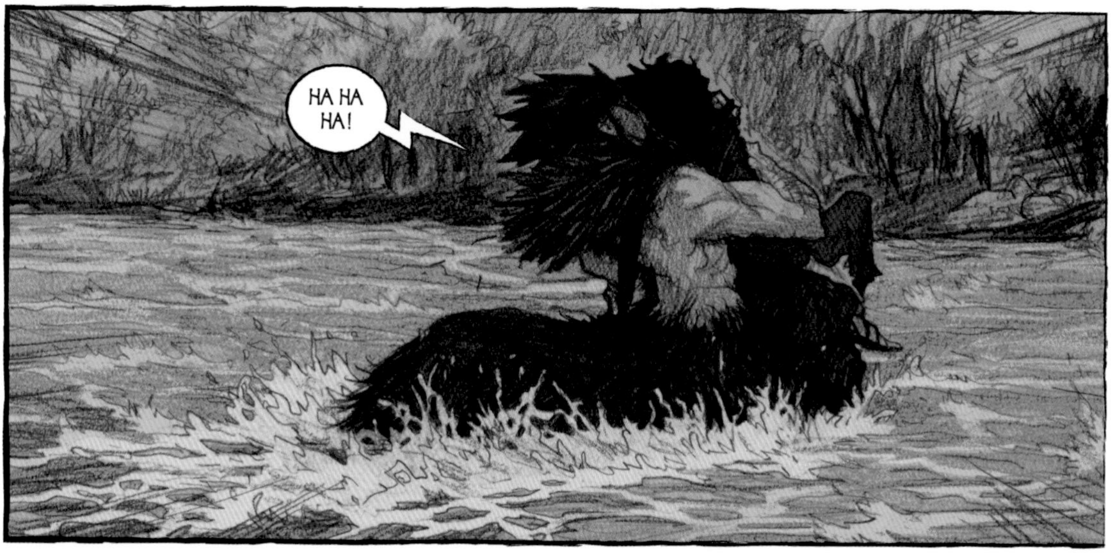
HA HA HA!

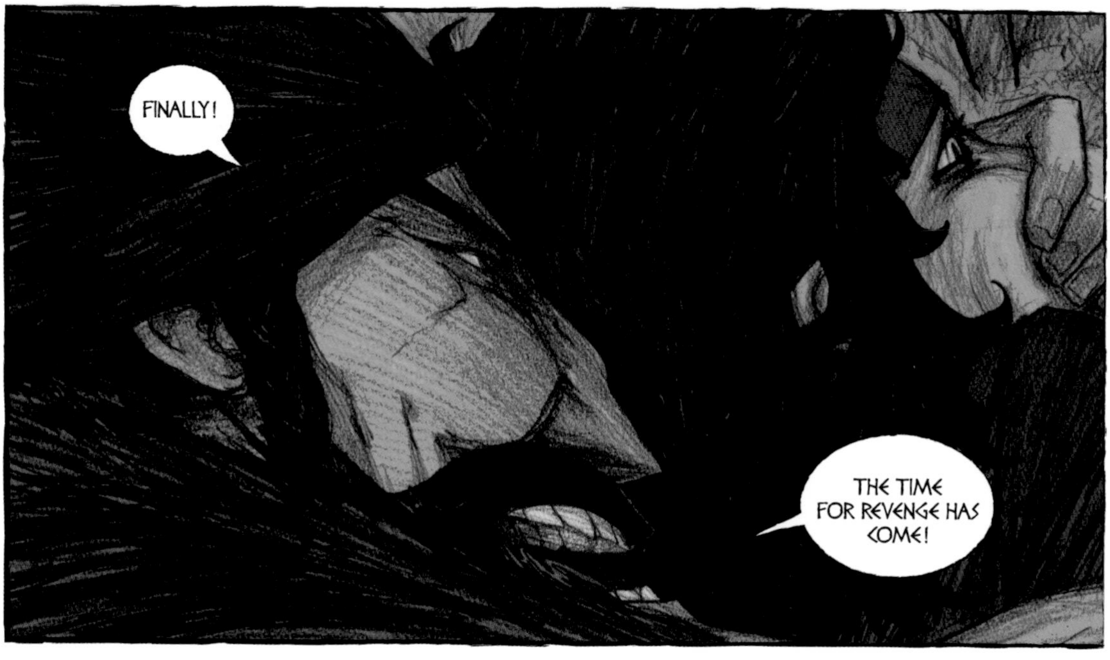
FINALLY!
THE TIME FOR REVENGE HAS COME!

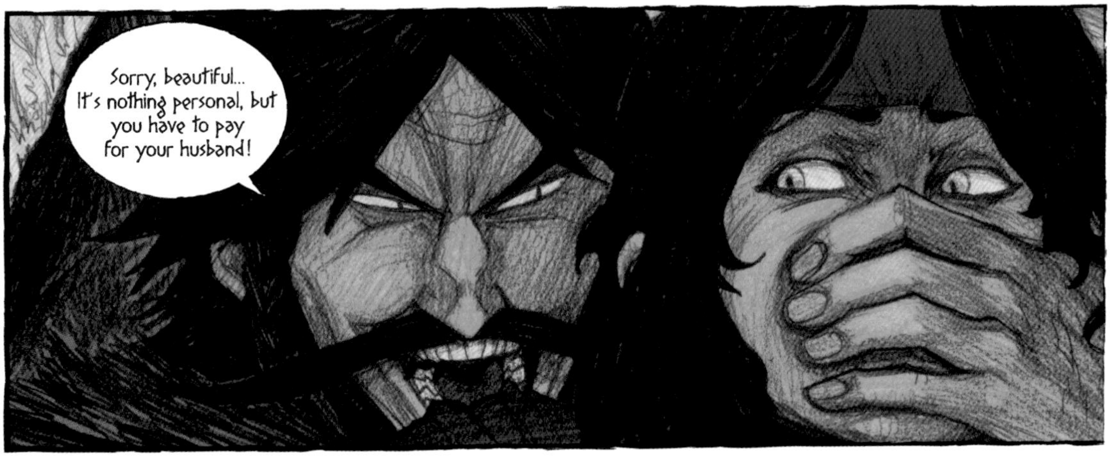
Sorry, beautiful... It's nothing personal, but you have to pay for your husband!

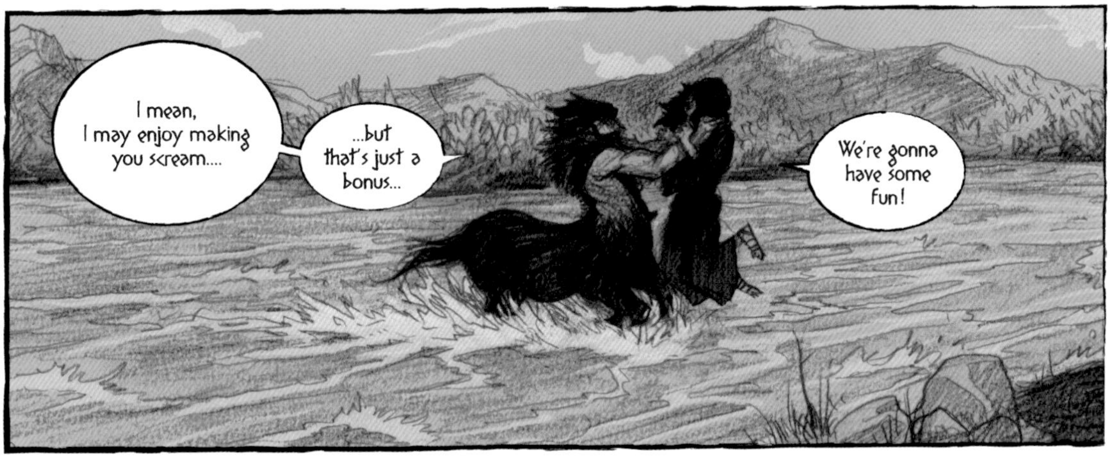
I mean, I may enjoy making you scream....
...but that's just a bonus...
We're gonna have some fun!

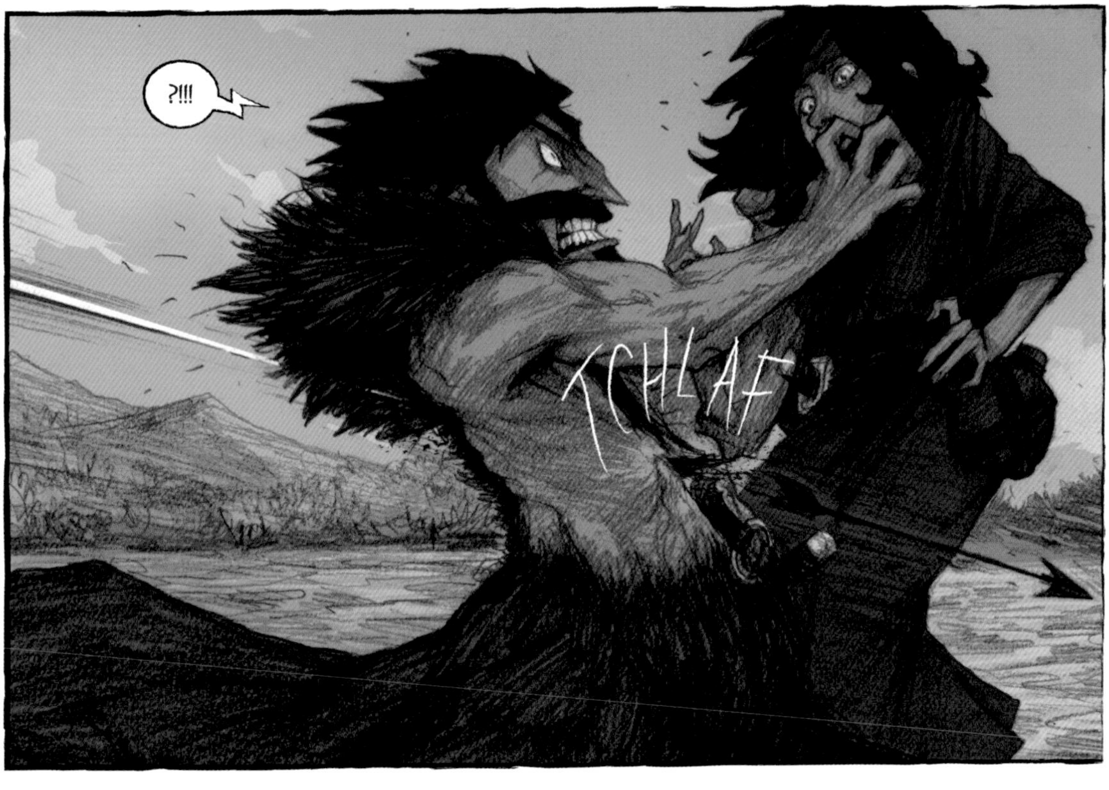
?!!!
TCHLAF

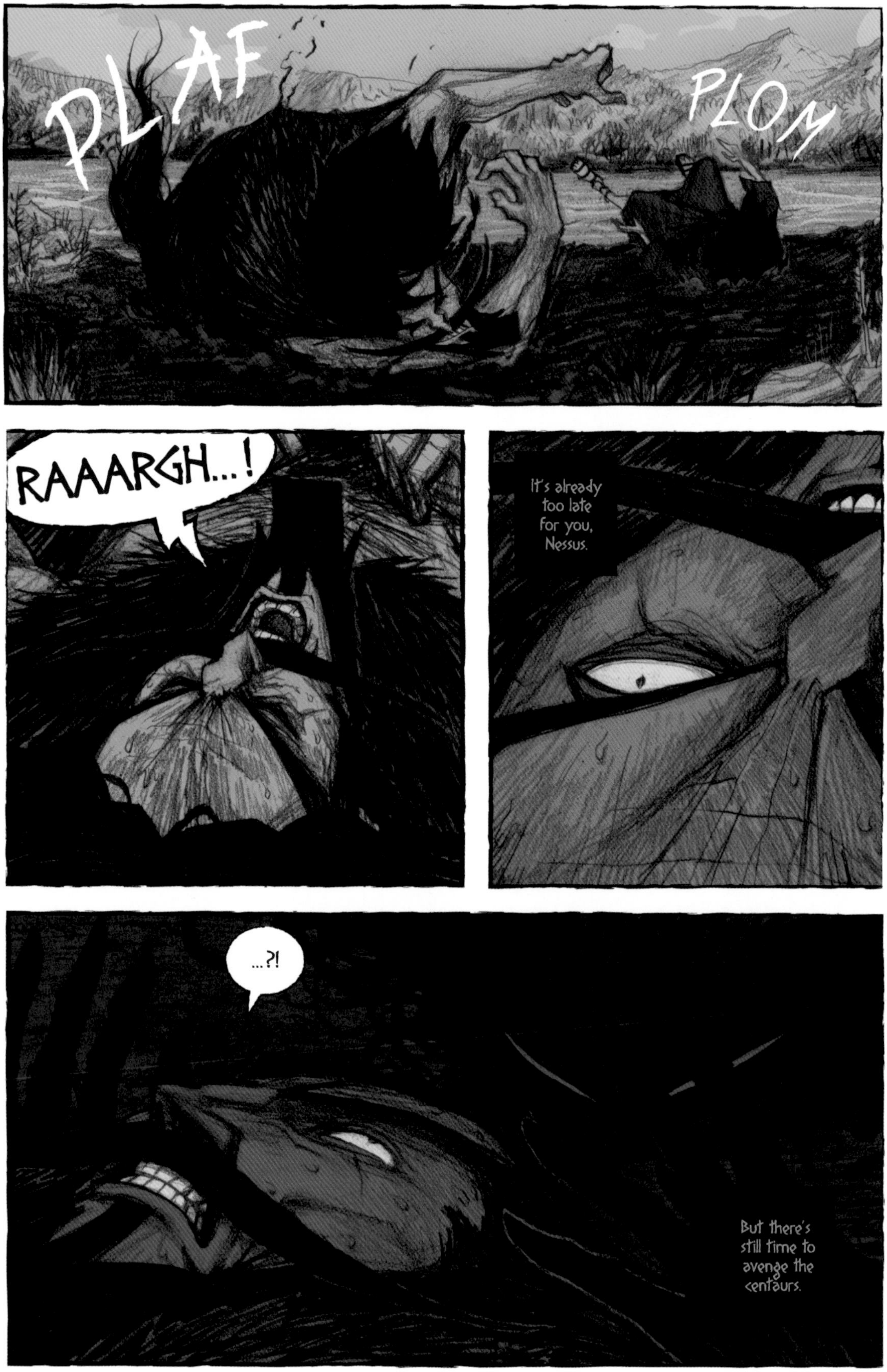
PLAF
PLOM
RAAARGH...!
It's already too late for you, Nessus.
...?!
But there's still time to avenge the centaurs.

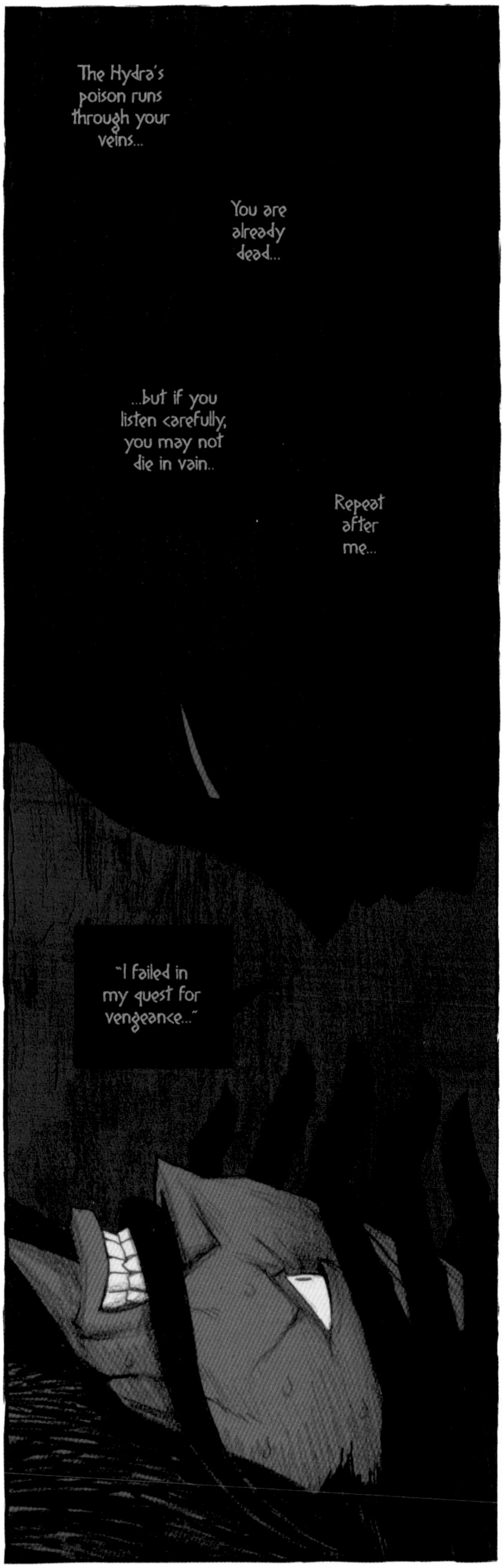
The Hydra's poison runs through your veins...
You are already dead...
...but if you listen carefully, you may not die in vain..
Repeat after me...
"I failed in my quest for vengeance..."

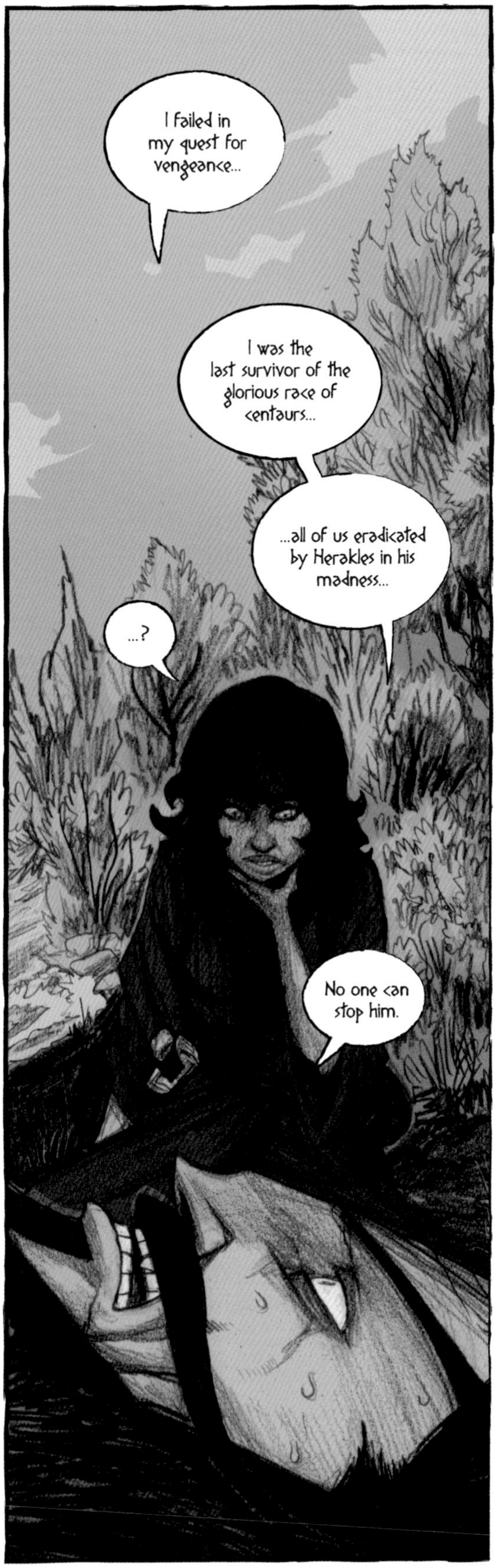
I failed in my quest for vengeance...
I was the last survivor of the glorious race of centaurs...
...all of us eradicated by Herakles in his madness...
...?
No one can stop him.

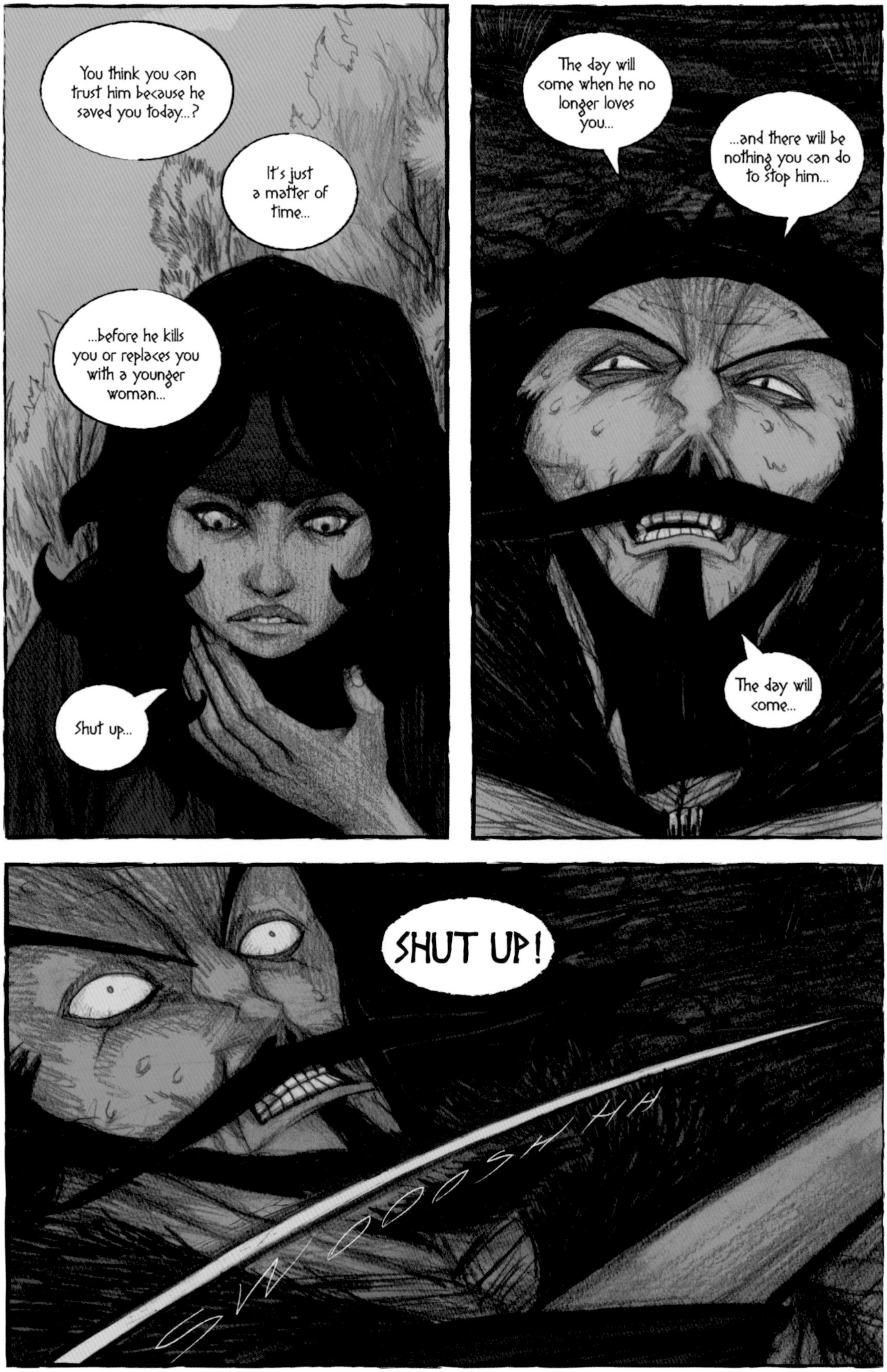
You think you can trust him because he saved you today...?
It's just a matter of time...
...before he kills you or replaces you with a younger woman...
Shut up...
The day will come when he no longer loves you...
...and there will be nothing you can do to stop him...
The day will come...
SHUT UP!
SWOOOSHHH

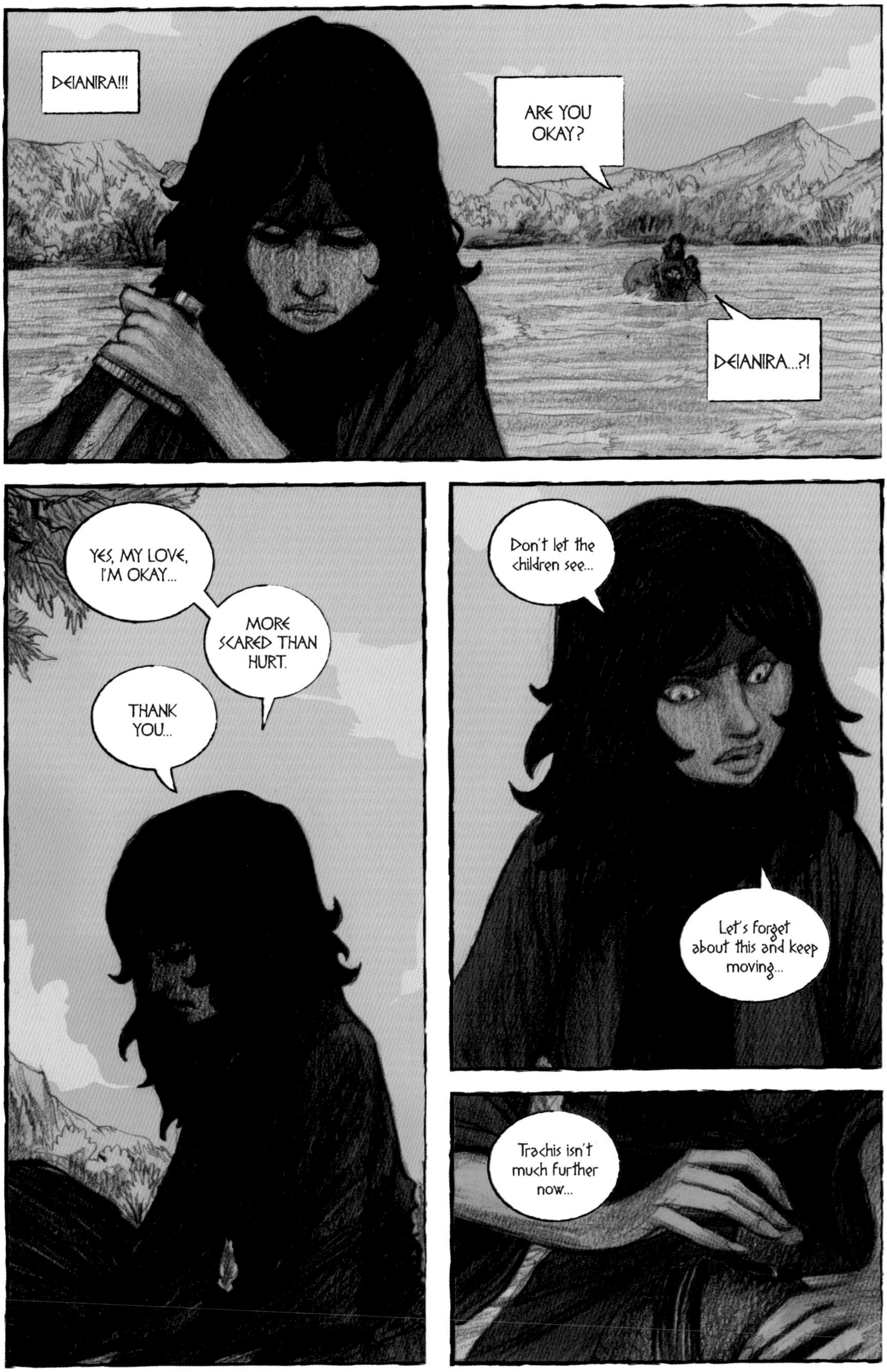
DEIANIRA!!!
ARE YOU OKAY?
DEIANIRA...?!
YES, MY LOVE, I'M OKAY...
MORE SCARED THAN HURT.
THANK YOU...
Don't let the children see...
Let's forget about this and keep moving...
Trachis isn't much further now...

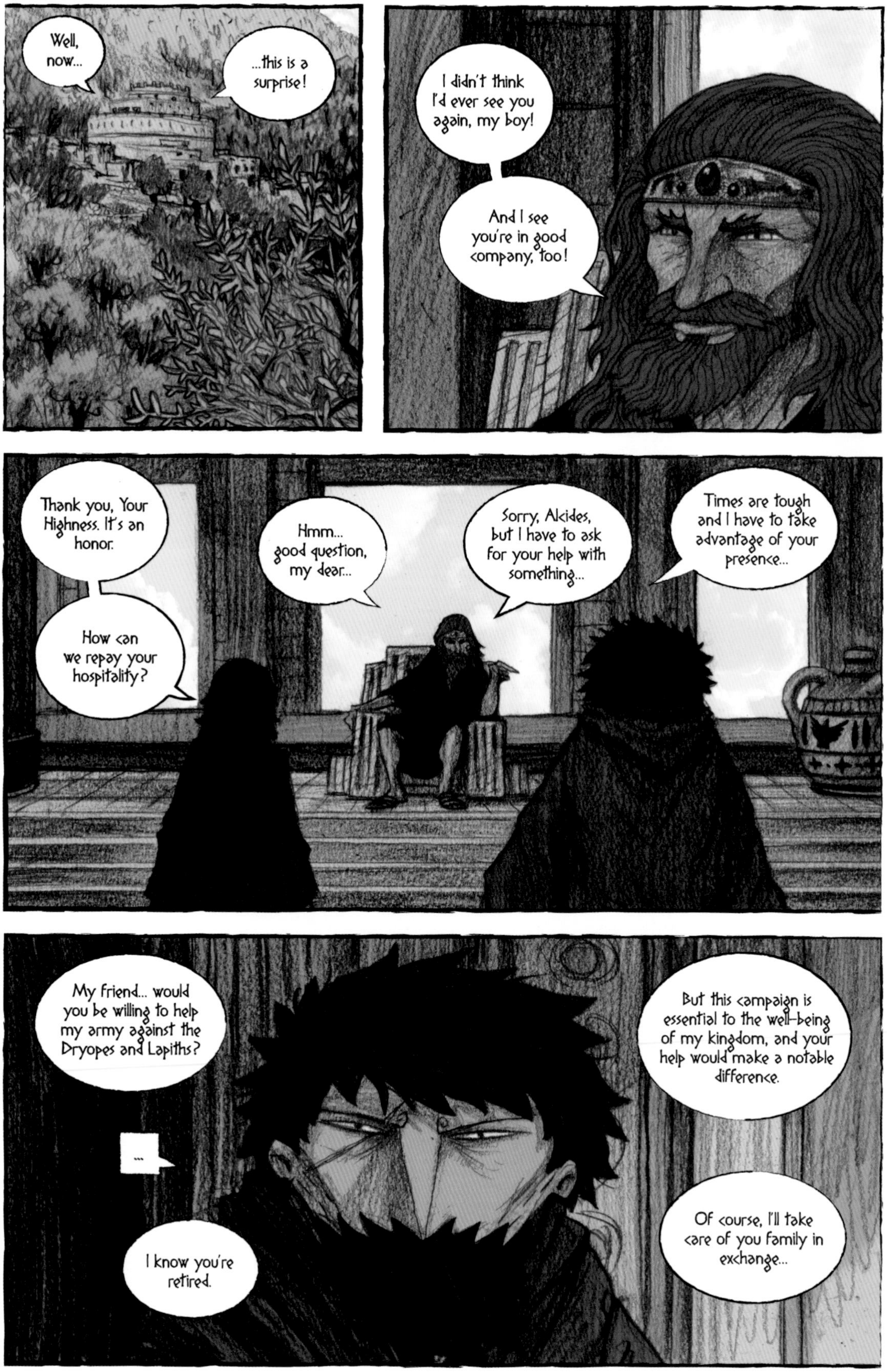
Well, now...
...this is a surprise!
I didn't think I'd ever see you again, my boy!
And I see you're in good company, too!
Thank you, Your Highness. It's an honor.
How can we repay your hospitality?
Hmm... good question, my dear...
Sorry, Alcides, but I have to ask for your help with something...
Times are tough and I have to take advantage of your presence...
My friend... would you be willing to help my army against the Dryopes and Lapiths?
...
I know you're retired.
But this campaign is essential to the well-being of my kingdom, and your help would make a notable difference.
Of course, I'll take care of you family in exchange...

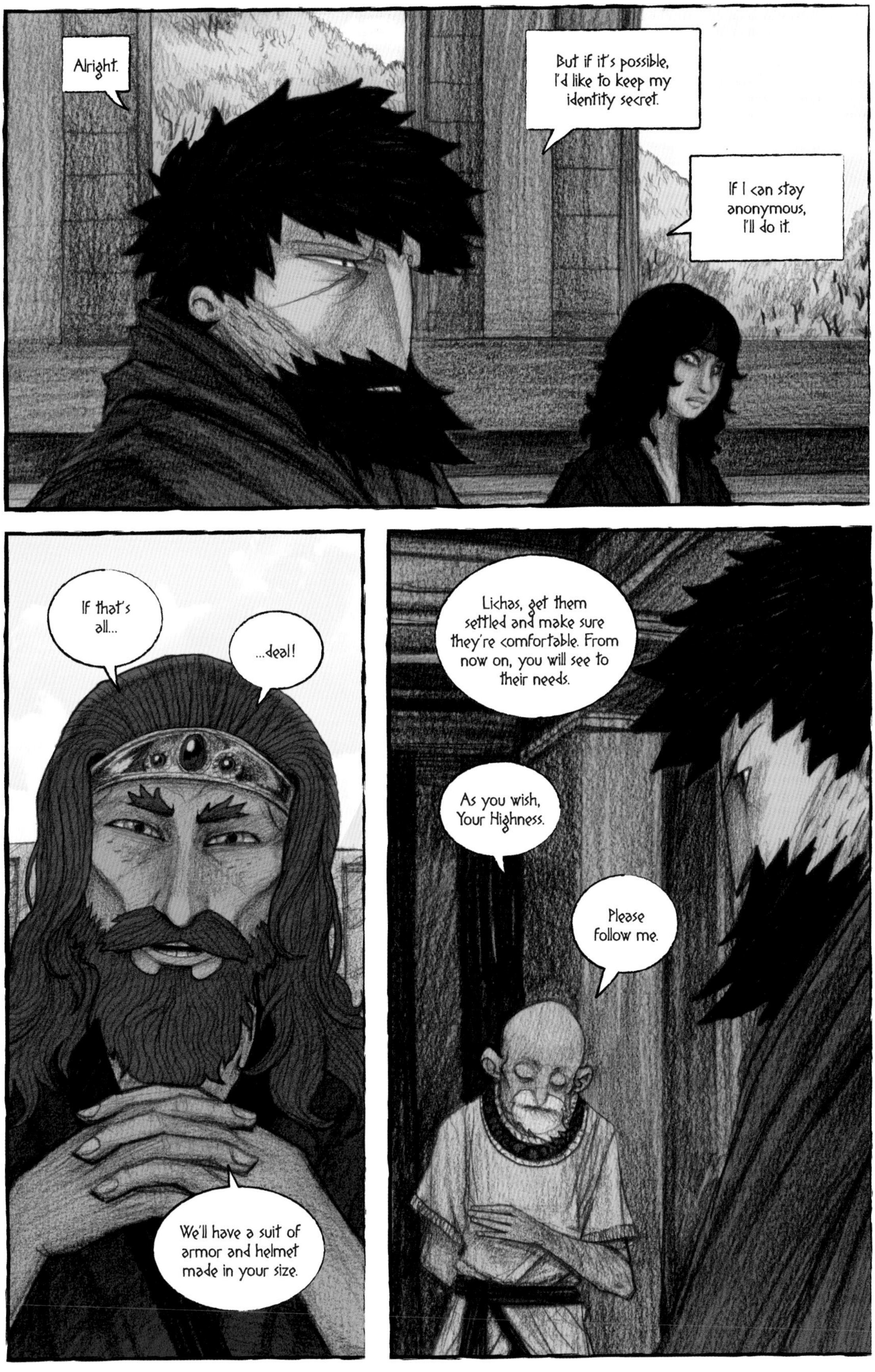

Alright.
But if it's possible, I'd like to keep my identity secret.
If I can stay anonymous, I'll do it.
If that's all...
...deal!
We'll have a suit of armor and helmet made in your size.
Lichas, get them settled and make sure they're comfortable. From now on, you will see to their needs.
As you wish, Your Highness.
Please follow me.

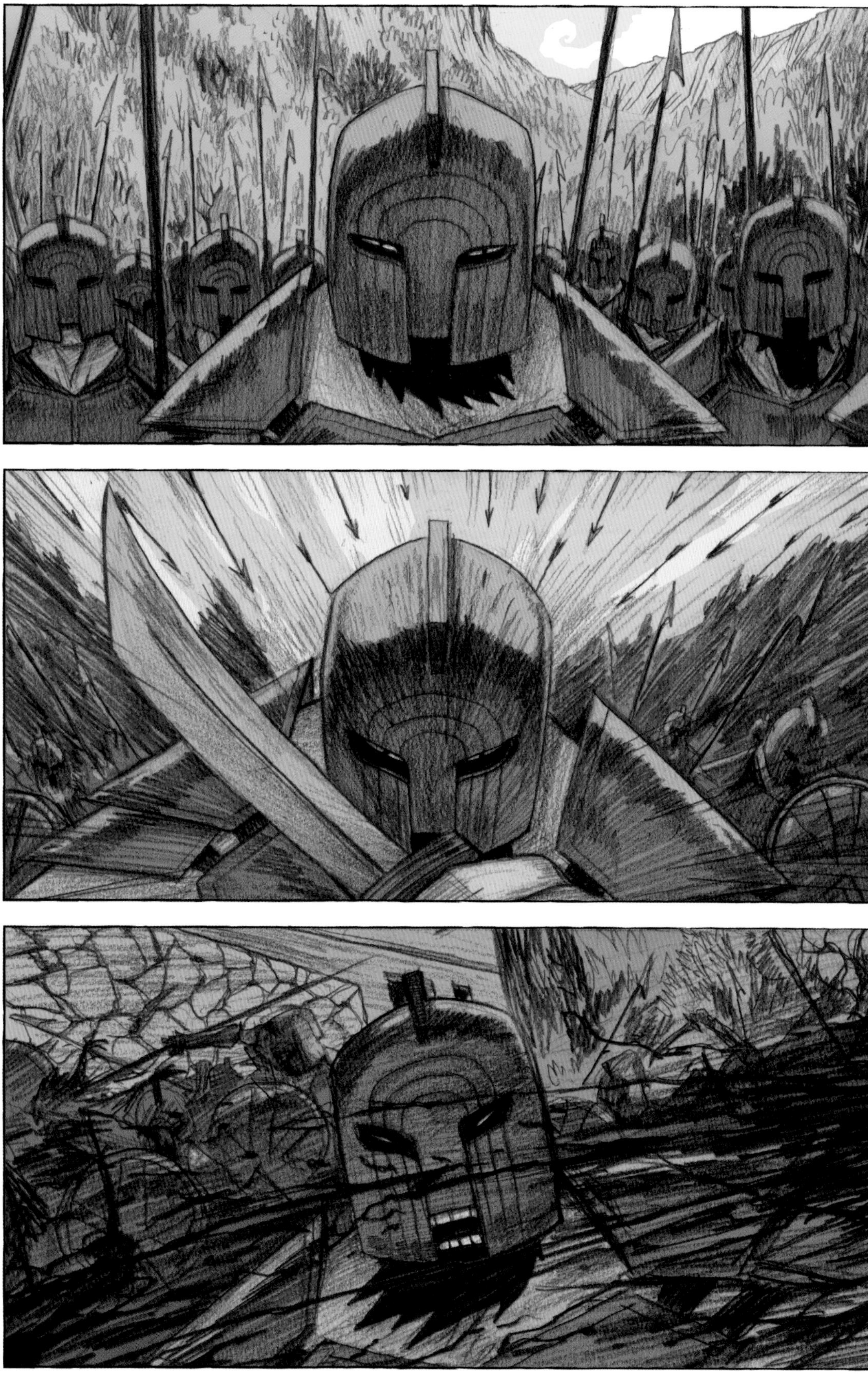

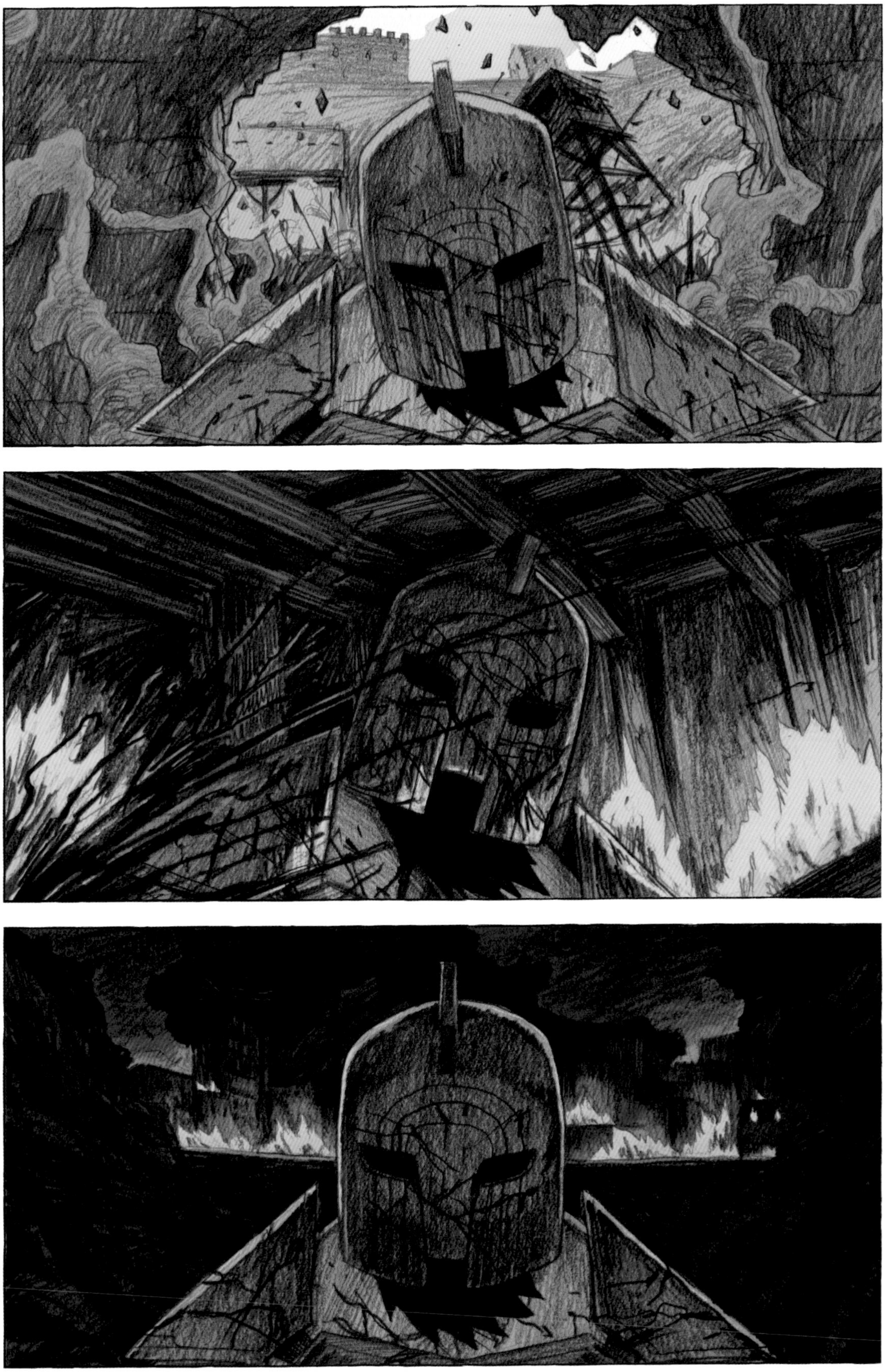

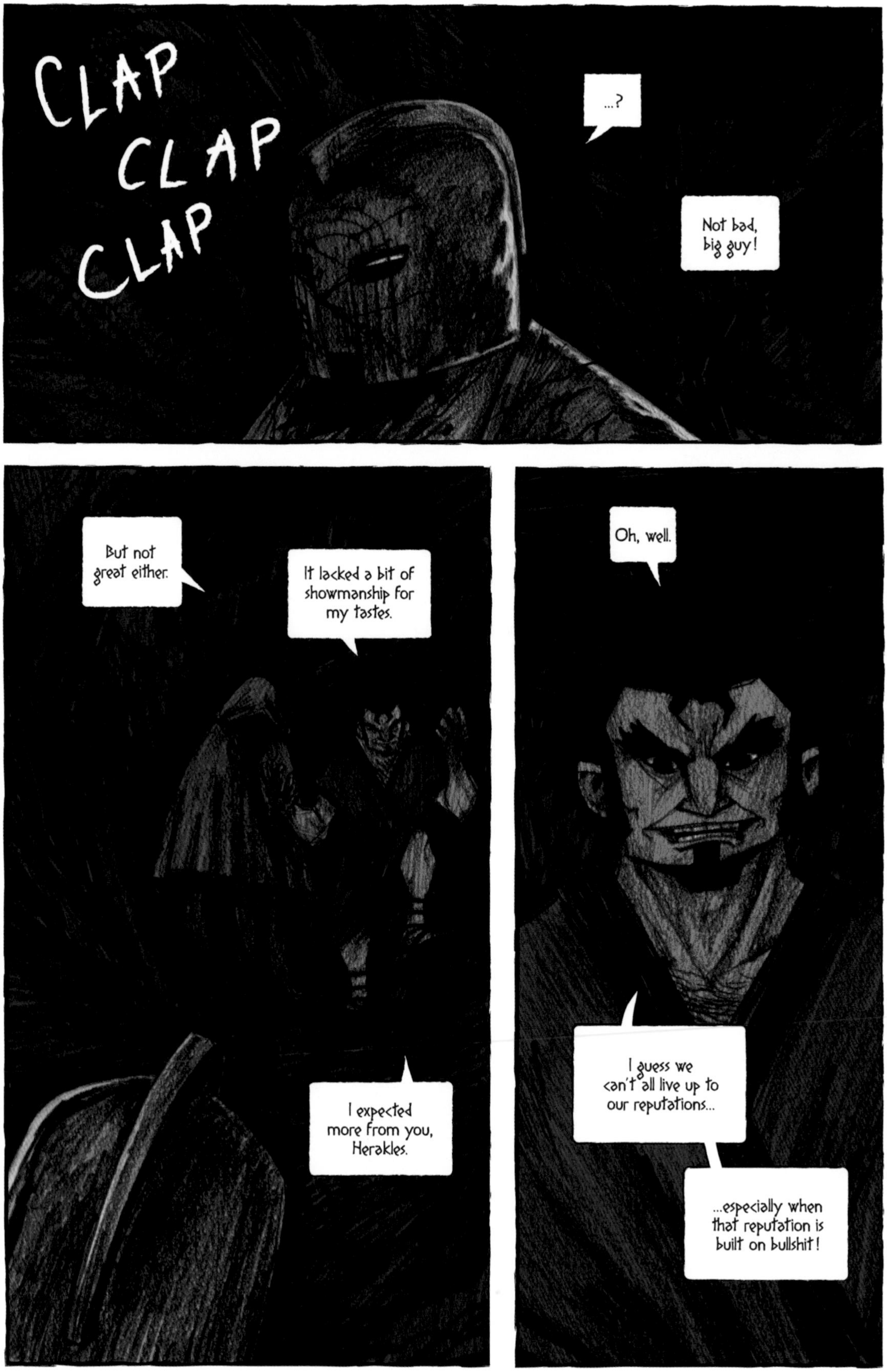

CLAP CLAP CLAP
...?
Not bad, big guy!
But not great either.
It lacked a bit of showmanship for my tastes.
I expected more from you, Herakles.
Oh, well.
I guess we can't all live up to our reputations...
...especially when that reputation is built on bullshit!

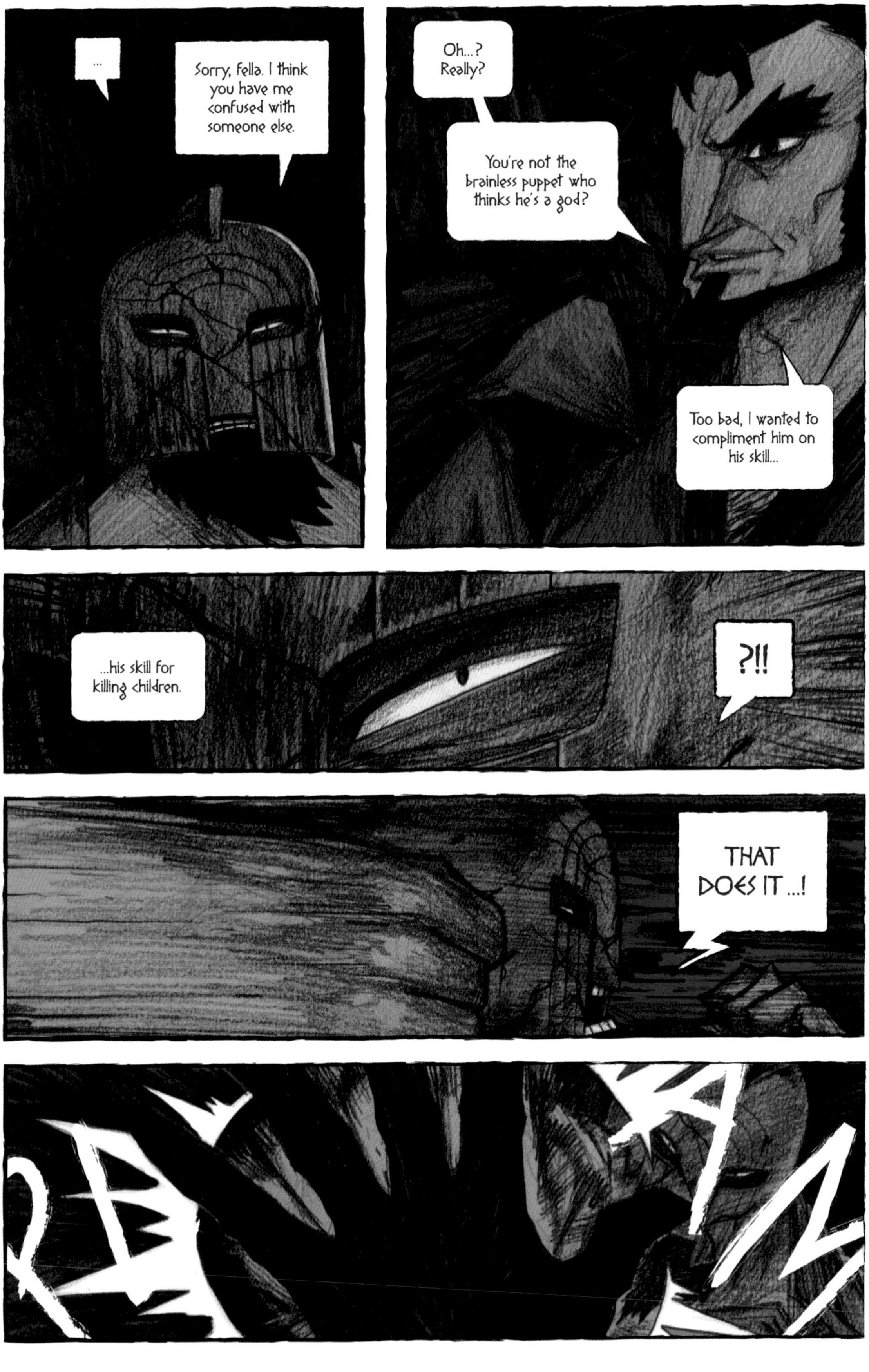
...
Sorry, fella. I think you have me confused with someone else.
Oh...? Really?
You're not the brainless puppet who thinks he's a god?
Too bad, I wanted to compliment him on his skill...
...his skill for killing children.
?!!
THAT DOES IT ...!

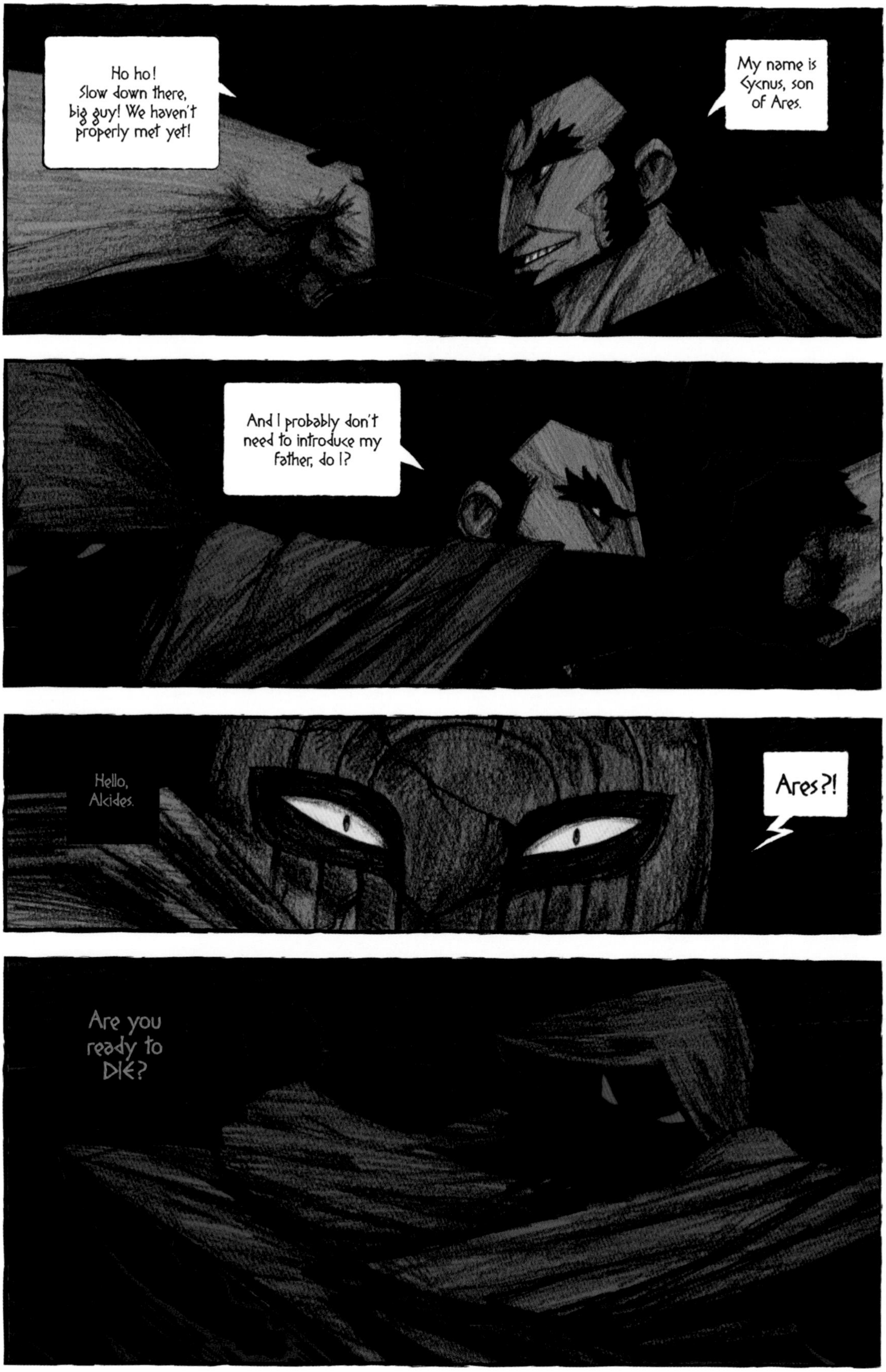
Ho ho! Slow down there, big guy! We haven't properly met yet!
My name is Cycnus, son of Ares.
And I probably don't need to introduce my father, do I?
Hello, Alcides.
Ares?!
Are you ready to DIE?

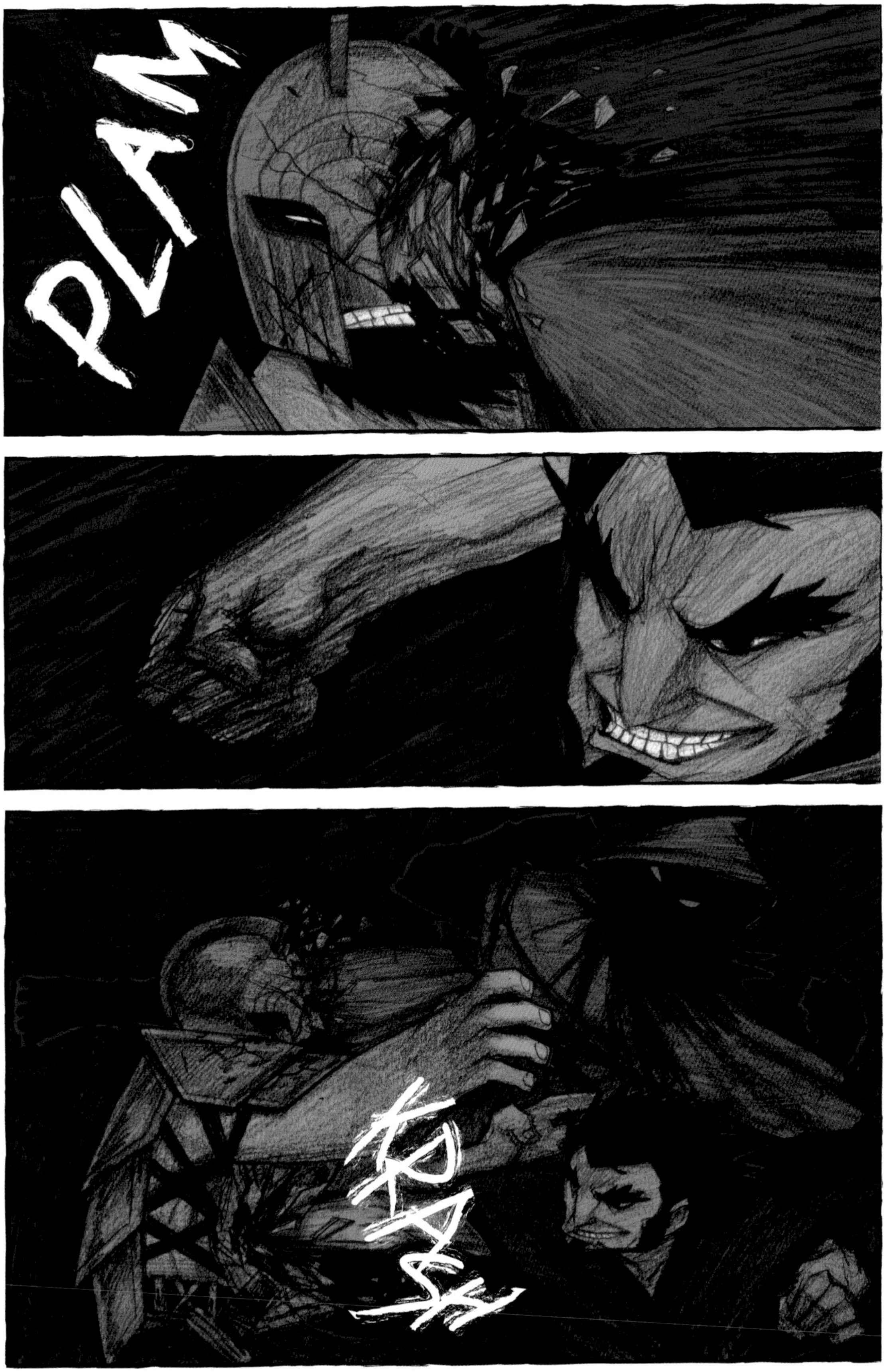
PLAM
KRASH

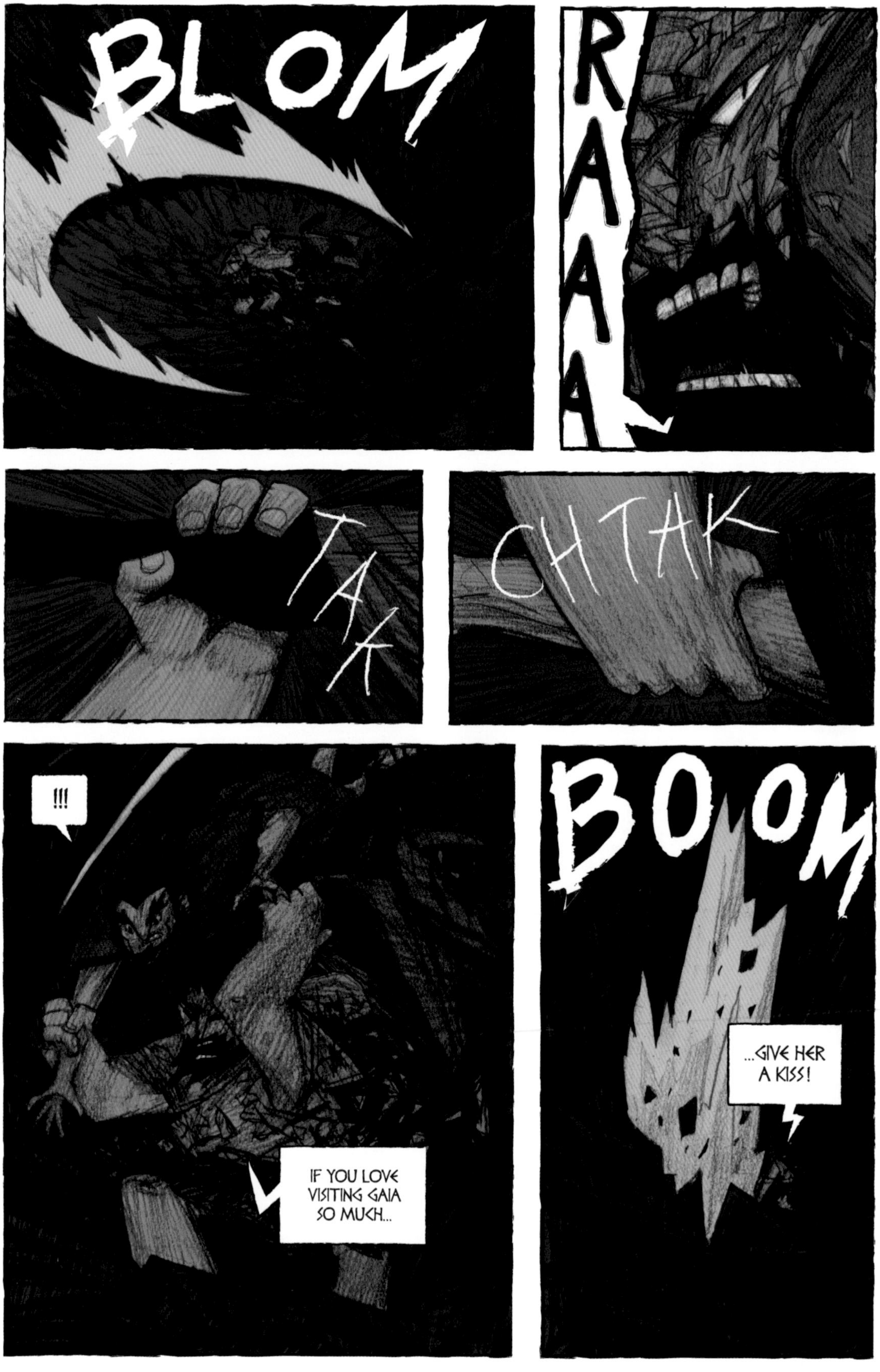
BLOM
RAAAA
TAK
CHTAK
!!!
IF YOU LOVE VISITING GAIA SO MUCH...
BOOM
...GIVE HER A KISS!

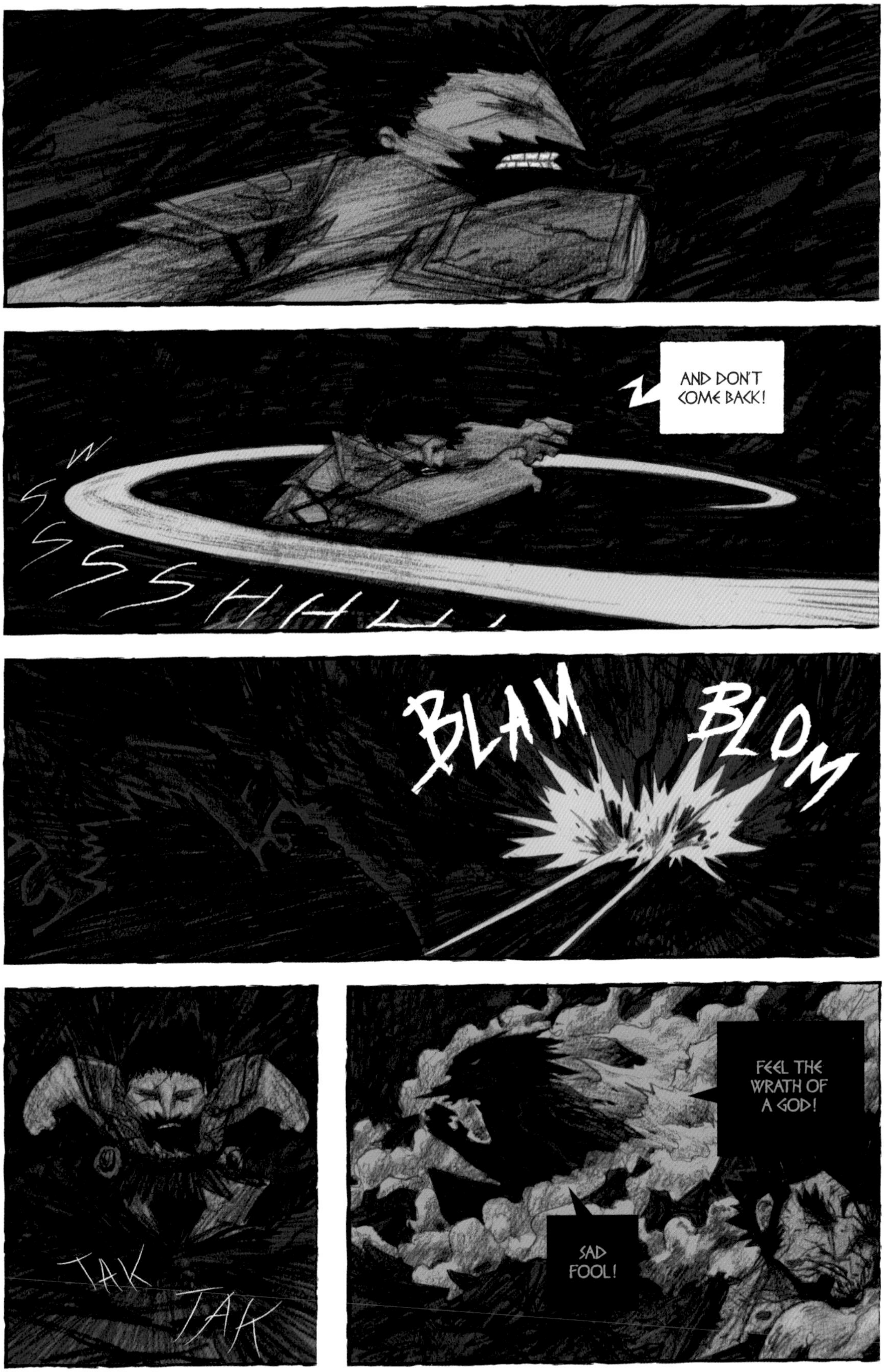
AND DON'T COME BACK!
WSSSSHH
BLAM
BLOM
TAK
TAK
FEEL THE WRATH OF A GOD!
SAD FOOL!

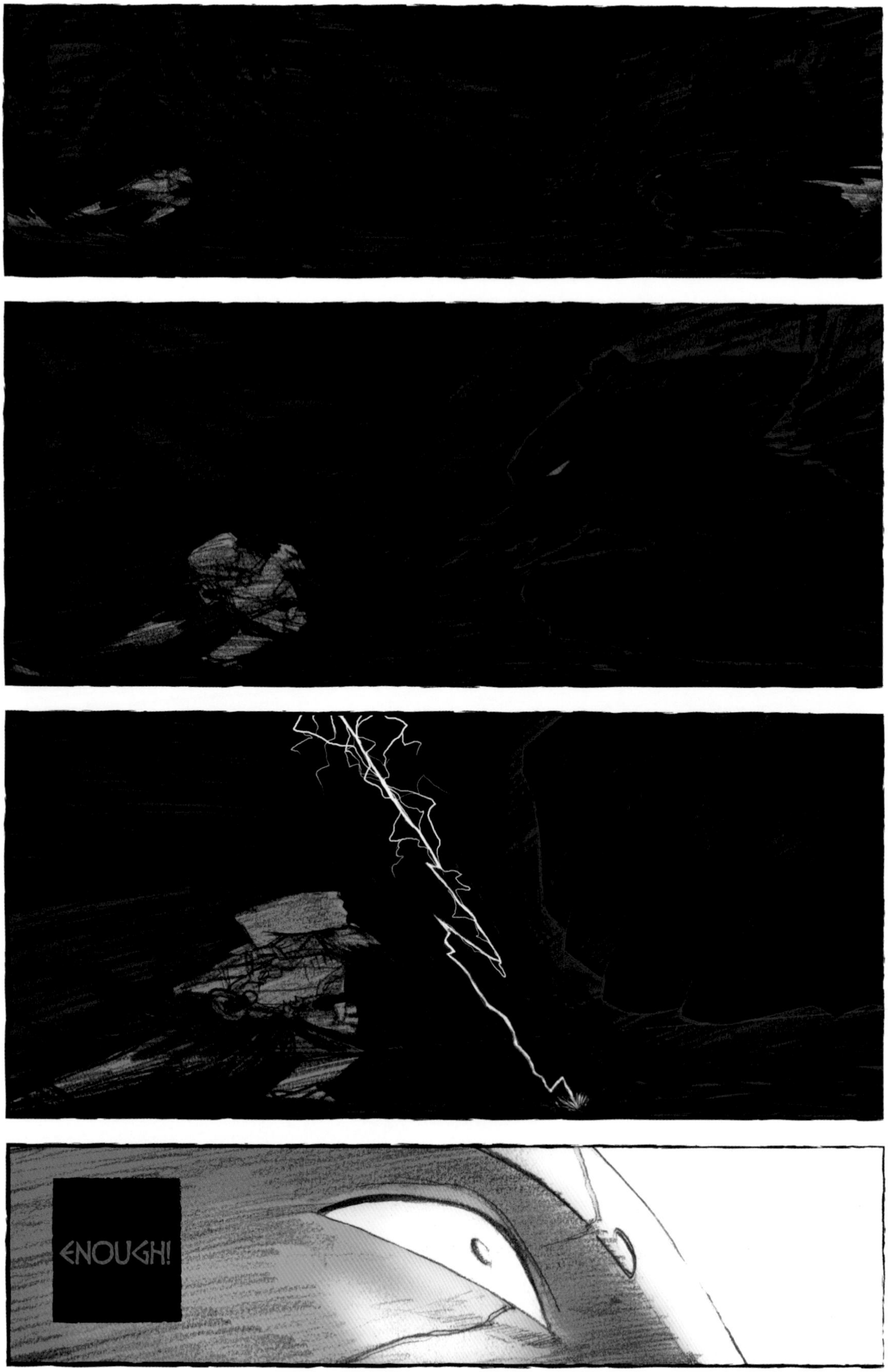
ENOUGH!

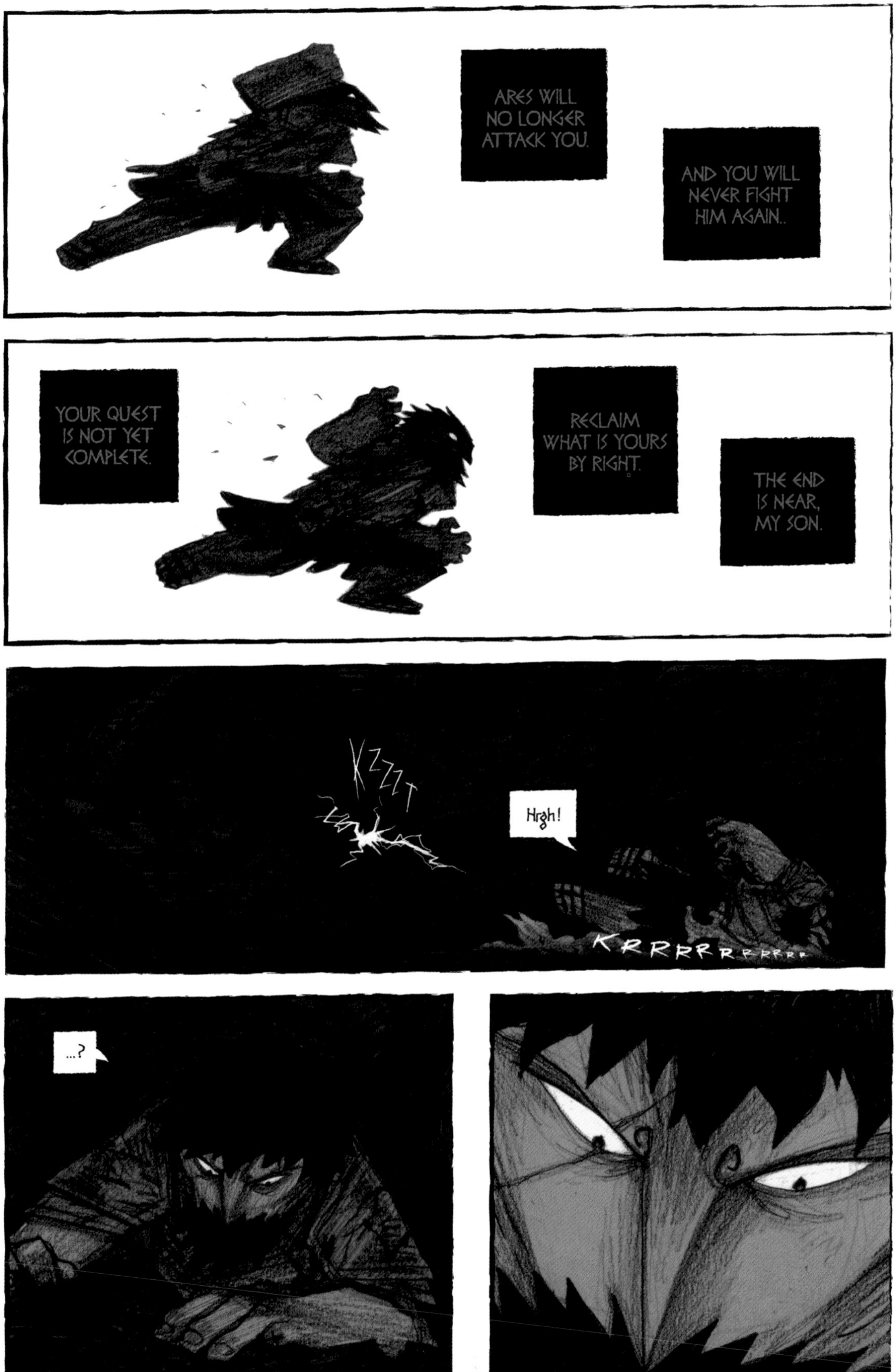

ARES WILL NO LONGER ATTACK YOU.
AND YOU WILL NEVER FIGHT HIM AGAIN..
YOUR QUEST IS NOT YET COMPLETE.
RECLAIM WHAT IS YOURS BY RIGHT.
THE END IS NEAR, MY SON.
KZZZT
Hrgh!
KRRRRRRRRRR
...?

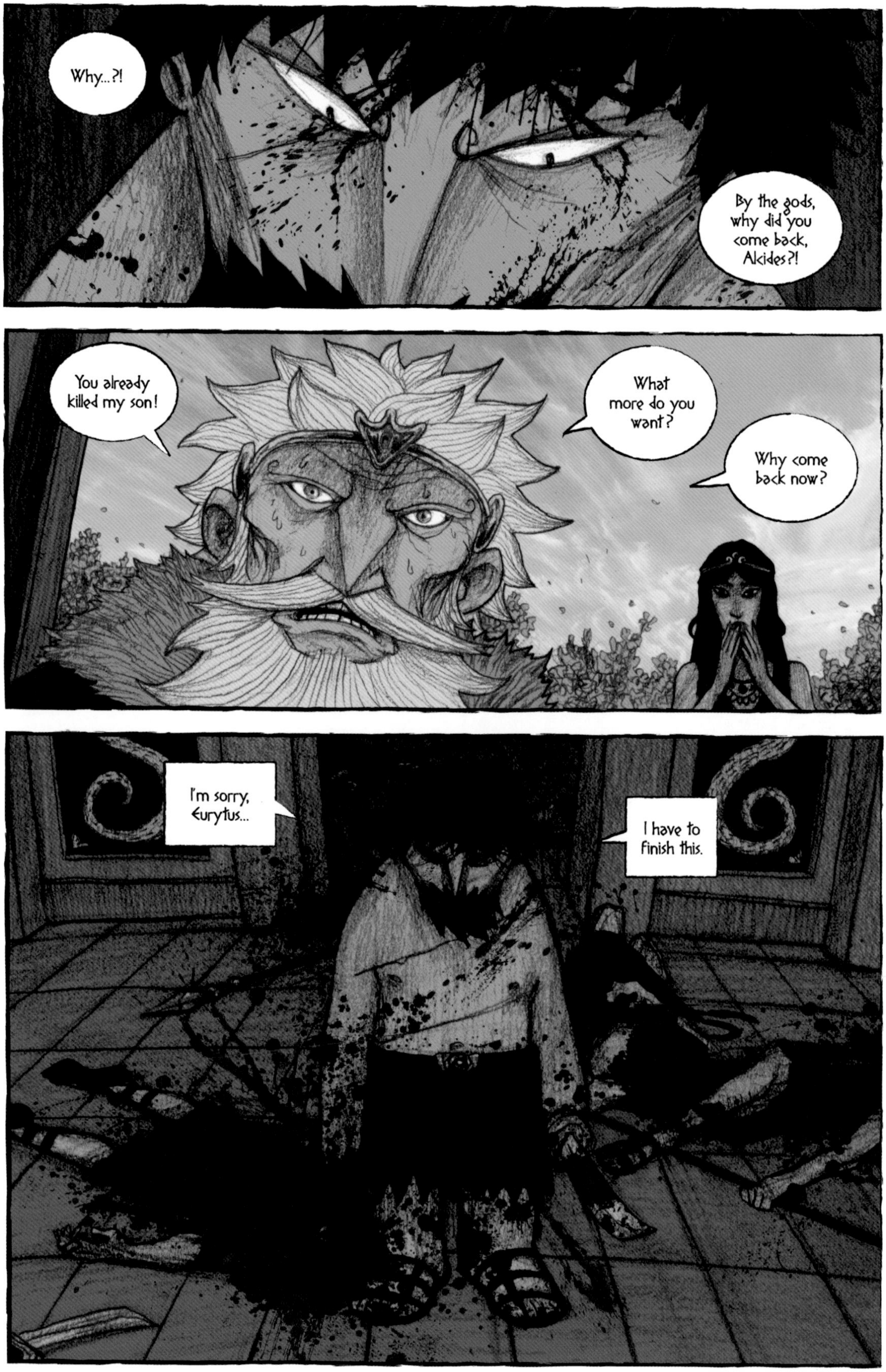
Why...?!
By the gods, why did you come back, Alcides?!
You already killed my son!
What more do you want?
Why come back now?
I'm sorry, Eurytus...
I have to finish this.

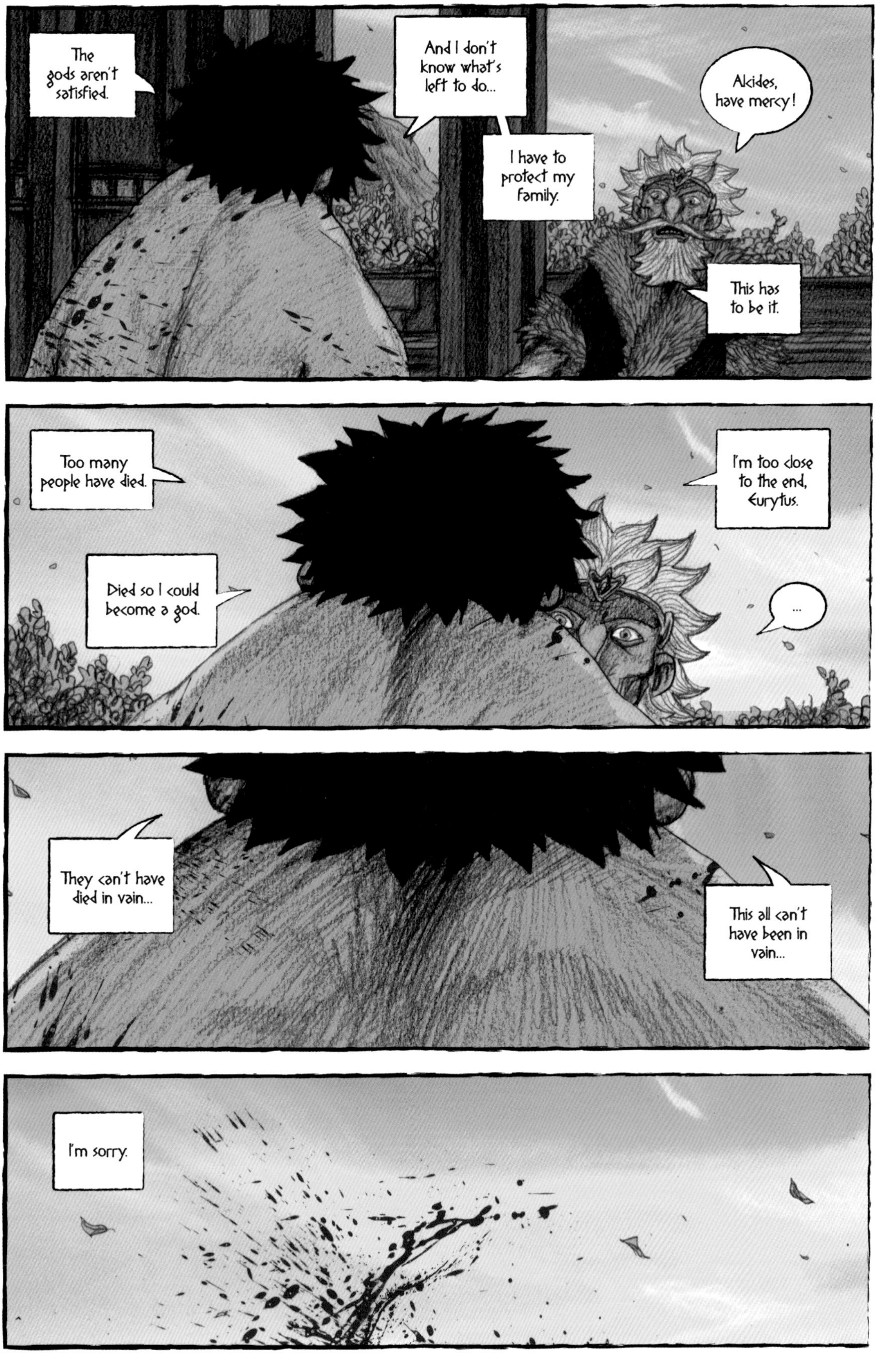
The gods aren't satisfied.
And I don't know what's left to do...
I have to protect my family.
Alcides, have mercy!
This has to be it.
Too many people have died.
Died so I could become a god.
I'm too close to the end, Eurytus.
...
They can't have died in vain...
This all can't have been in vain...
I'm sorry.

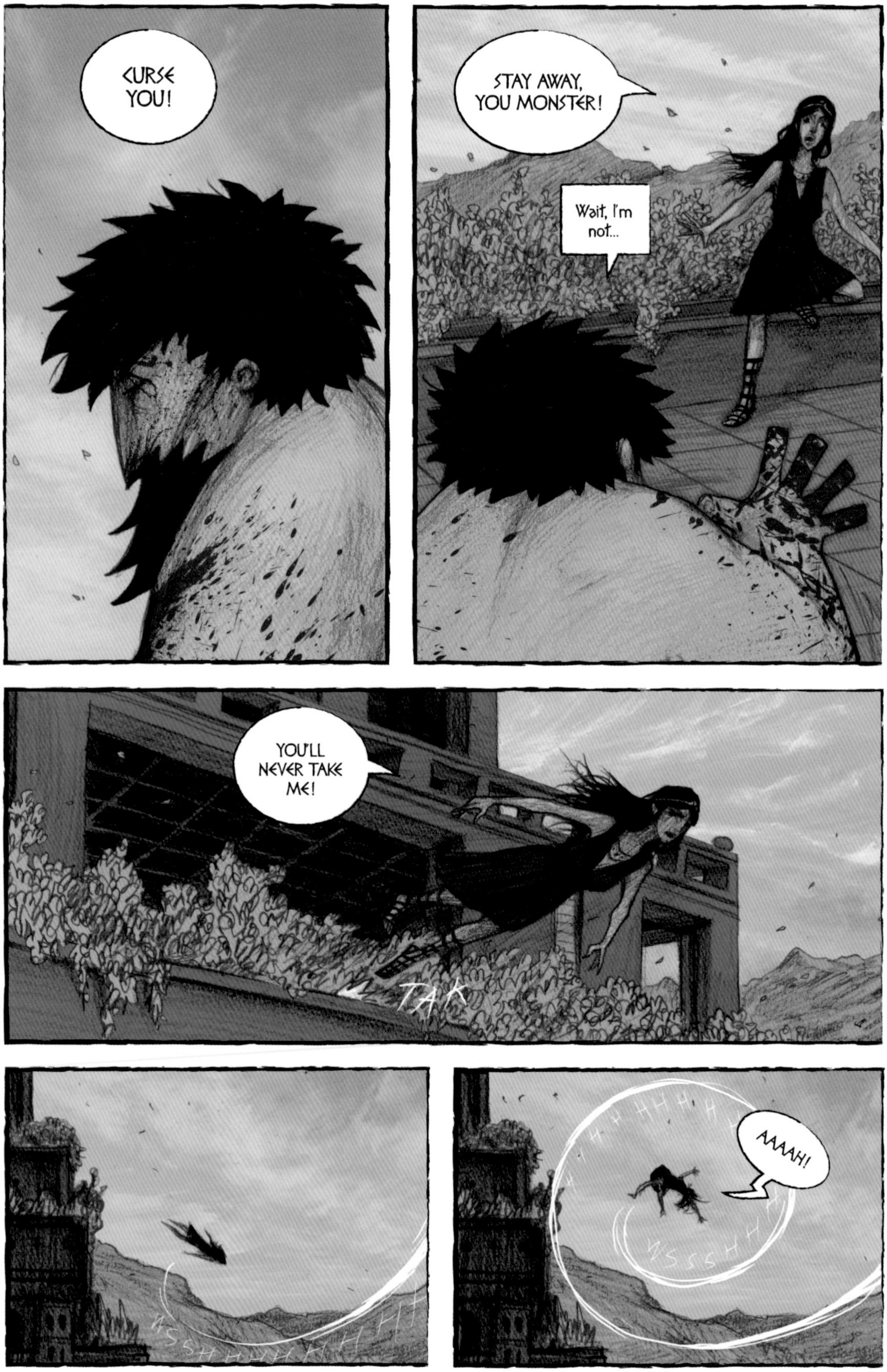
CURSE YOU!
STAY AWAY, YOU MONSTER!
Wait, I'm not...
YOU'LL NEVER TAKE ME!
TAK
AAAAH!

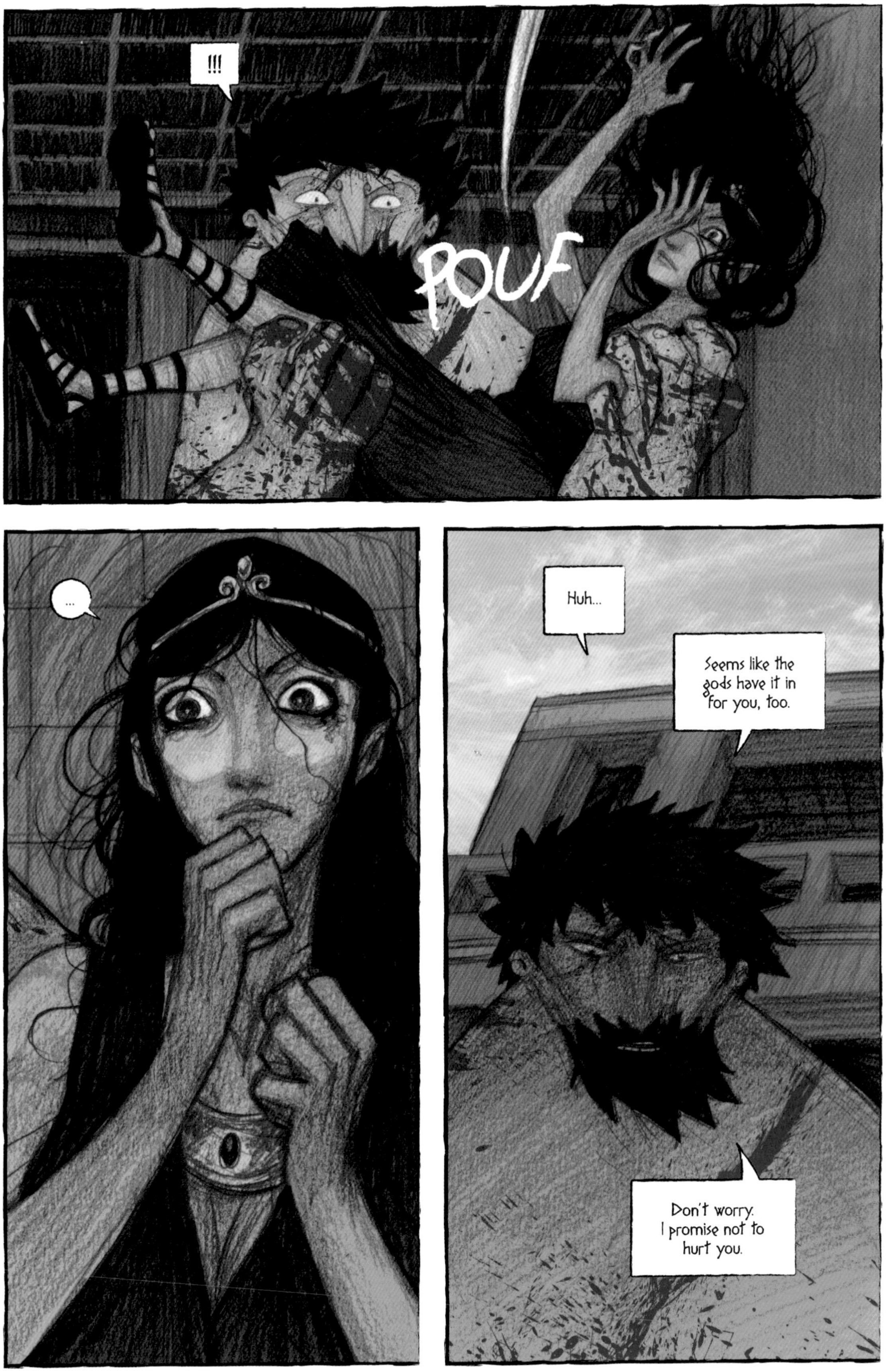
!!!
POUF
...
Huh...
Seems like the gods have it in for you, too.
Don't worry. I promise not to hurt you.

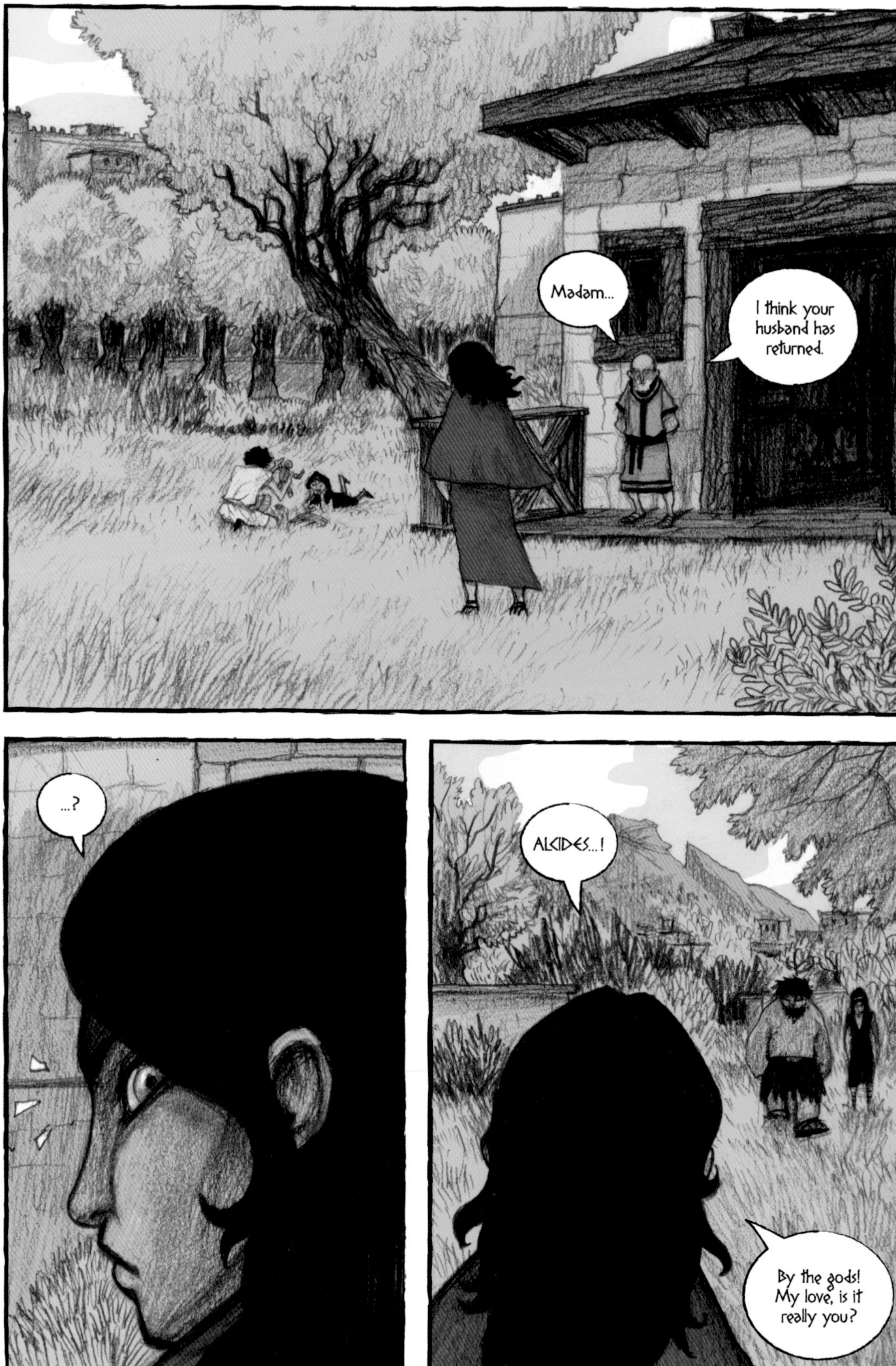
Madam...
I think your husband has returned.
...?
ALCIDES...!
By the gods! My love, is it really you?

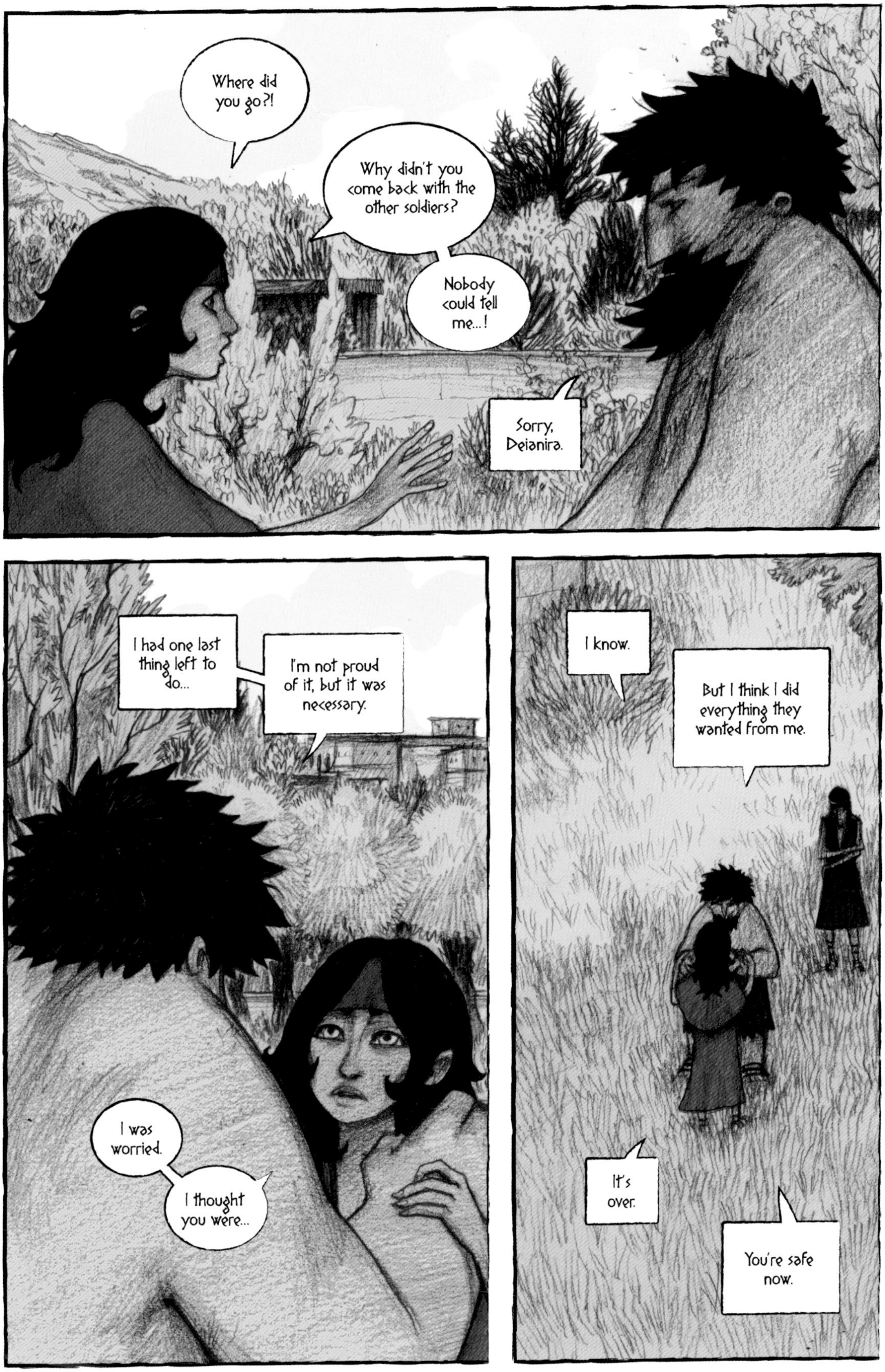

Where did you go?!
Why didn't you come back with the other soldiers?
Nobody could tell me...!
Sorry, Deianira.
I had one last thing left to do...
I'm not proud of it, but it was necessary.
I was worried.
I thought you were...
I know.
But I think I did everything they wanted from me.
It's over.
You're safe now.

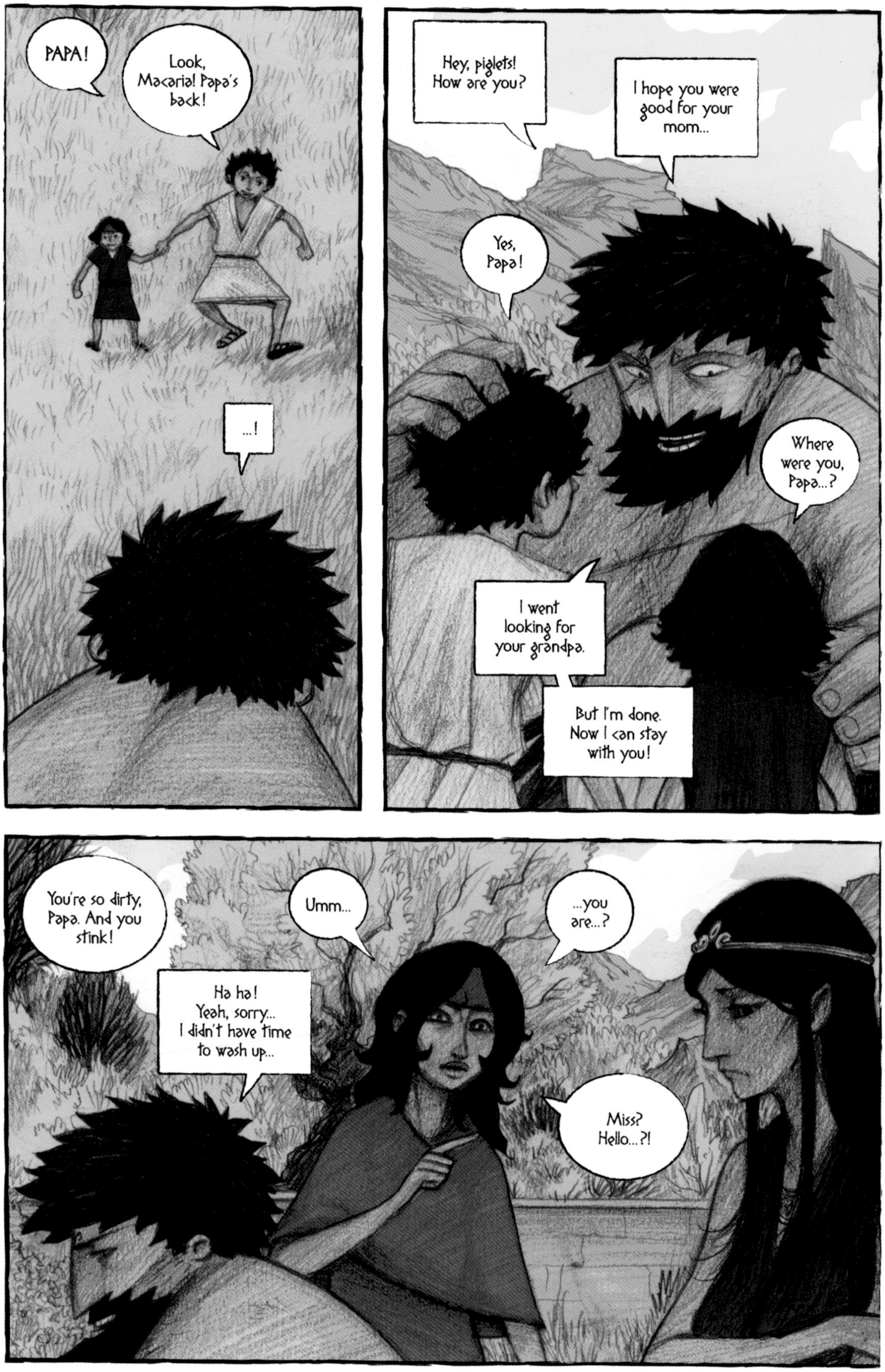
PAPA!
Look, Macaria! Papa's back!
...!
Hey, piglets! How are you?
I hope you were good for your mom...
Yes, Papa!
Where were you, Papa...?
I went looking for your grandpa.
But I'm done. Now I can stay with you!
You're so dirty, Papa. And you stink!
Ha ha! Yeah, sorry... I didn't have time to wash up...
Umm...
...you are...?
Miss? Hello...?!

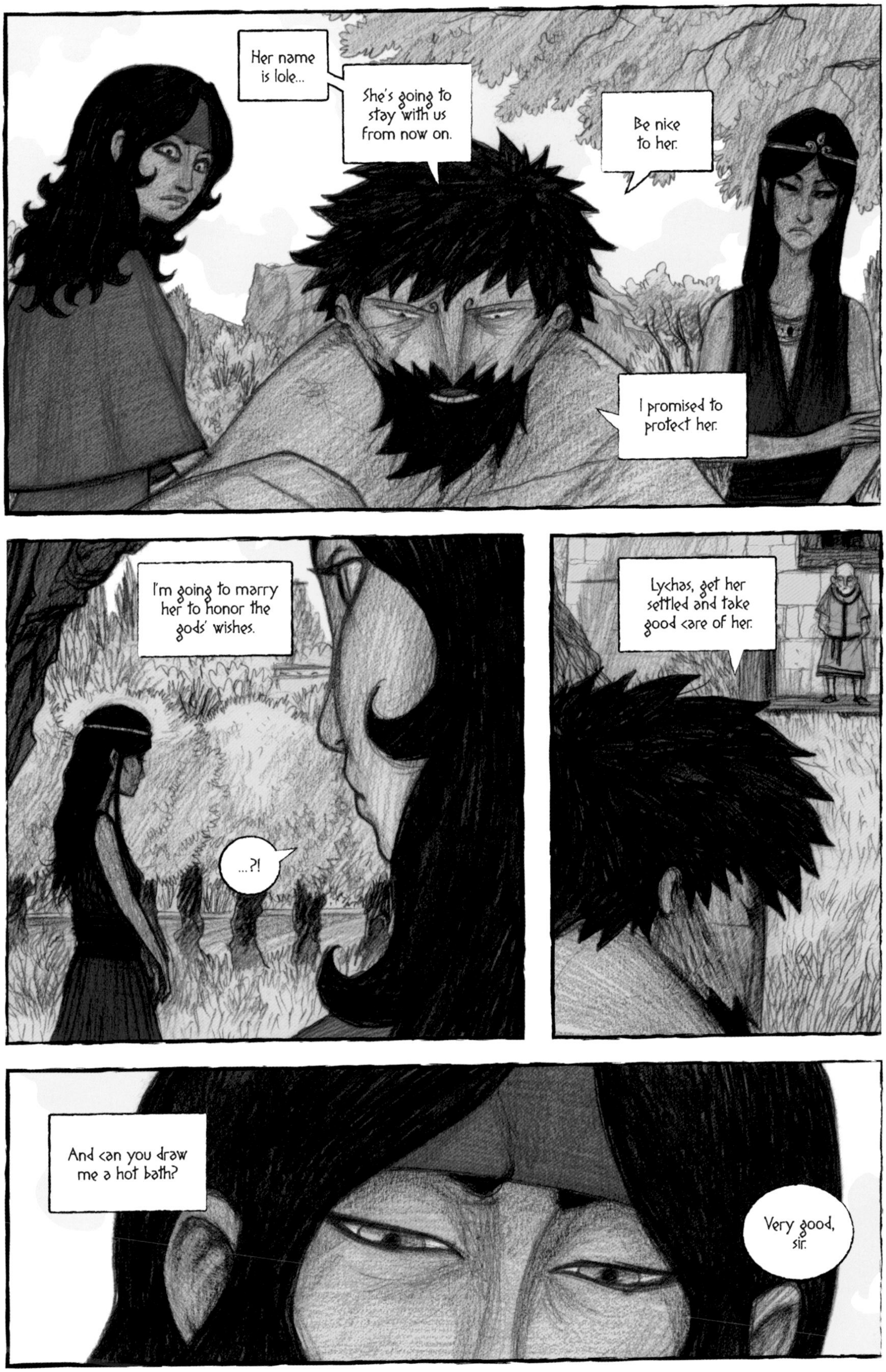
Her name is Iole...
She's going to stay with us from now on.
Be nice to her.
I promised to protect her.
I'm going to marry her to honor the gods' wishes.
...?!
Lychas, get her settled and take good care of her.
And can you draw me a hot bath?
Very good, sir.

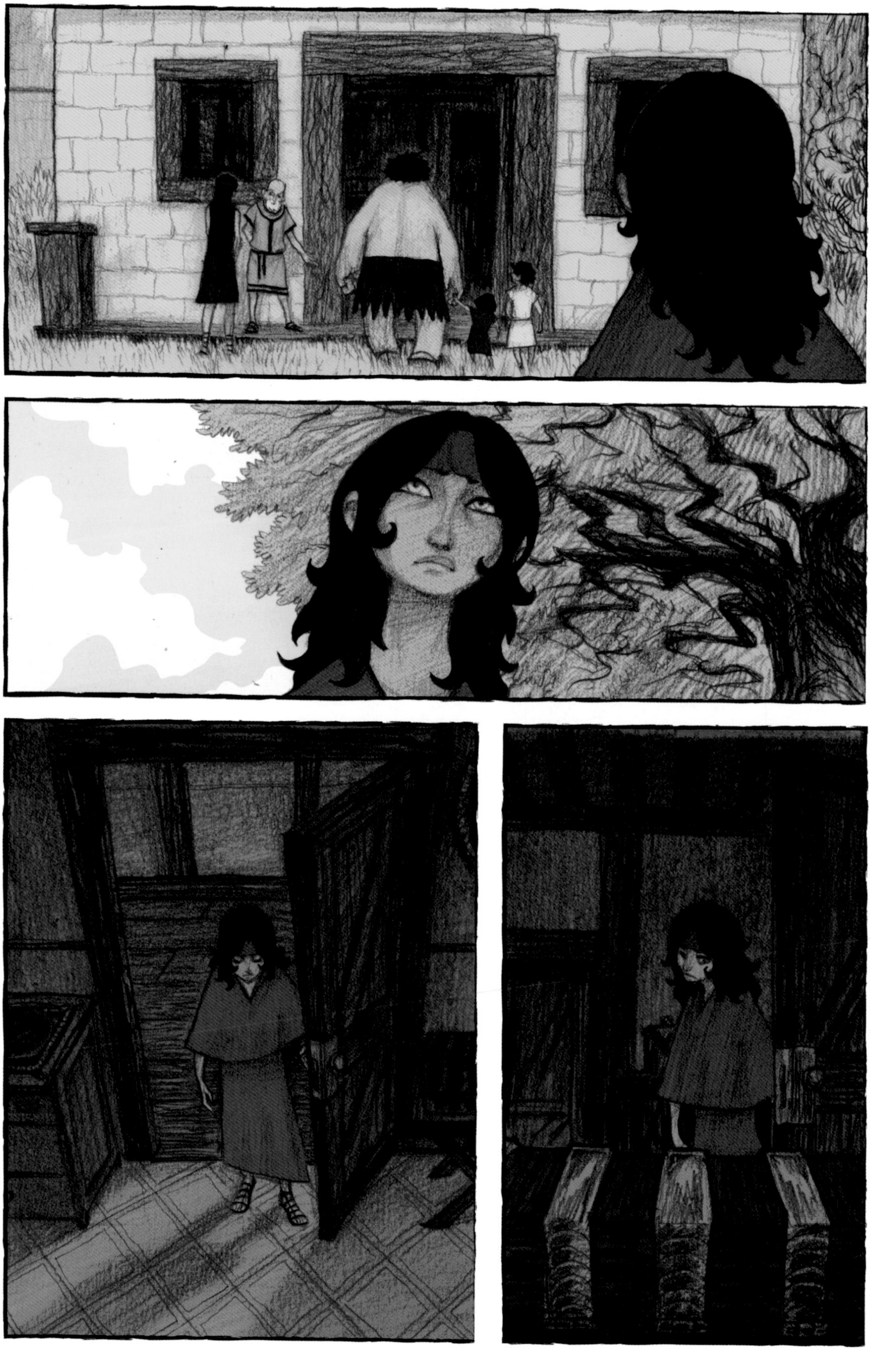

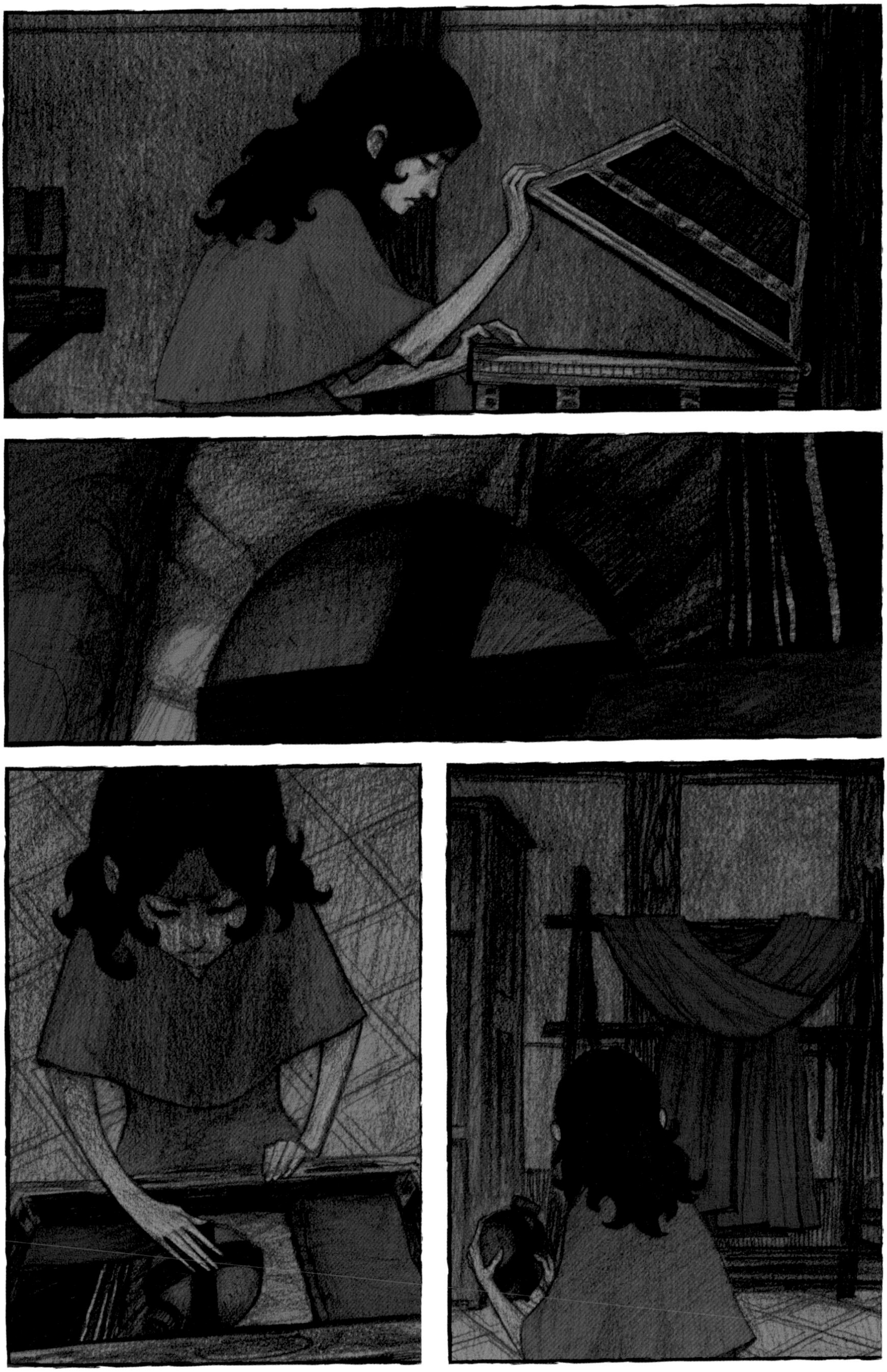

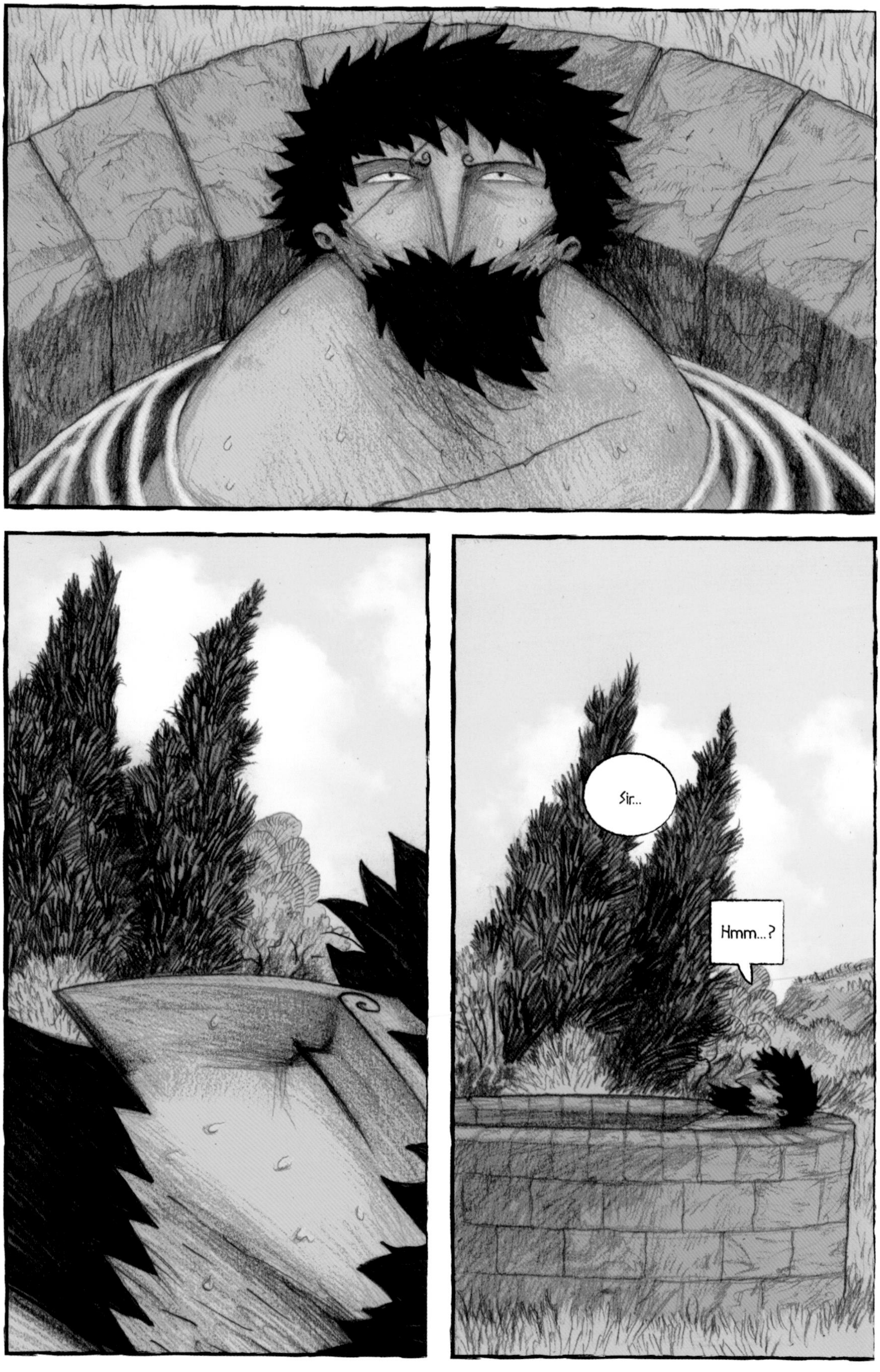
Sir...
Hmm...?

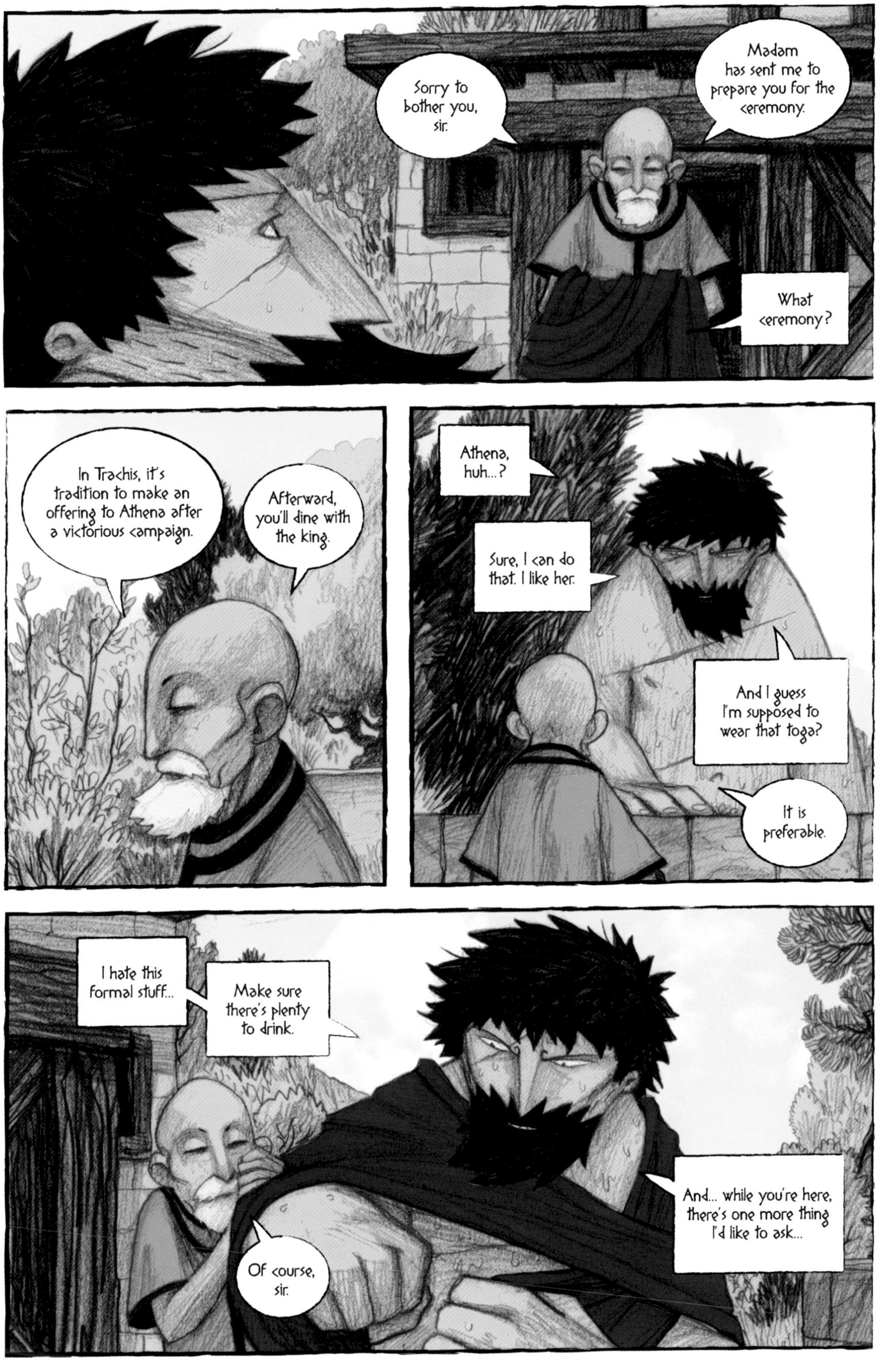
Sorry to bother you, sir.
Madam has sent me to prepare you for the ceremony.
What ceremony?
In Trachis, it's tradition to make an offering to Athena after a victorious campaign.
Afterward, you'll dine with the king.
Athena, huh...?
Sure, I can do that. I like her.
And I guess I'm supposed to wear that toga?
It is preferable.
I hate this formal stuff...
Make sure there's plenty to drink.
And... while you're here, there's one more thing I'd like to ask...
Of course, sir.

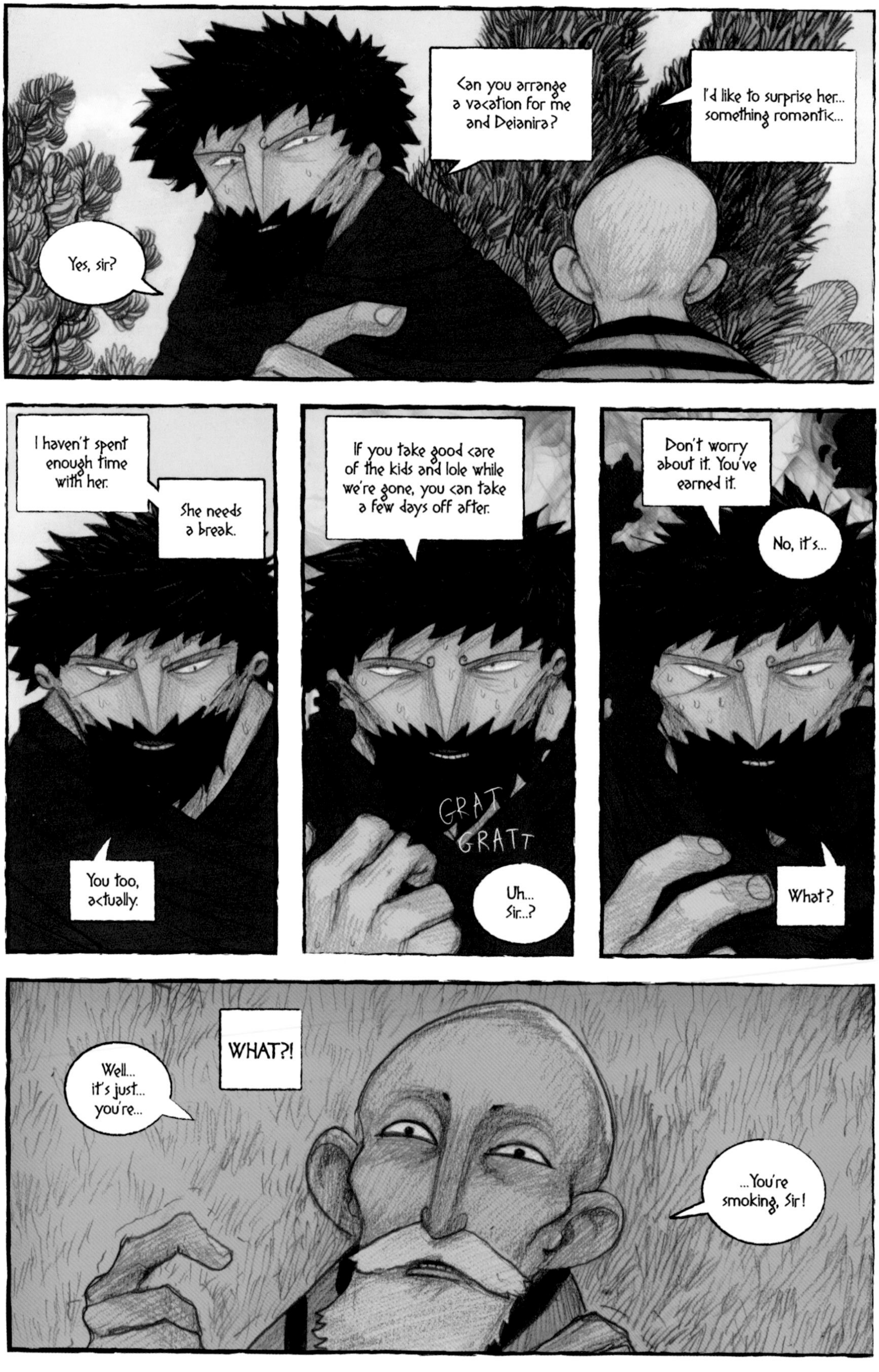
Yes, sir?
Can you arrange a vacation for me and Deianira?
I'd like to surprise her... something romantic...
I haven't spent enough time with her.
She needs a break.
You too, actually.
If you take good care of the kids and Iole while we're gone, you can take a few days off after.
GRAT GRATT
Uh... Sir...?
Don't worry about it. You've earned it.
No, it's...
What?
Well... it's just... you're...
WHAT?!
...You're smoking, Sir!

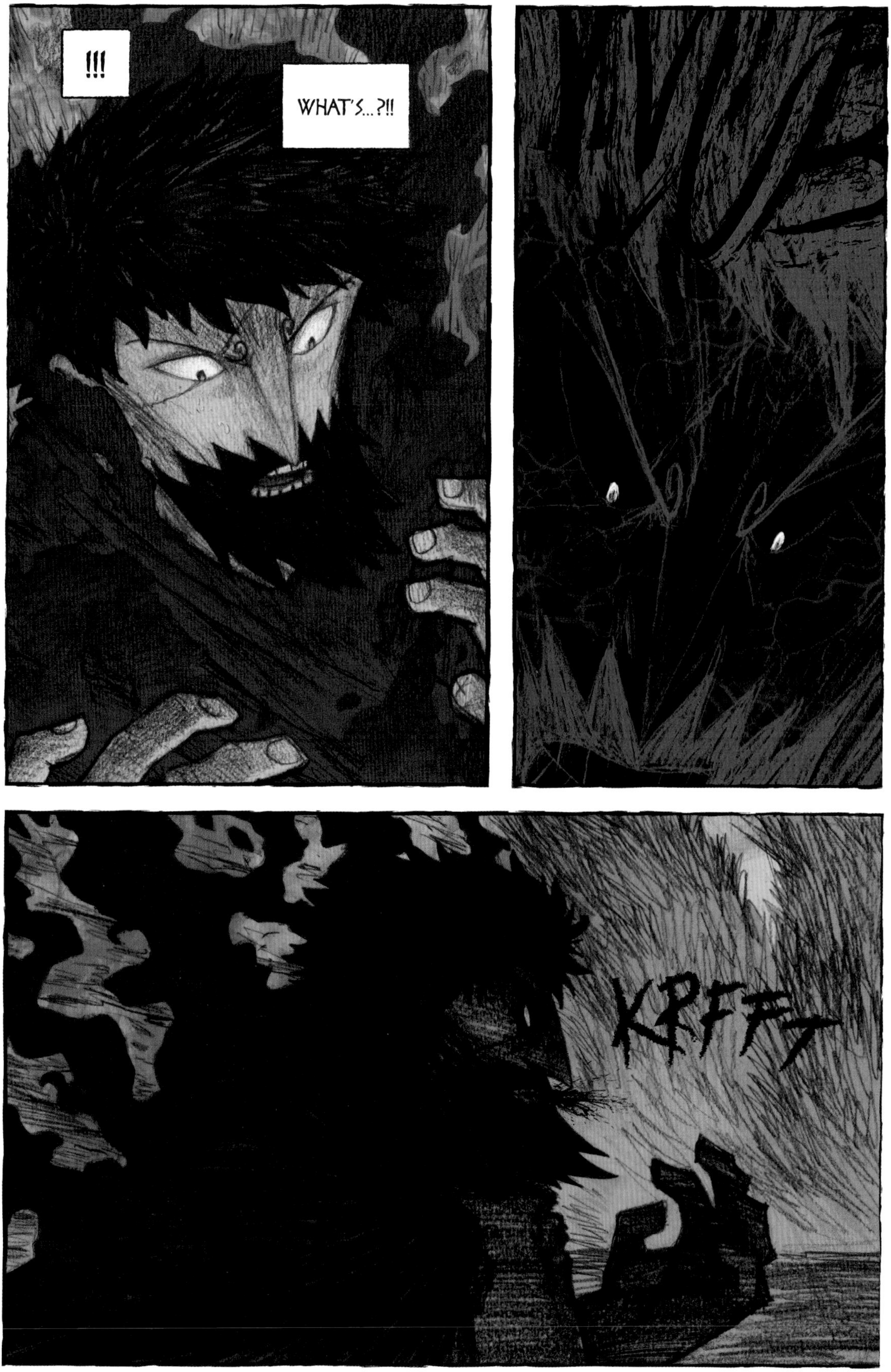
!!!
WHAT'S...?!!
KRFFT

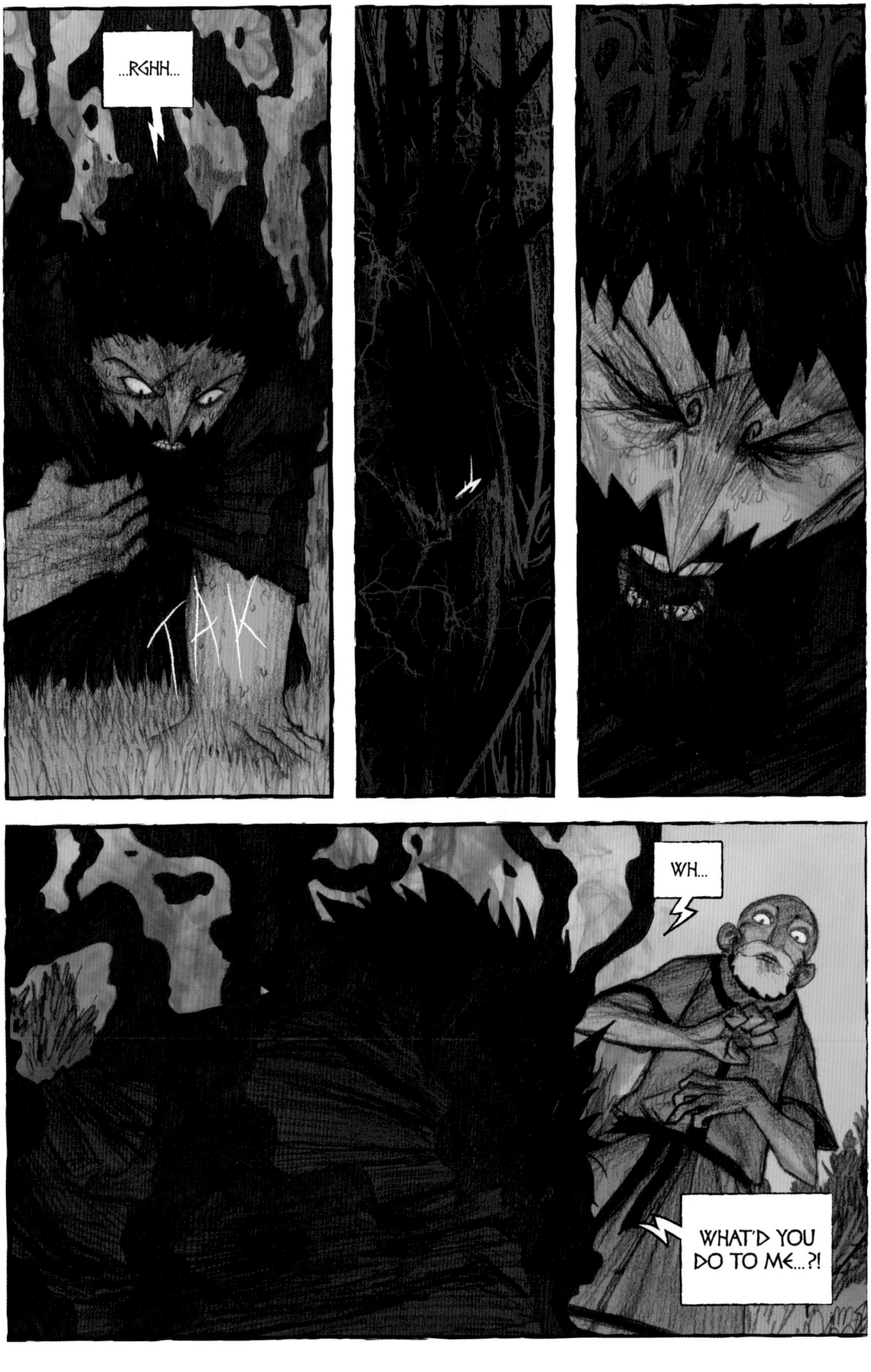
...RGHH...
TAK
BLARG
WH...
WHAT'D YOU DO TO ME...?!

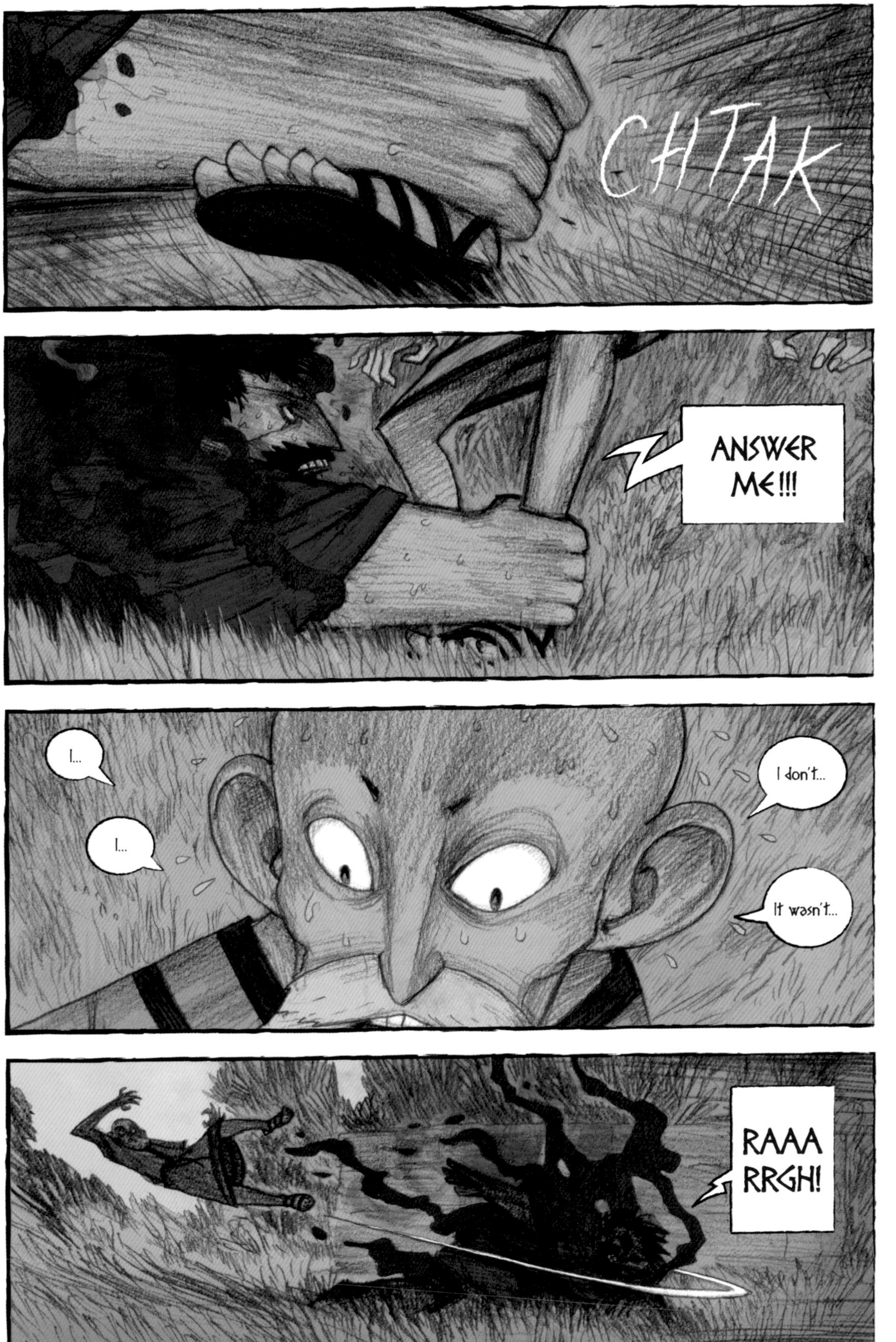
CHTAK
ANSWER ME!!!
I...
I...
I don't...
It wasn't...
RAAA RRGH!

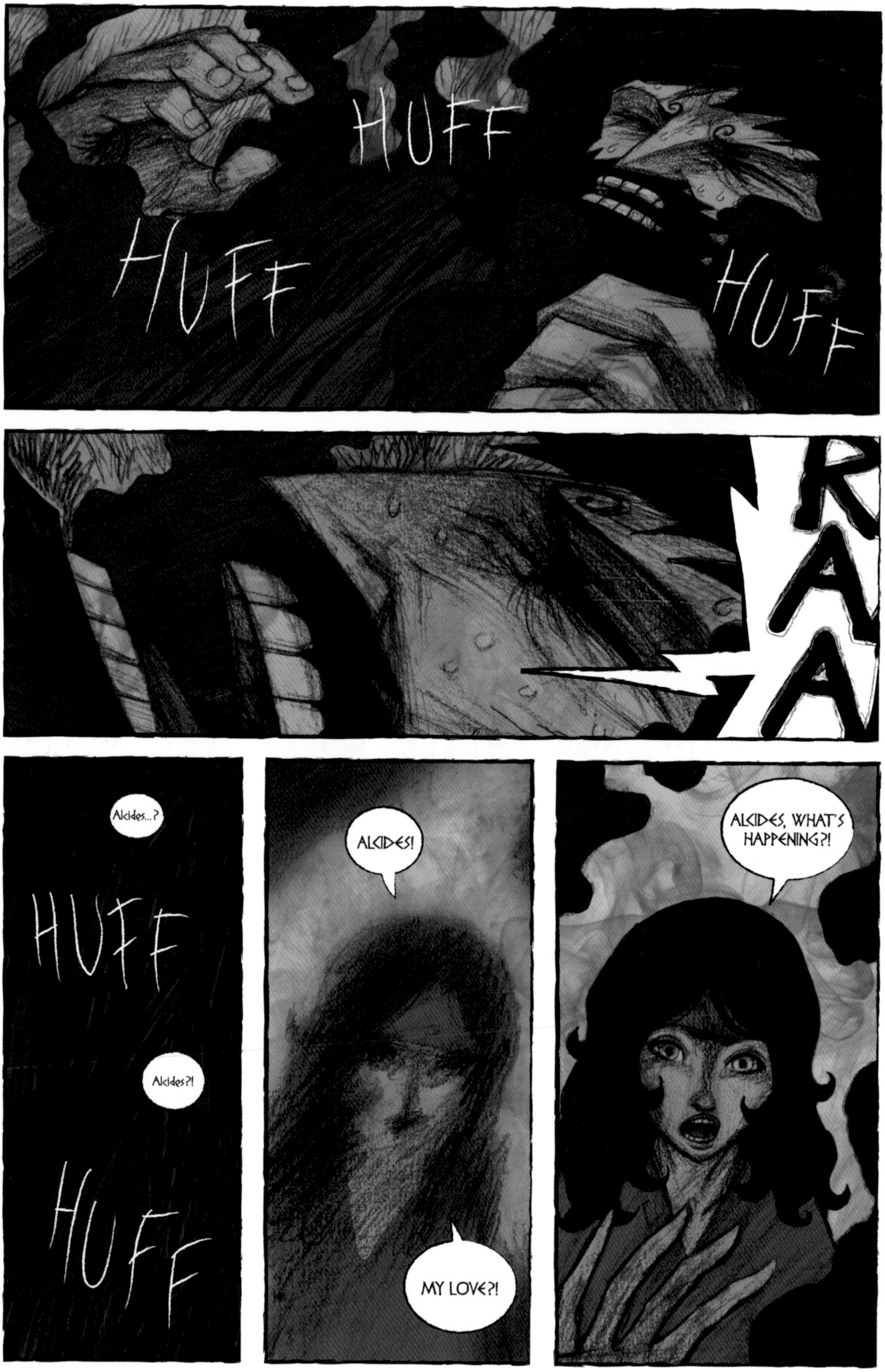
HUFF
HUFF
HUFF
RAAA
Alcides...?
HUFF
Alcides?!
HUFF
ALCIDES!
MY LOVE?!
ALCIDES, WHAT'S HAPPENING?!

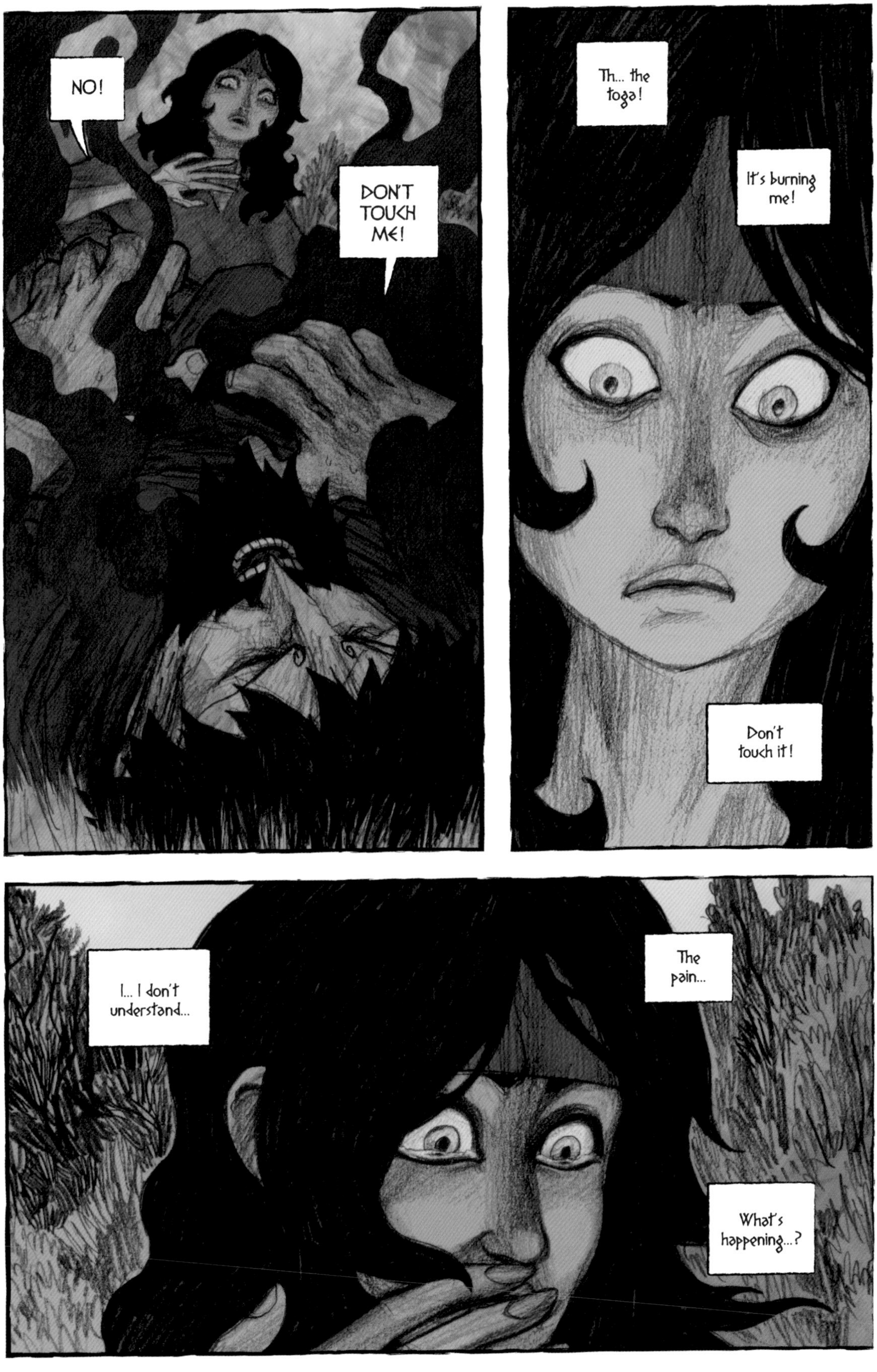
NO!
DON'T TOUCH ME!
Th... the toga!
It's burning me!
Don't touch it!
I... I don't understand...
The pain...
What's happening...?

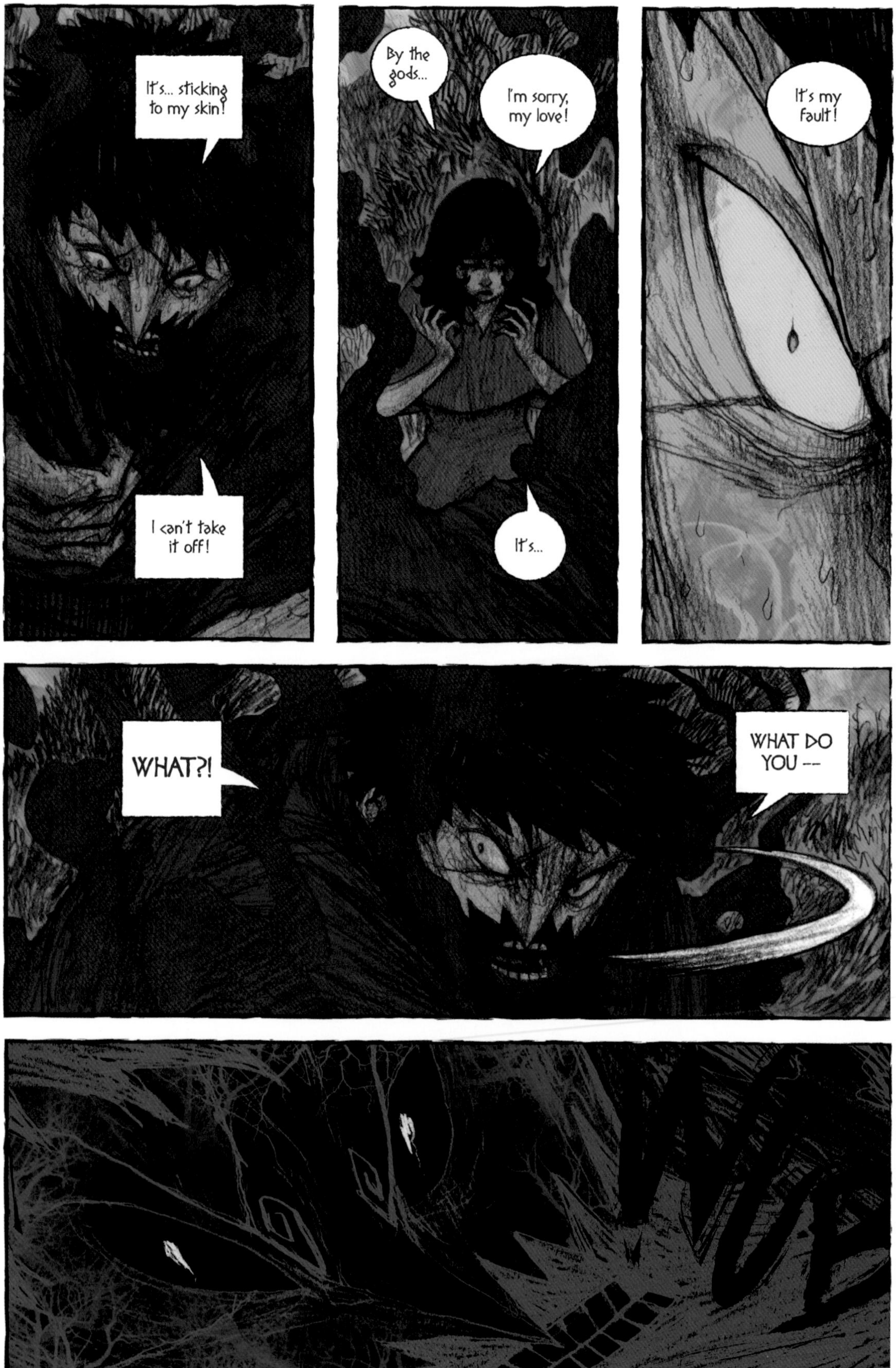
It's... sticking to my skin!
I can't take it off!
By the gods...
I'm sorry, my love!
It's...
It's my fault!
WHAT?!
WHAT DO YOU --

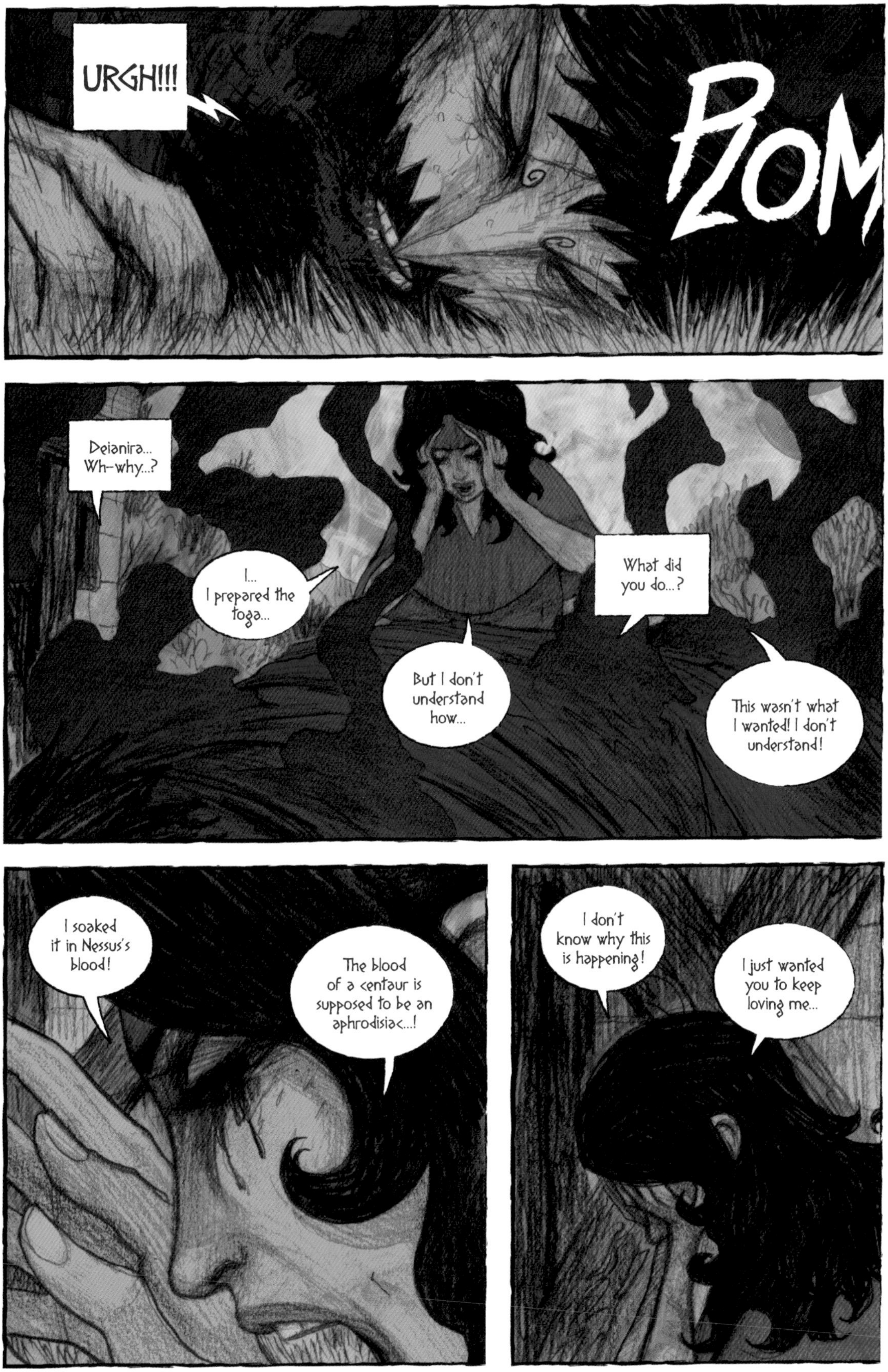
URGH!!!
PLOM
Deianira... Wh-why...?
I... I prepared the toga...
What did you do...?
But I don't understand how...
This wasn't what I wanted! I don't understand!
I soaked it in Nessus's blood!
The blood of a centaur is supposed to be an aphrodisiac...!
I don't know why this is happening!
I just wanted you to keep loving me...

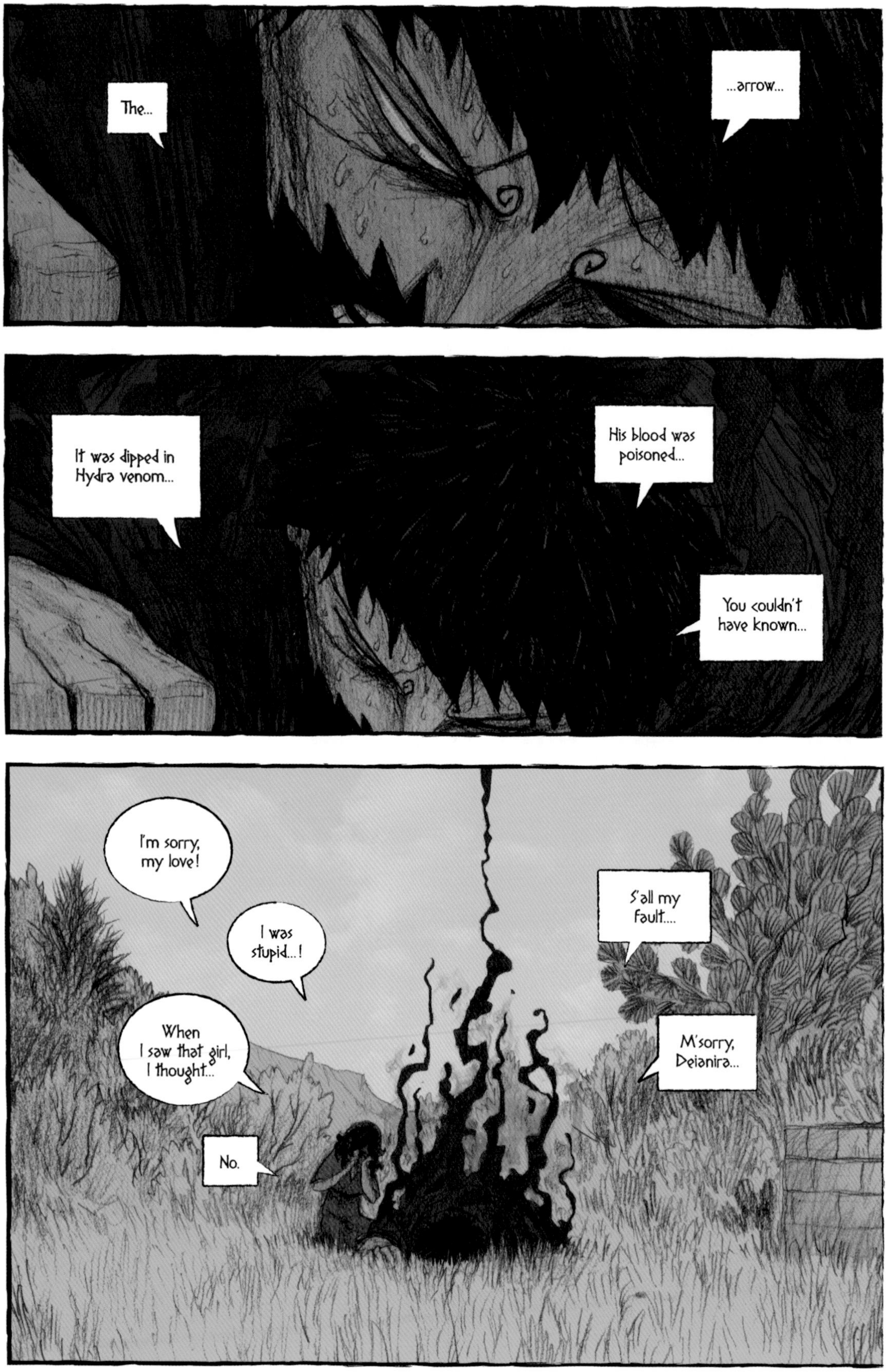

The...
...arrow...
It was dipped in Hydra venom...
His blood was poisoned...
You couldn't have known...
I'm sorry, my love!
I was stupid...!
When I saw that girl, I thought...
No.
S'all my fault....
M'sorry, Deianira...

You deserved
a better life...

...and I probably
deserve this
suffering...

...I should
thank you...

...before I met you, I
thought I'd never find
happiness again...

...you
gave my life...
meaning...

...don't cry,
sweetie...

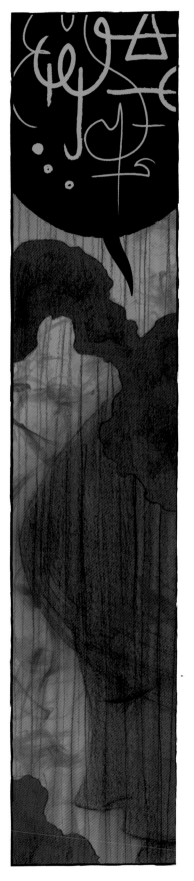

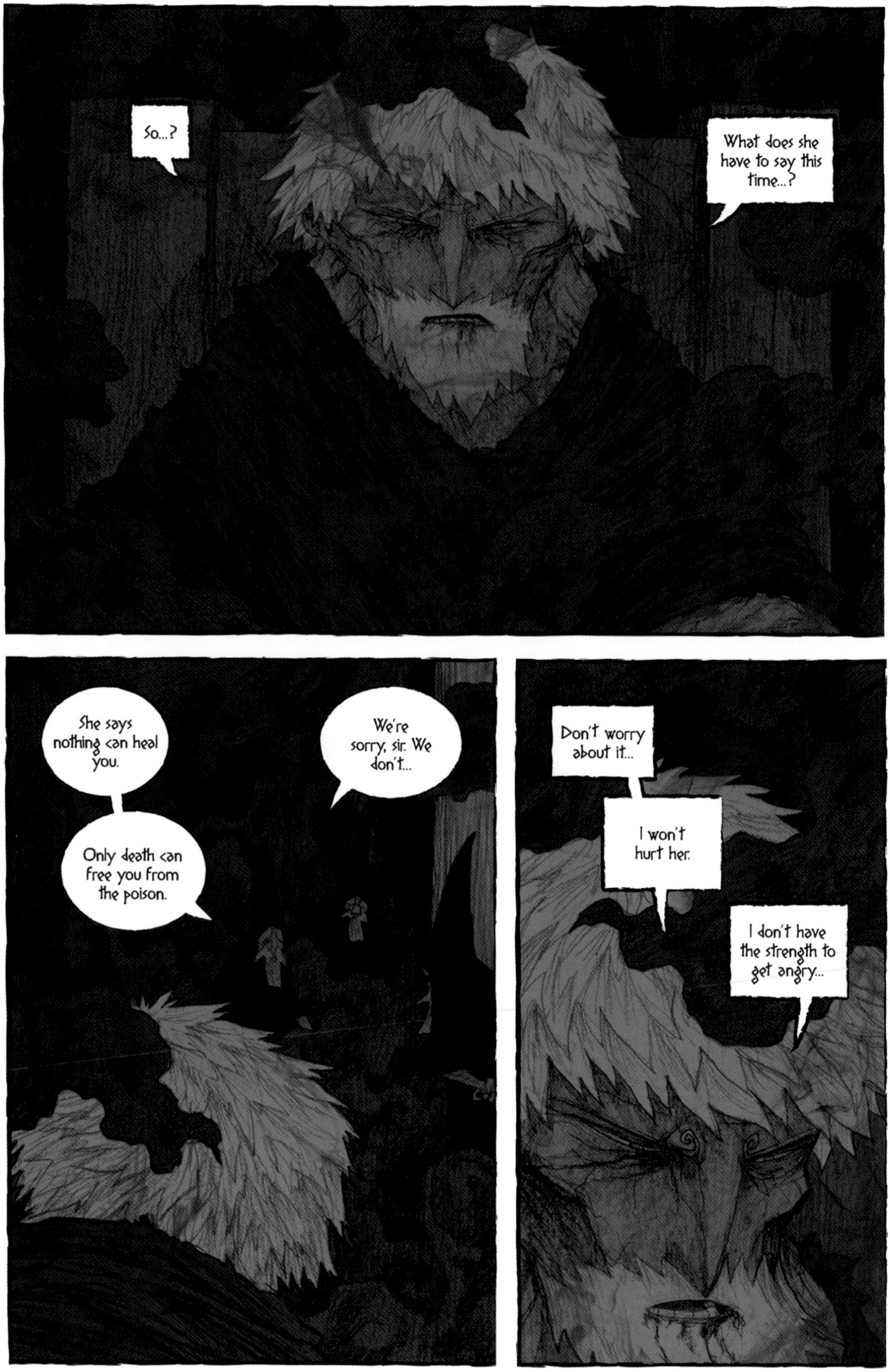

So...?
What does she have to say this time...?
She says nothing can heal you.
Only death can free you from the poison.
We're sorry, sir. We don't...
Don't worry about it...
I won't hurt her.
I don't have the strength to get angry...

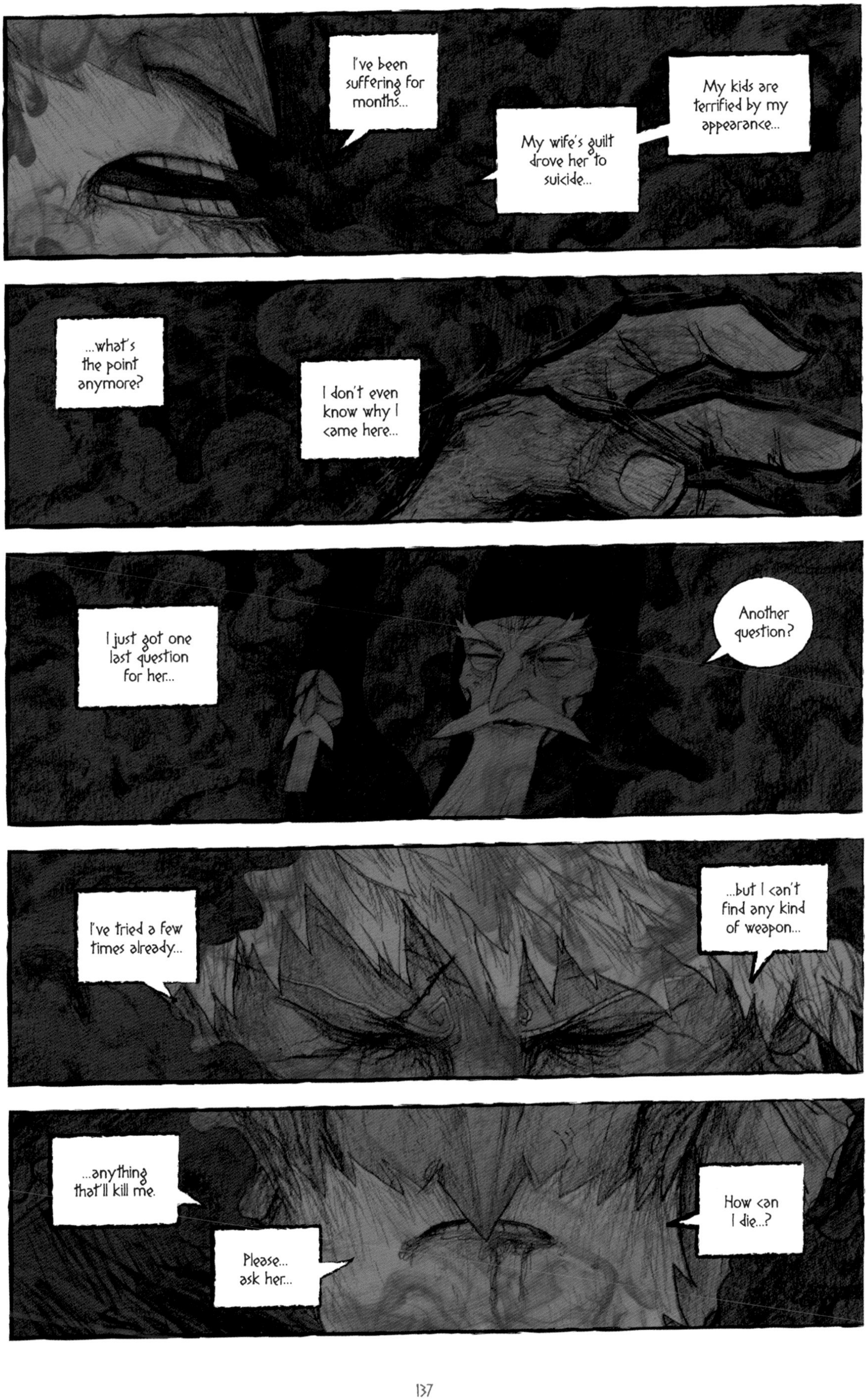
I've been suffering for months...
My kids are terrified by my appearance...
My wife's guilt drove her to suicide...
...what's the point anymore?
I don't even know why I came here...
I just got one last question for her...
Another question?
I've tried a few times already...
...but I can't find any kind of weapon...
...anything that'll kill me.
Please... ask her...
How can I die...?

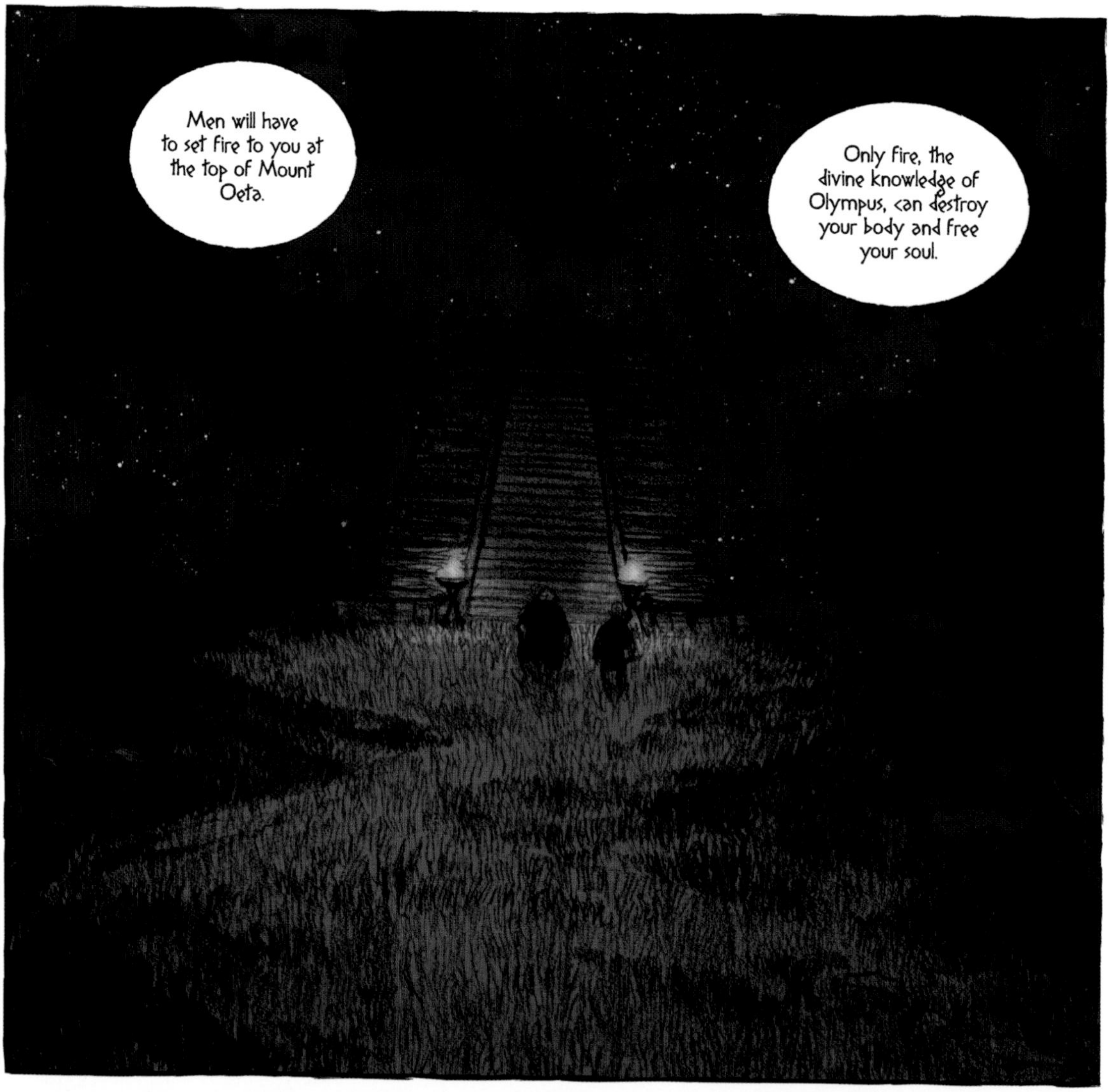
Men will have to set fire to you at the top of Mount Oeta.
Only fire, the divine knowledge of Olympus, can destroy your body and free your soul.

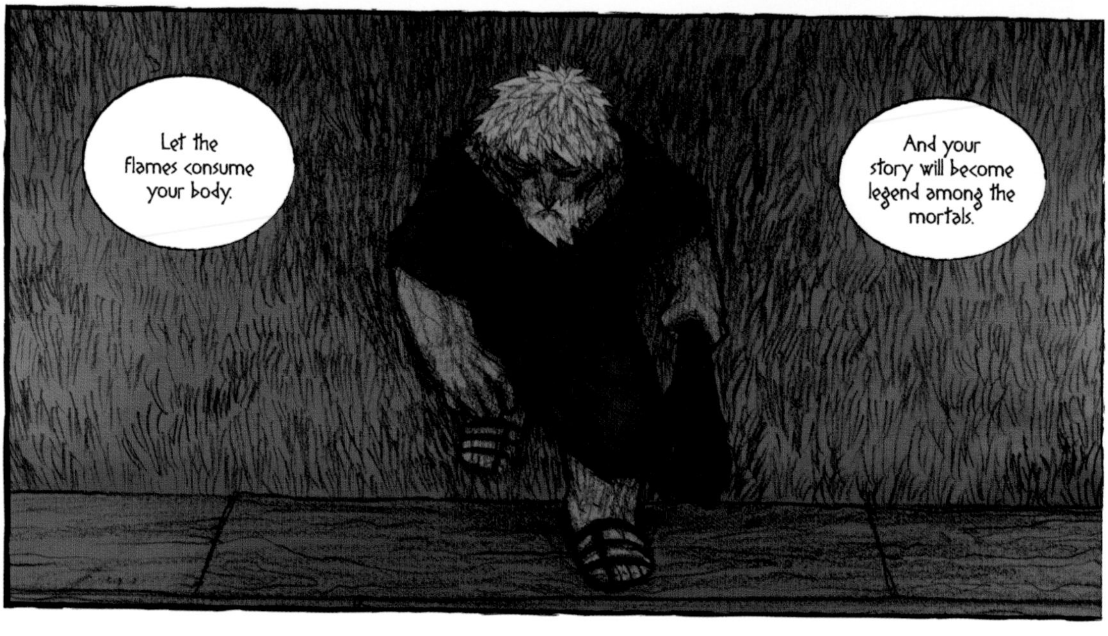
Let the flames consume your body.
And your story will become legend among the mortals.

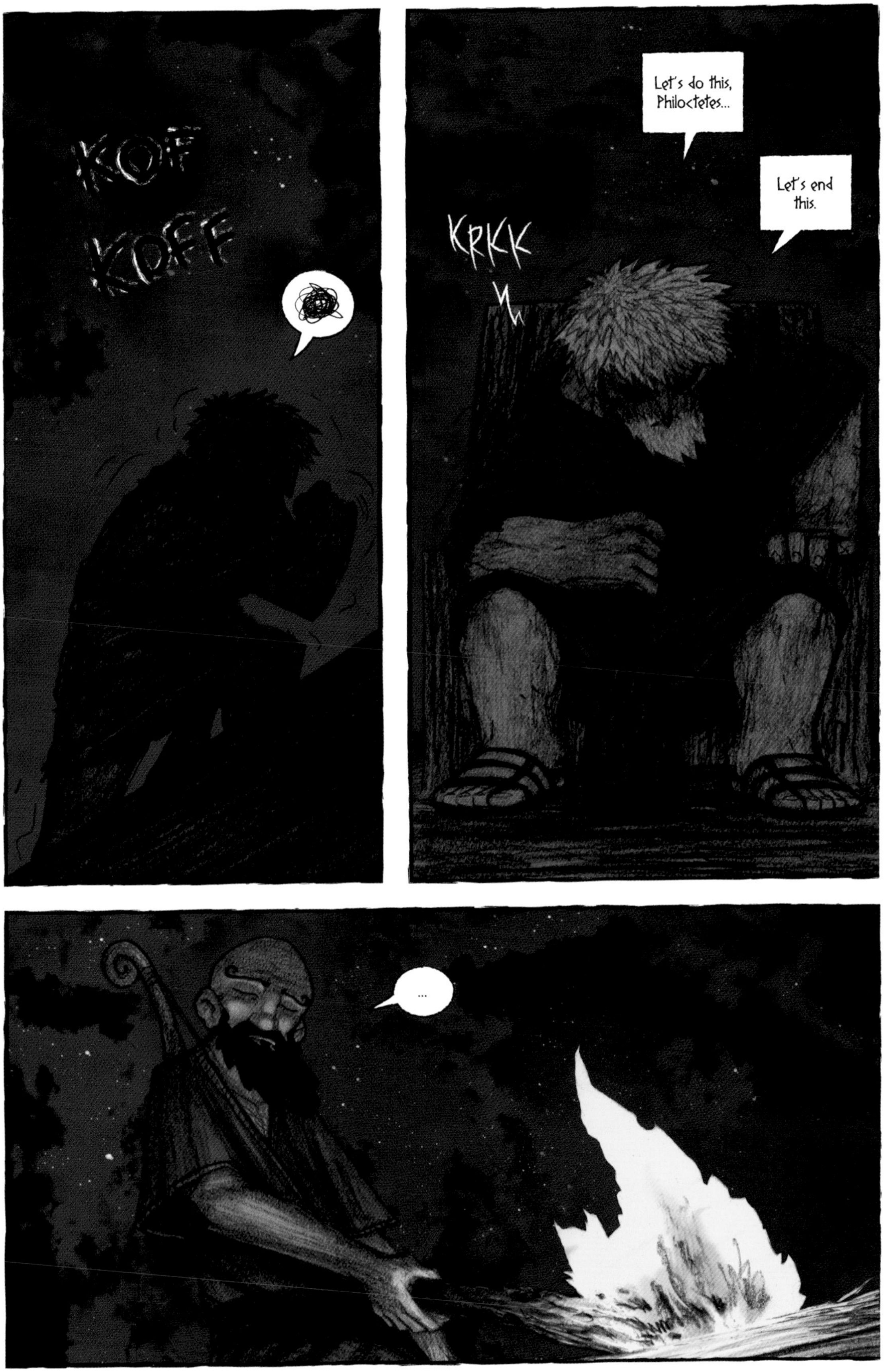
KOF
KOFF
Let's do this, Philoctetes...
Let's end this.
KRKK
...

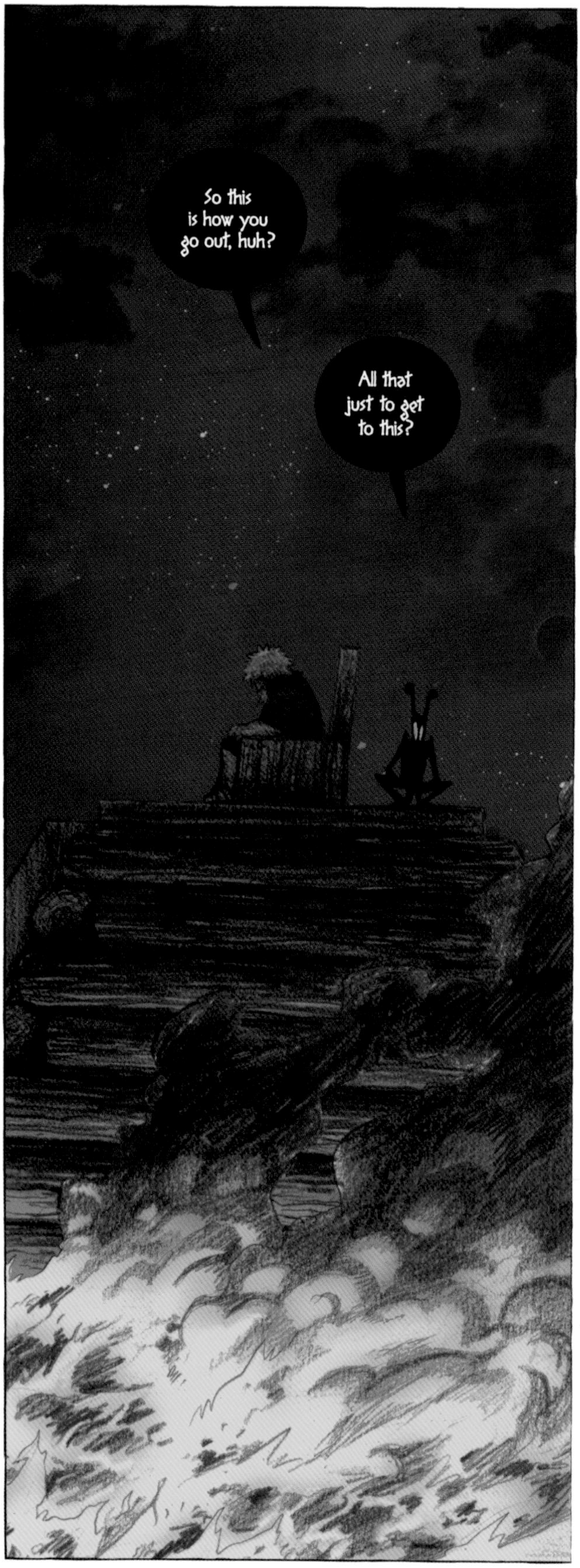
So this is how you go out, huh?
All that just to get to this?

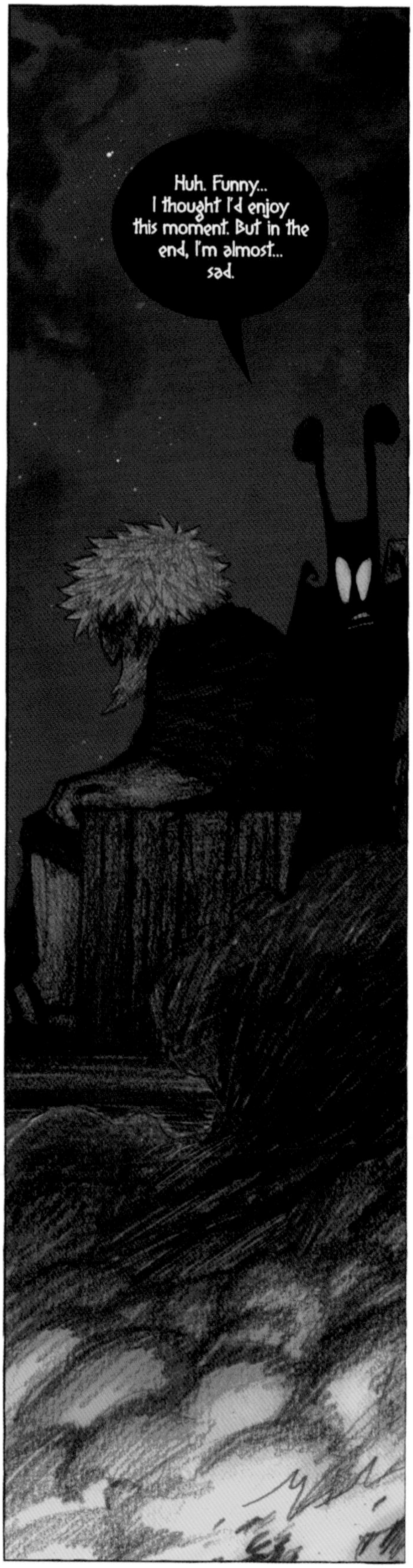
Huh. Funny... I thought I'd enjoy this moment. But in the end, I'm almost... sad.

Well... I guess there's nothing left to say but Godspeed, Alcides!

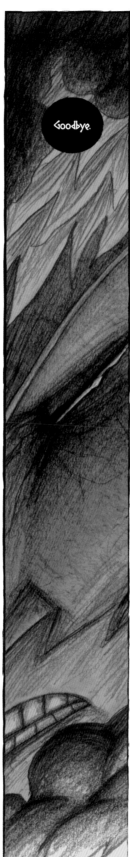

Goodbye.

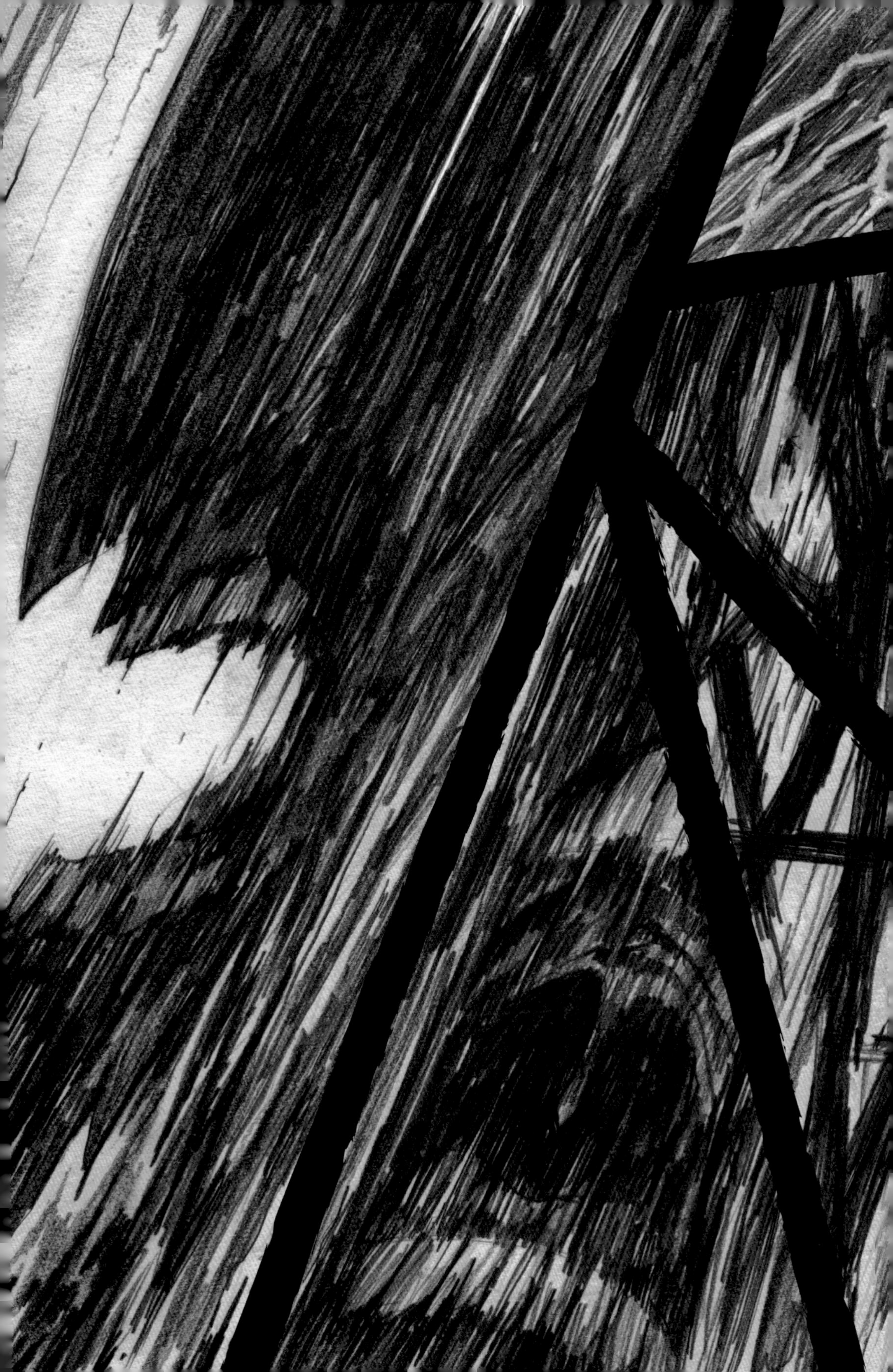

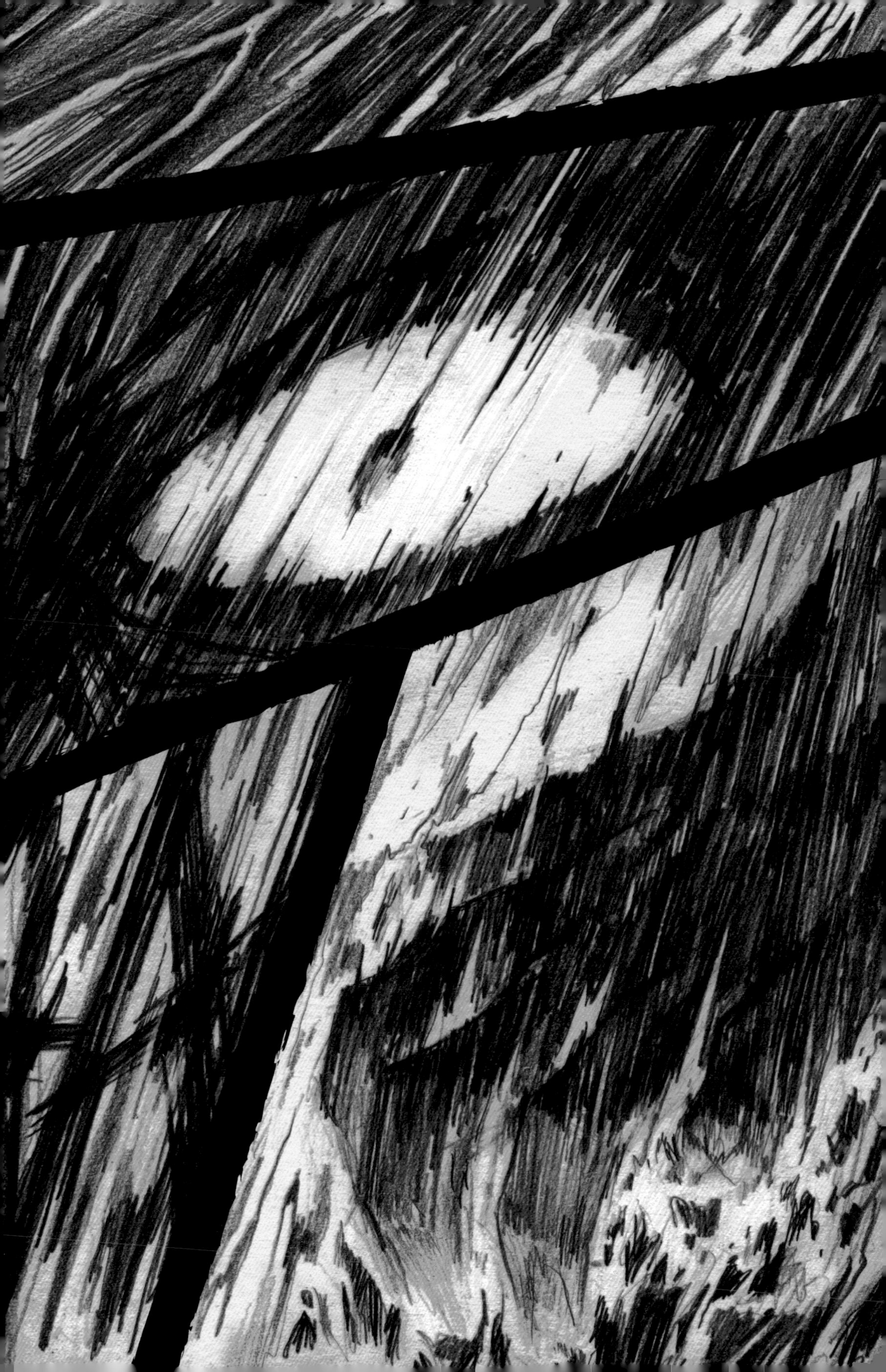

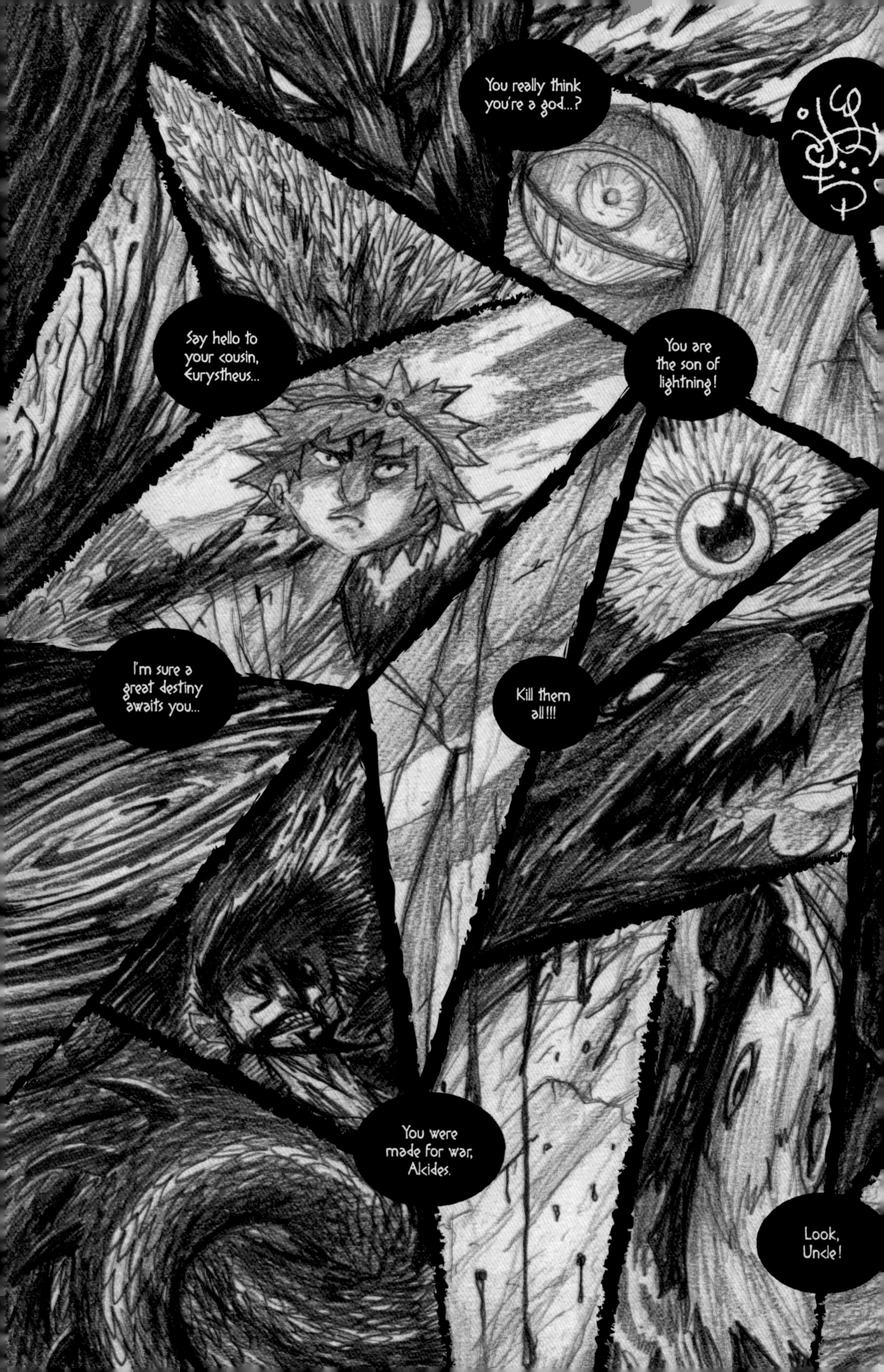
You really think you're a god...?
Say hello to your cousin, Eurystheus...
You are the son of lightning!
I'm sure a great destiny awaits you...
Kill them all!!!
You were made for war, Alcides.
Look, Uncle!

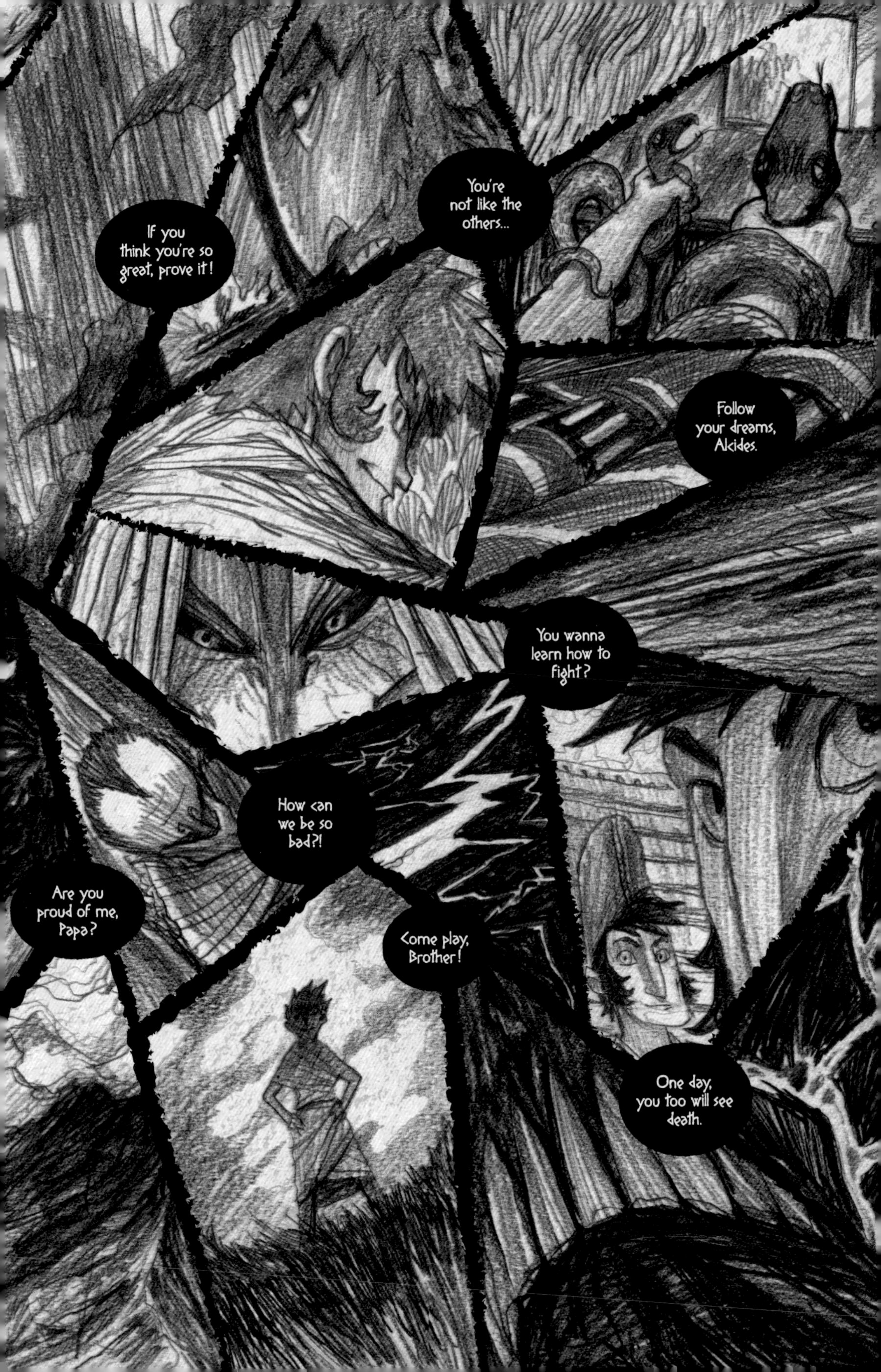
If you think you're so great, prove it!
You're not like the others...
Follow your dreams, Alcides.
You wanna learn how to fight?
How can we be so bad?!
Are you proud of me, Papa?
Come play, Brother!
One day, you too will see death.

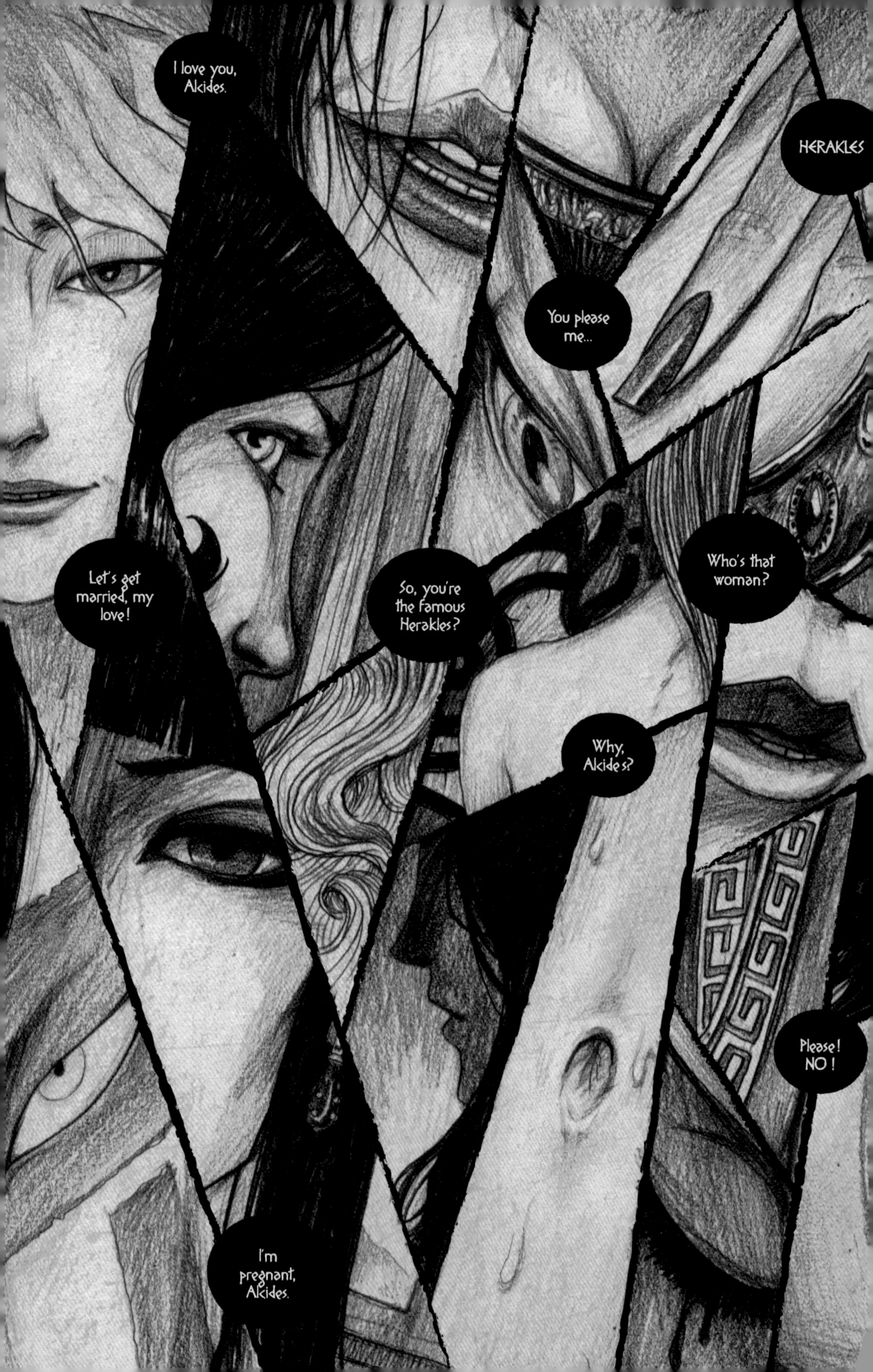
I love you, Alkides.
HERAKLES
You please me...
Let's get married, my love!
So, you're the famous Herakles?
Who's that woman?
Why, Alkides?
Please! NO!
I'm pregnant, Alkides.

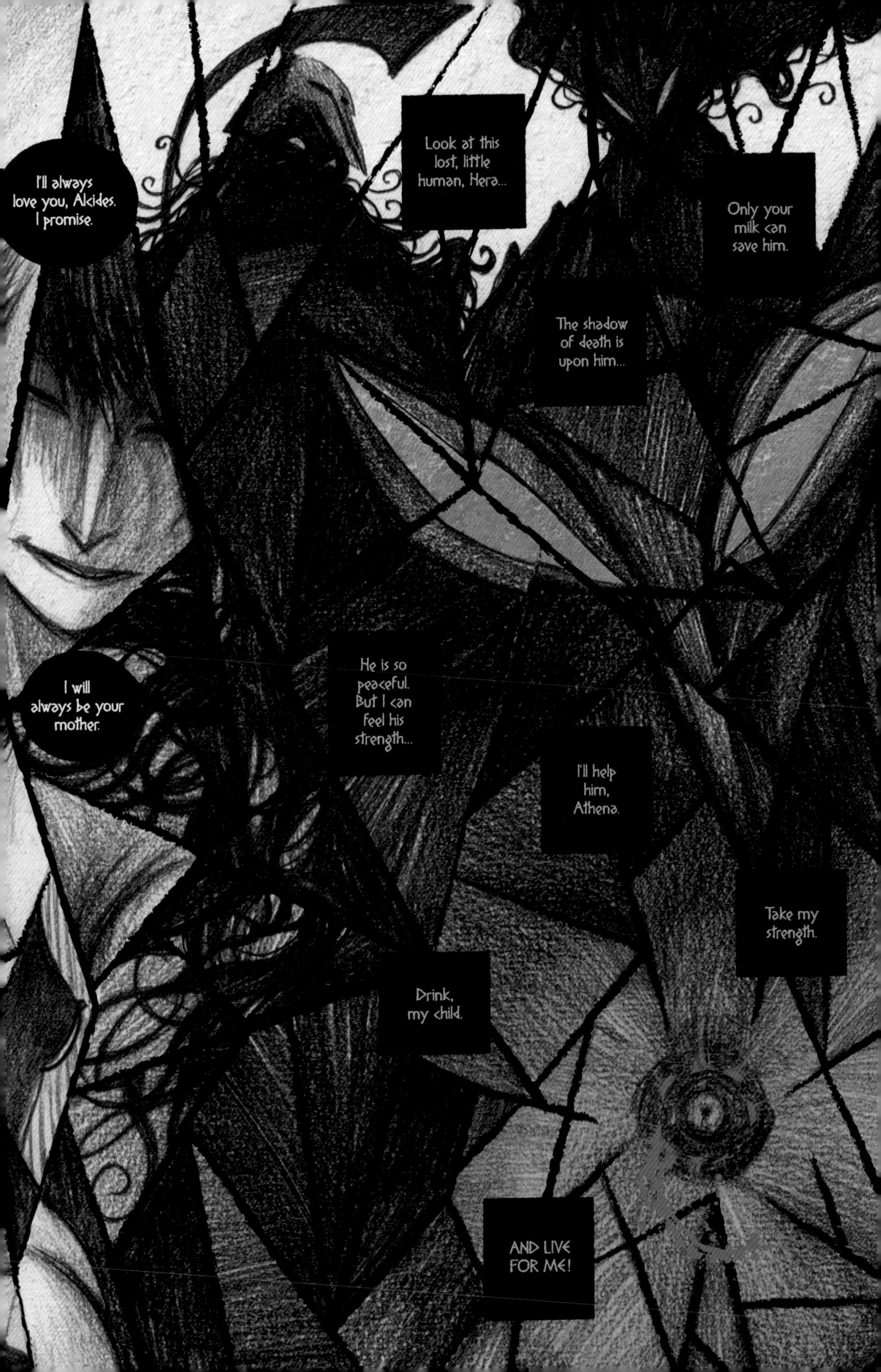
I'll always love you, Alcides. I promise.
Look at this lost, little human, Hera...
Only your milk can save him.
The shadow of death is upon him...
I will always be your mother.
He is so peaceful. But I can feel his strength...
I'll help him, Athena.
Take my strength.
Drink, my child.
AND LIVE FOR ME!

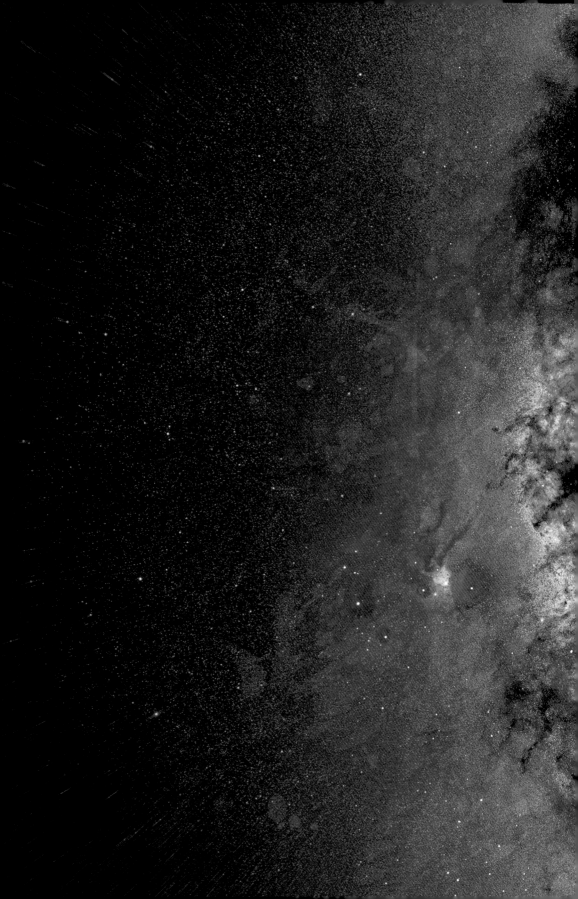

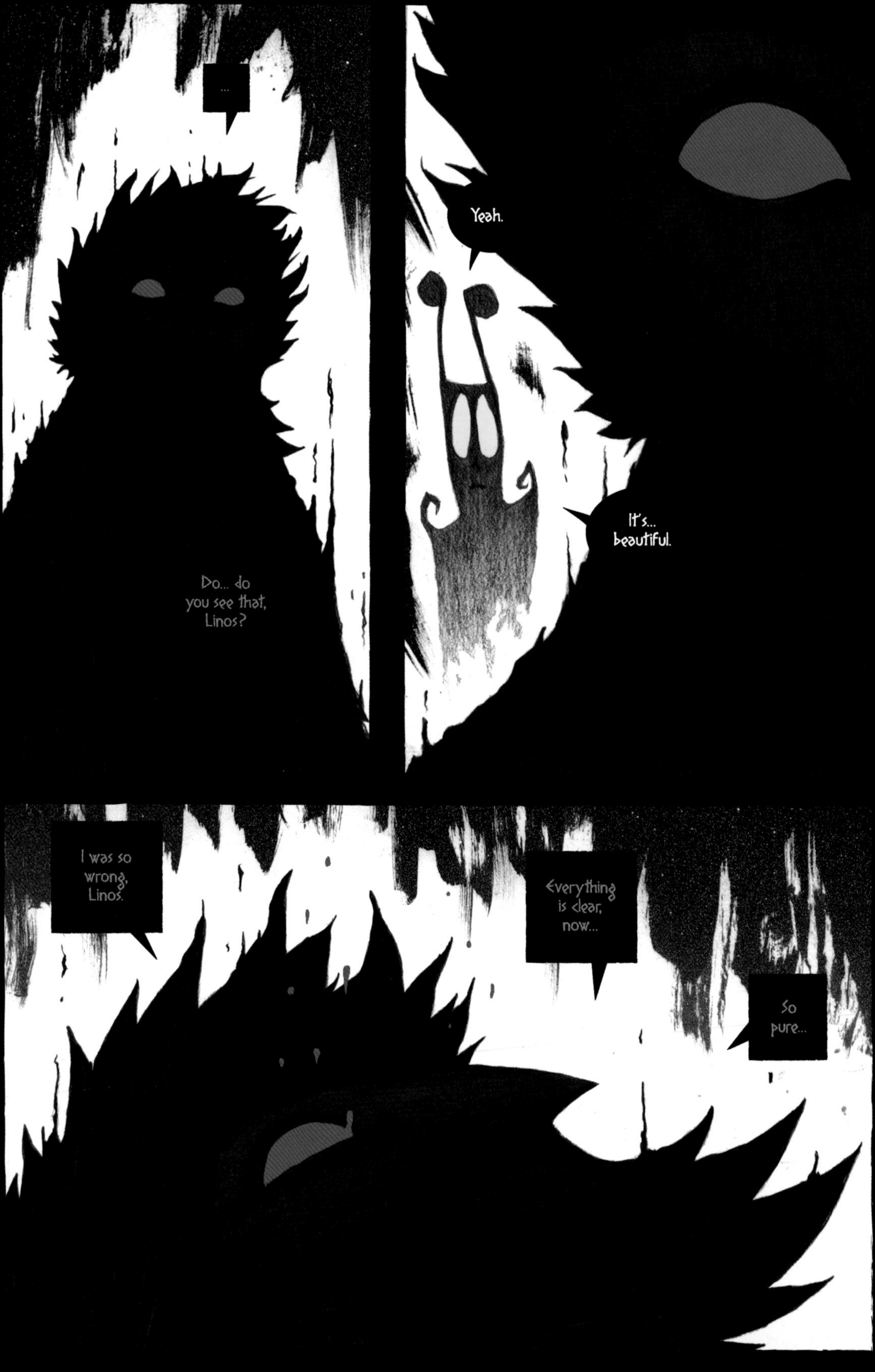
...
Do... do you see that, Linos?
Yeah.
It's... beautiful.
I was so wrong, Linos.
Everything is clear, now...
So pure...

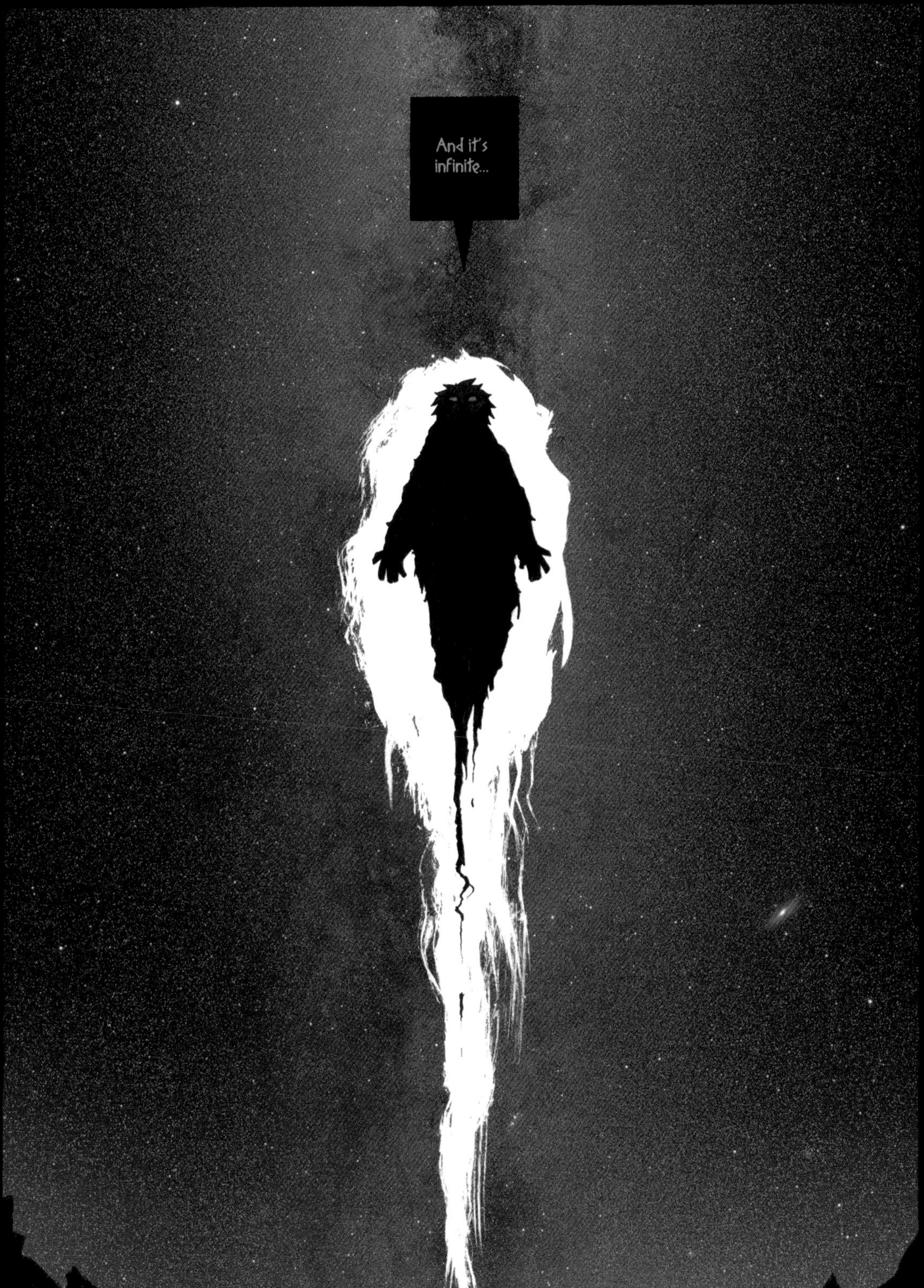
And it's
infinite...

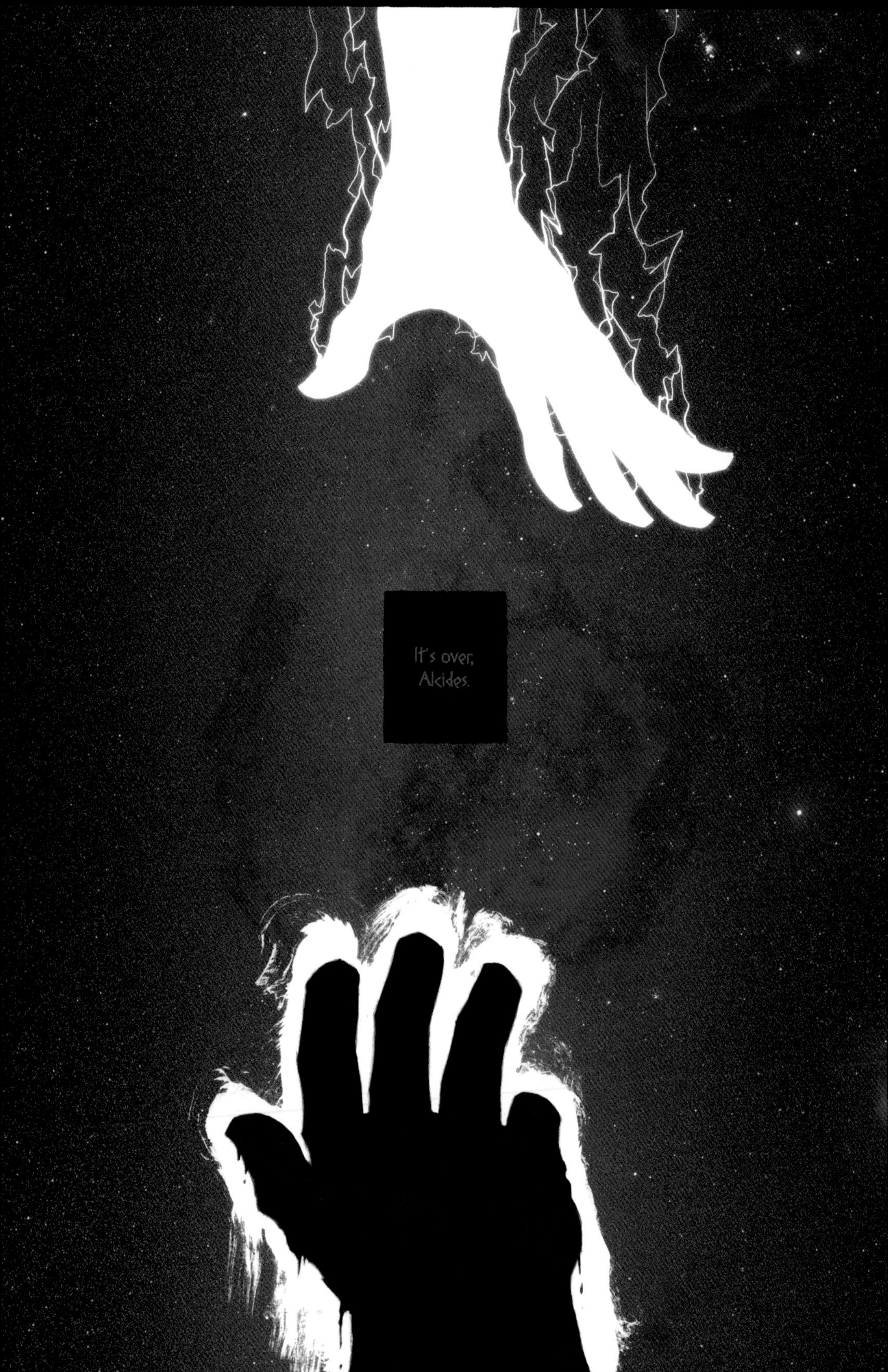
It's over, Alcides.

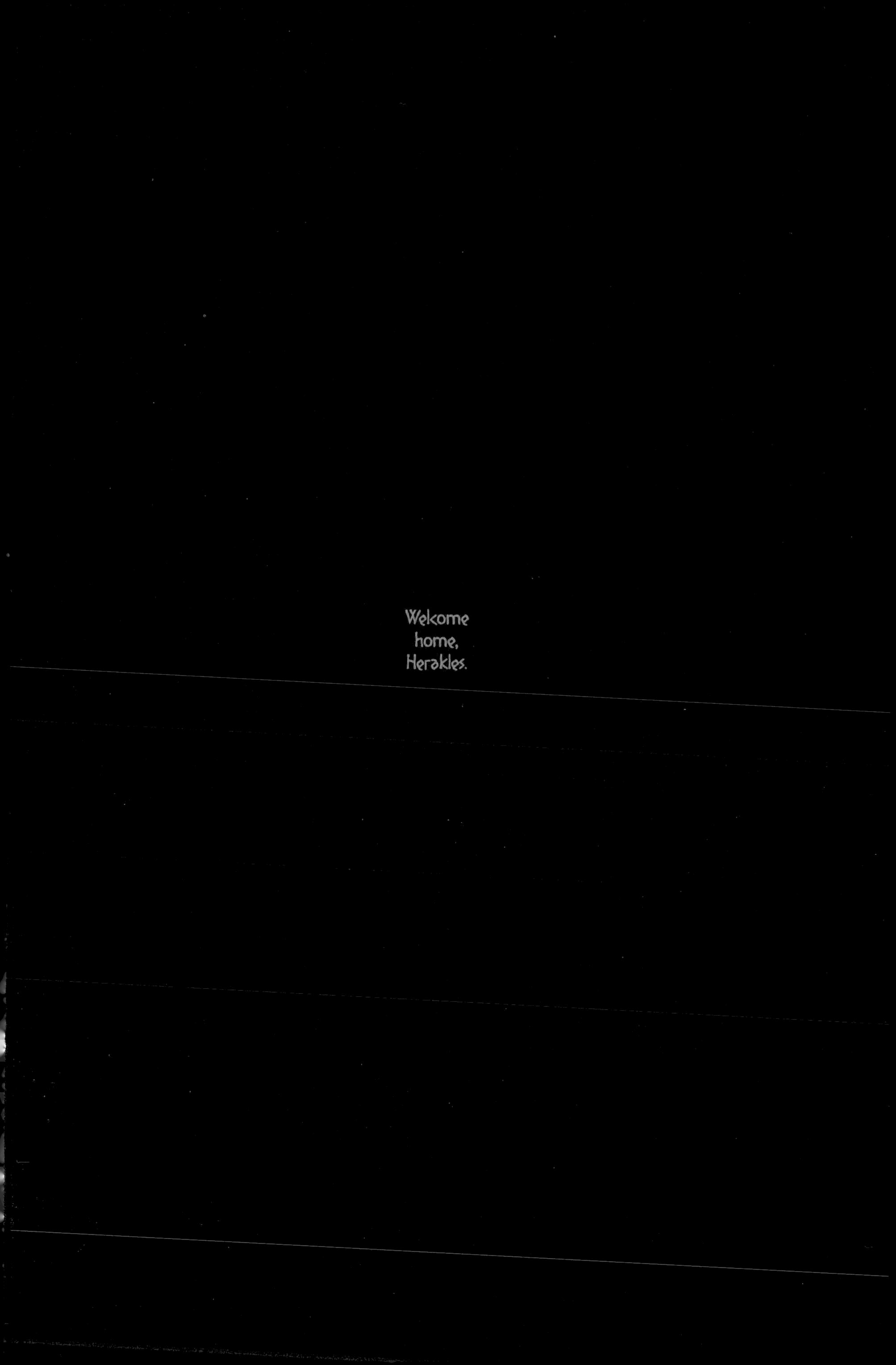
Welcome home, Herakles.

END.

APPENDIX

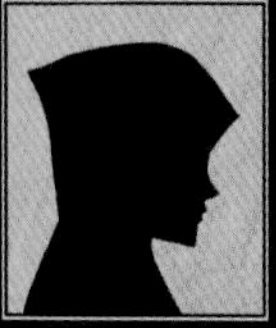

THE PYTHIA

Virgin chosen by the priests of Delphi to serve as their oracle and to speak Apollo's prophecy. She goes into a trance by breathing in pneuma, the vapor that comes from Gaia's entrails, from which state the Gods speak through her.

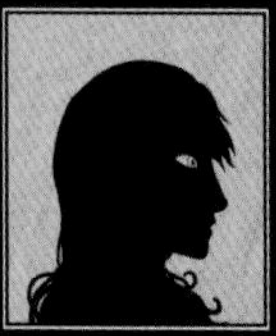

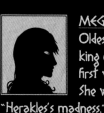

MEGARA

Oldest daughter of Creon, the king of Thebes. She was Herakles's first wife and gave him three sons. She was also the first victim of "Herakles's madness."

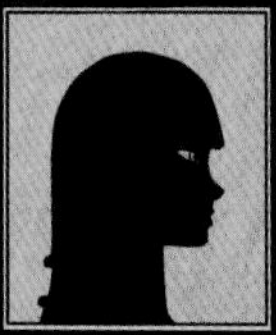

OMPHALE

Queen of Lydia, daughter of King Iardanus. She had two sons with Herakles, Agelaus and Alcaeus. Nobody ever learned what happened to the three coins she paid Hermes.

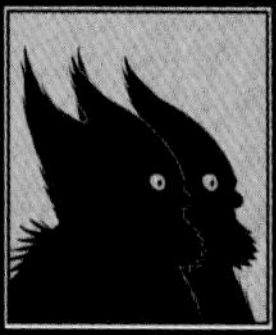

PASSALOS AND AKMON (KERKOPES)

The sons of Oceanus and the Oceanid, Theia. During their childhood, they were often warned of the legendary Melampygos, who would punish them if they fooled around too much.

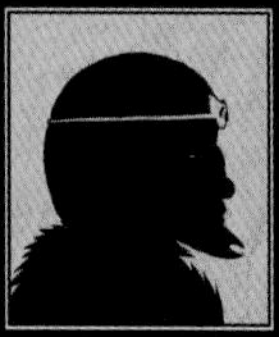

NELEUS

King of Pylos and Poseidon's son. After Iphitos's death on his land, Herakles asked him for absolution. Herakles's revenge after he refused cost Neleus the life of all his sons, except Nestor, a future Argonaut and hero of the Trojan War.

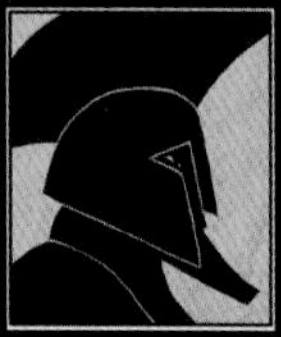

HIPPOCOON

King of Sparta and son of Oebalus, he ascended to the throne after chasing his brother Tyndareus from the kingdom with the help of his twenty sons. After Herakles attacked, Tyndareus reclaimed his place.

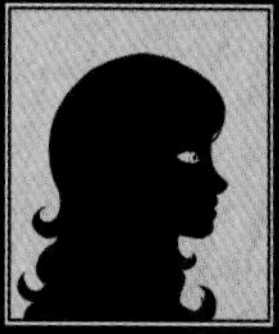

DEIANIRA

Daughter of Althaea and Oeneus, the king of Calydon. Before meeting Herakles, she had run away from her kingdom to escape her suitors and the tournament meant to determine her husband. She hung herself to escape the guilt she felt for inadvertently poisoning Herakles.

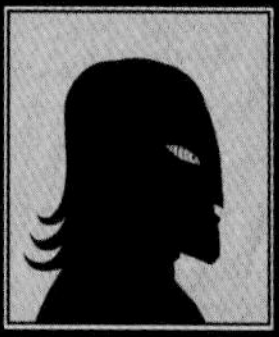

ACHELOUS

A river god who was the son of Oceanus and Tethys. The horn he lost to Herakles became the legendary Horn of Plenty.

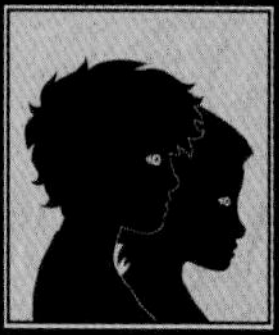

HYLLUS AND MACARIA

Herakles's last children, born to Deianira. Together, they killed Eurystheus to avenge their father. Macaria was Herakles's only daughter.

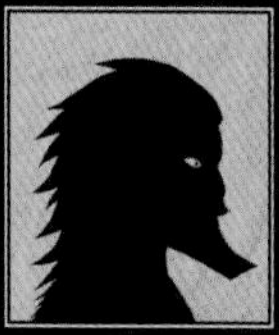

NESSUS

Last of the centaurs, born from the union of Ixion and Nephele. He had set himself up as the ferryman of the Euenos river after having escaped the battle his brothers fought against Herakles.

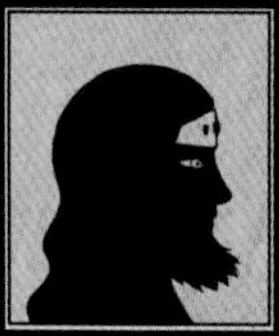

CEYX

King of Trachis, son of Eosphorus. After Herakles's death, he tutored the hero's children and later entrusted them to Theseus.

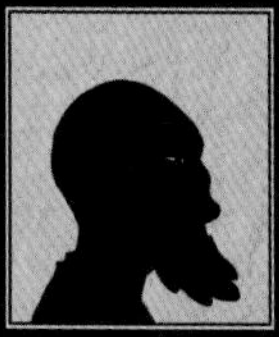

LICHAS

Loyal servant of Herakles and Deianira during the war against the Dryopes and Lapiths. He drowned in the Euboean Sea after Herakles threw him in.

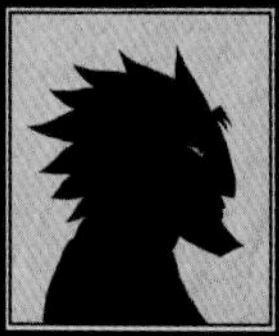

CYCNUS

Son of Ares and Pelopia, renowned for his cruelty and bloodthirstiness. He didn't survive the injuries Herakles inflicted on him.

IOLE
Princess of Oechalia, daughter of Eurytus. Before climbing onto the pyre, Herakles asked Hyllus to marry her.

PHILOCTETES
Berger, son of Poeas and friend of Heracles. He was the only one who agreed to light the pyre in exchange for the hero's bow and arrows.

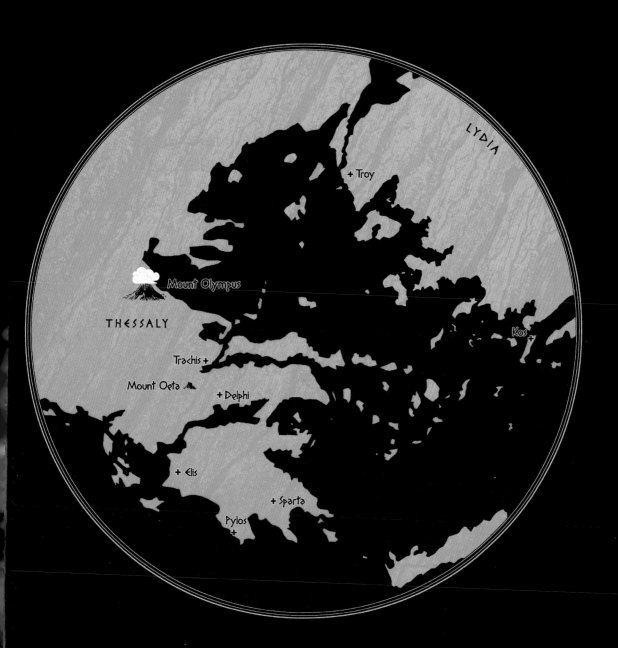

LYDIA

+ Troy

Mount Olympus

THESSALY

Kos +

Trachis +

Mount Oeta

+ Delphi

+ Elis

+ Sparta

Pylos +